Disclaimer

This is a work of fiction. The names, characters, places, events, locales, and incidents are either the outcome of the author's imagination and/or are used in a fictitious manner. Any resemblance to actual persons, living or dead, or actual events is purely coincidental.

THE MAN WITHOUT PERSONALITY

The Life and Struggle of the Family of a Special Child in the World of Uncertainty

Lester Laoagan

Bucharest, Romania
2022

Table of Contents

Lester Laoagan

Ordering Information:
For details, contact the publisher at the address below.

Laoagan, Lester
The Man Without Personality

ISBN - 978-973-0-36931-1 (PDF)
ISBN - 978-973-0-36925-0 (Paperback)

https://900street.com/

First Published (2022) 900 ST. Incorporated
Drumul Valea Furcii 71A, Bucharest
Sector 6, Romania 061985

info@900street.com
+40754509600

Acknowledgement

First and foremost I thank God because without him none of this is possible.

To my family for believing in my writing journey.

Miss. Divina Sayaan and company for helping me with the editing process.

To **Mr.** Christian Malinias for the front cover.

The Author

Dedication

For my brother Clarence, who this novel is loosely based from.

PREFACE

Growing in a family with a "special child" was the term called for someone like "Bart" as portrayed in this story. The experience I had with my "special brother" as I call him made me appreciate the simple thing in life that matters most. On how lucky I am to be alive, on how lucky I am to have loving parents, on how lucky I am to have a "special brother" that I never got to appreciate with my journey called life when I was younger. In fact, there were many questions I threw at life in general. "Why is my brother different from the rest of us?" "Why is my brother given a condition?" "Why is life unfair with the presence of my brother with a condition?" "Why are people indifferent to my brother?" and many questions that until now are not answered and could never be answered in my lifetime.

I have experienced the environment of having a "special brother" in a country such as the Philippines. A country considered as third world or developing where people are not well informed as compared to the first world countries or the developed countries or what we call "The West". And having a condition that involves the brain that affects one's behavior seen in public or talk in public is considered in the culture of Taboo. Also the difficulty of having to fend for ourselves and families similar to us with the absence of services or programs catered to people with special needs.

I viewed several movies that were global such as the "Rain Man", "I am Sam", "Forest Gump" and others. Moreover, I read articles about autism, Asperger's syndromes, learning disabilities and others. I observed that the main subjects had the verbal mild types and the stories were transpired in western settings. I couldn't help but make a comparison from what I viewed and read as opposed to the reality of my "special brother". "They call those people with special needs? They are normal compared to my brother." Those are the words that keep bugging my thoughts every time I encounter stories of "people with special needs". I felt I had to tell the world about my "special brother" but I didn't know the method on how to narrate the story. I also presume I didn't have the means to execute such an undertaking. I can't say that writing this book was without its obstacles. Writing in my home country of the Philippines is not taken seriously. The majority of the population are not readers. They prefer doing other stuff such as watching TV, the internet and even just hanging around doing nothing as in Filipino term "Tambay" than grabbing a book and reading. It is aggravated by the fact that I am from the Cordillera region. The people are more focused on fulfilling their basic needs than being involved in the arts. I witnessed artists in all aspects such as musicians, painters, sculptors, dancers, writers and the like struggle so much in life economically. They could hardly pay for rent, for food, for clothing, shelter, medicines and basic needs.

Those factors had a big impact on my writing. My first attempt was never supported. Everybody was advising me to focus on my work or having a sideline that generates income rather than wasting my effort on inserting writing on my extra time. Writing this book was on my mind. However, I believed what others said. I was trying to erase it from my mind but I was reminded from time to time. I even imagined that scenario of my book as a best-selling novel and acquiring wealth out of it. It was the initial motivation as any other first time writer. I assumed that it would be a breeze. Extracting memories from my head and putting it into writing. "How hard could it be." As I thought it was. I could never be wrong. I wrote a few chapters of my manuscript and tried to interview my loved ones on what they remember about my "special brother' but they were no help. I gave up and went on with my life. Until the 2020 coronavirus pandemic came. The lockdown left me with nothing to do at home. I again reviewed my unfinished manuscript and completed it bit by bit.

There were moments that I could not extract the memories. It took for only a couple of minutes to an hour to hours and days. Interviewing loved ones could have been a tremendous help. I was dismayed with the situation and again left my writing. In a random way, I imagine the writers in the past who were in difficult situations and without the luxury of technology but still were successful with their writings. I began watching youtube videos on "How to write a book/novel" and researching more about autism when I incur "the writer's block". I tried to apply what I learned the best of my abilities when I resumed my writing until the manuscript was completed.

Finding a beta reader and a critic partner was a difficult task for me. The lockdown for the pandemic was lifted in most of the provinces. People were already allowed to get out of their houses with few restrictions and health protocol. First, I tried social media but those I contacted did not respond or were not willing to be my beta readers for they claimed they were not knowledgeable about grammar or writing. I approached English and grammar teachers but none seemed to be available. I again contacted some of my friends on social media and one responded. She requested a copy of my manuscript and she informed me to wait until she claimed to know somebody who can help me with the editing. All I had to do was wait for her message. So I waited with follow-ups in between through the messenger. It took more than nine months before the editing was completed. I was searching for a book publisher in my locality with the hope of polishing my manuscript by a professional but it was non-existent. I pitched my manuscript in social media posting my concerns until a publishing company expressed their interest. I hope this book will shed a light to the consciousness and understanding of those who will read this book through the story of my brother with autism and the people around him.

Chapter I

The entire country of the Philippines was in turmoil. It was a sense embedded in the people's mind, hearts and spirits. Their passions were like the precious gems flowing through their beings, igniting the desire for liberty. The expressions were so strong that it got the attention of the whole world. The public places were full of protests and concerts against the powerful regime. The government troops composed of the military and the police were ready to strike at any cost. The stand-off tensions between the two opposing sides were felt on the ground. What will prevail? Who will win? Those were the questions. Anticipations were rising. The world was at a standstill. Mrs. Santos' eyes were glued on the television as the news camera caught his husband Mr. Santos with his fellow police officers on standby.

The military and police forces were equipped for battle as tanks and fully armed troops moved towards the rally, met by the people decorating the tanks with the abundance of flowers while singing songs of peace and patriotism. Mr. Santos, as part of the government troop with some of his colleagues, was defiant with the shoot-to-kill order from their superiors. Mr. Santos was as blank as a white paper with his gun pointing at the people. "Am I in a dream state?" "Is this really happening?" His consciousness went back into the reality by a young girl putting necklace flowers around his neck. In a slow motion, he dropped his weapon and looked at the young girl, and everything below him was showered by tears from his eyes. He saw most troops stood their ground while doing nothing to prevent the people from ever forwarding to the President. The loyalists retreated to the Presidential Palace only to find it was empty. Some of them were captured while others joined the people's side to save their own thick skins.

The great news of the President and the first family's exile sparked massive celebrations all over the country. People were making noises in every possible manner. Cars were honking with the sound system set on the highest volume. Everybody was dancing. It was a fiesta. Mrs. Santos could not believe her senses. Am I dreaming? Is this for real? She took a deep breath of relief and her eyes welling with joy when her husband was again visible from being momentarily lost in the crowd.

The noise woke the children from their afternoon nap puzzled and unaware of what was happening to the country. Mrs. Santos hugged them and put them back to bed. She peeked from the window and saw many familiar and unfamiliar entities having a party or celebration of some sort. Suddenly, someone was knocking on the door. She was reluctant to open. It could be anybody, a burglar, a loyalist of the former president or even one of the criminals her husband arrested. She tried to find out who it was without being detected. It put a smile on her face when the one knocking was her next-door- neighbor holding a beer on his right hand.

"Open the door and join us. You're the only one absent at the party!" She said.

"Uhmm, but, I am pregnant and my kids," Mrs. Santos said.

"Don't worry. Just lock the door. They will be fine. It won't take long. Just let the others know that you are with us, I mean with us with the new found freedom. Stay for a while then you can go back to your kids." The next-door-neighbor said.

Mr. Santos arrived in the apartment after to check on his family. He saw the kids without his wife.

"Honey, where are you?" Mr. Santos asked.

He heard the deafening music and noise of the next- door- neighbor while searching for his wife. There was Mrs. Santos sitting alone on the corner sipping a juice box while watching the drunk and unruly citizens. Mr. Santos had a little nip of the punch displayed on the service table. It was to show that they were one in spirit with the neighborhood. The celebration continued while Mr. and Mrs. Santos left. The Santoses were alert all-night due to the party that seemed to last forever. The children were synchronized with the party and played through-out the night.

There was utter silence as the sun rose into the horizon. The outdoor was empty with the exception of a few people striding on the street. It was like another worldly place full of peace and silence. It was a great chance for them to explore the rest. The city center was another story. Public places such as the streets and parks were packed that they could hardly move forward. Nevertheless, Mr. Santos tried to find a parking space, but there was no vacancy. He tried to find restaurants or fast-food or any establishments offering meals but met the same fate. They had no other choice but to return home.

"Honey, I'm having the baby." Mrs. Santos said after a few minutes of arriving.

"Are you sure?" Mr. Santos said.

"Yes, to the hospital. Please." Mrs. Santos said.

Mr. Santos begged their next-door-neighbor to watch over the kids because he had to rush his wife to the hospital. Due to the influx of vehicles and people to the city center, the traffic situation became so horrible. It was great timing that an on-duty motorcycle policeman recognized Mr. Santos. He rendered a police escort service with loud sirens for the other vehicles to clear the way. Their vehicles were speeding disregarding everybody around them. Their only focus was for Mrs. Santos to arrive at the hospital on time. Mr. Santos was a brave member of the Police force and he had two kids prior but nothing prepared him for the untimely birth of his third child. They almost reached their destination but the baby was already out. The police escort informed the hospital's emergency personnel when he noticed the baby in the car.

"Relax, sir, everything is fine. Your son and wife are safe without any complications. You can now see them. They are in room 205." The nurse said to Mr. Santos who can't keep still in the hallway.

People were coming from everywhere bearing gifts or greetings of congratulations while others donated cash for the hospital expenses. Some were even unfamiliar to Mr. and Mrs. Santos until they were reminded of who they were during their conversations. Mr. and Mrs. Santos were overwhelmed by the love given by the people that a simple thank you was not enough to express their gratitude.

They drew a blank when asked what name should be registered on their baby's birth certificate. Then, it clicked on Mr. Santos' memory. He remembered a brand-new cartoon TV show entitled The Simpsons with the son's character named "Bart". It was agreed upon that Bart would be the name of their third and last child.

Later that day, the media came to interview the Santos family.

"We are here in the Hospital of Manila to interview one of the heroes of the Philippine revolution, Senior Police Officer IV Pete Santos," the reporter said on air.

"Thank you, Madam, for the publicity directed to us which I still don't understand." Mr. Santos said.

"Sir, the news footage and the headline picture on the newspapers of you intercepting your colleague from shooting a girl has gotten immense popularity. It got so popular that people regarded you as a hero for doing such noble act. What is your reaction to that?" The reporter asked.

"Well, I did what must be done at that moment but I had no idea it would get this big. Thank you; I appreciate the sentiments of the people who have seen the video and photo. Thank you also to the media for publishing it or playing the video on the news. For me, the real heroes are the people who sacrificed and risked their lives fighting for our liberty. I mean, yes, those are the real heroes. I am just doing my job, to serve and protect and it is just commonsense that we must help one another just like what I did for the little girl and for our country," Mr. Santos said.

"Well said sir, but in our eyes, you are still a hero and by the way, how are your wife and baby?" The reporter asked.

"They are both okay. They just needed to be admitted to rest and for further observation as advised by the doctor to make sure of the absence of any complications." Mr. Santos answered.

"That's great, Sir. Congratulations." The reporter said.

"Thank you very much for your concern," Mr. Santos said.

"Sir any final message for our televiewers?" The reporter asked.

"My fellow Filipinos, what I will say are just simple reminders and pleas. Please don't waste the freedom that we fought for. Cherish it. Take advantage of it to make good to your compatriots and for our country. Use it to do things that will make you a better person. Don't ever forget what happened and learn from it. Thank you, and God bless us all," Mr. Santos said.

"Thank you, sir, and God bless your family," the reporter said.

The media was supposed to include Mrs. Santos in the interview but, instead, they gave her time to rest. Mr. Santos shook the reporter and cameraman's hands and thanked them for the interview.

Mrs. Santos did an excellent job being a homemaker but with an addition to the family, she could use all the help she needed. Several relatives' stay with the Santoses with the main purpose of babysitting Bart was short-lived. Some had no place to stay while applying for work abroad, while others had to leave due to emergency reasons. Mrs. Santos' cousin Sam was a lifesaver for his arrival was a great timing for the Santoses. One of the relatives' applications for overseas work was approved and to leave the Santoses. His stay with the Santoses was also intended for a temporary basis only. However, his stay was longer than expected. Babysitting Bart was a breeze which he very much enjoyed.

"Bart's demeanor is unique compared to the other babies I encountered. Other babies cry a lot and nothing seems to work to make them stop. It is the opposite of him. A gentle sway or a bottle feeder on his mouth is enough to make him fall asleep." What prevail on Sam's mind when it came to Bart.

Mr. and Mrs. Santos had many questions on why Bart was different from the majority of babies they encountered. Nonetheless, they never attempted to find the answers. They were only alarmed when they observed that Bart wasn't communicating or at least trying to communicate as he grew. He also uttered words without making any sense at any given moment. He also seemed to prefer to be alone while playing or whatever he was doing.

Mr. Santos arrived home from work. He turned the television on to take a glimpse of the evening news. Mrs. Santos was in the kitchen preparing for a snack and went to join Mr. Santos.

"Dad, I prepared us some snack." Mrs. Santos said.

"Thank you, mama." Mr. Santos said.

A few minutes of watching the news turned into a conversation.

"Dad, what is happening to Bart? He is already six years old, but he could not even say mama or papa." Mrs. Santos said

"Yes, I am worried about him also. Irene and Martin could already say simple words at the age of five. He is already six, but nothing." Mr. Santos said.

"I hope he will improve when he gets older. Let's hope and pray he will." Mr. Santos added.

"I really hope so. I am really worried about him. I am really worried if he could face the world with what is happening to him." Mrs. Santos said.

Mr. Santos smiled at Mrs. Santos and they went on watching the news.

Bart's condition did not improve as he got older. Mr. and Mrs. Santos attempted to find any answers they could. They consulted every doctor they could find. Unfortunately, it was the era of mullet and synth-pop. There were no available in-depth studies about Bart's condition. They were left with the doctor's hypothesis, other people's opinions and their own prejudices regarding Bart. Sam found a permanent job after staying with the Santos for roughly six years. He stayed with them full time in between side jobs. He was hired as a family driver for a businessman and the job required him to stay with them regularly.

"I want the job, but how can I tell "manong" and "manang?" I am a bit shy to tell them. I'm leaving despite of all the good things they did for me through these years." He told himself.

He struggled on disclosing it to Mr. and Mrs. Santos. He only had the courage to finally break the news when he realized that he had to leave the Santoses someday and live a life on his own.

"If not now, when?" was an encouraging statement he told himself.

He looked at each of the Santoses including Irene and Martin during dinner. He planned all along to tell them about his situation. As he was going to announce that he was leaving for a job, Mr. Santos handed Mrs. Santos a letter from the National Police Headquarters.

"You know what this means?" Mr. Santos asked.

"It means you are promoted?" Mrs. Santos asked.

"Yes and the confirmation of my appointment is on the letter and we are moving to my hometown of Kabayan and I am very thrilled to go back to my home town with you guys." Mr. Santos said.

"Congratulations, "manong" and I have been meaning to tell you this. I have to leave also for a job I found. I was hired as a family driver and I am required to stay with the family." Sam said.

"Okay, congratulations for the two of you." Mrs. Santos said.

"Manang, I should have informed you earlier but I was so ashamed to leave this family for the good things you have done for me during my time of stay." Sam said.

"No problem. We are all happy for you. You have to live your life on your own also. Stop worrying about us or what the people would think when you leave. We all understand." Mrs. Santos said.

"So, when will you start your job?" Mr. Santos asked

"Three weeks from now manong." Sam said.

"Okay, they are giving me two months to finalize everything in the office for the transition. I say this again, we are happy for you and you deserve to go on with your life. We are also very grateful for your years of stay with us. It meant a lot to us." Mr. Santos said.

Mrs. Santos was thrilled the moment she learned about the promotion. She wanted to experience the simple rural life similar of her childhood again. She also wanted her children to experience the simple lifestyle of the rural area. She was hoping that the change to a cleaner, fresher and more relaxed environment as she had expected would be a big help for the improvement of Bart.

Chapter II

The municipality of Kabayan presented a breath-taking beauty of the natural highland landscapes. Thick lustrous forests on top of gigantic mountains were filled with pine trees that emitted aromas pleasant to the senses. It was also home to several wildlife creatures from the cute and fuzzy cloud rat to the vicious wild dogs and strange creatures that appeared to be taken straight from science fiction movies. Aquatic creatures were visible from the fresh water. Native mountain cultures passed through generations were still robust in the lives of the locals. It was a natural paradise.

Mrs. Santos fell in love with the place with so much excitement. Mr. Santos never felt so relaxed with the easy living and the taste of nature. He was tired of the bustle and hassle of the polluted city life. Not much had changed since he left except for some evidence of progress. As they were settling, his mind wandered to a place full of memories. He was reminded of his childhood, him leaving his hometown in pursuit of higher education and how he became a family man.

They were provided with a house to stay. It was an old traditional "nipa" hut type of abode. The wooden flooring was elevated from the ground with lumber walls, hay roofing and boulders on the ground as the anchor of the wooden foundation. Some modern modifications were present, such as the concrete that supplemented the stability of the boulders, galvanized iron under the hay roof and the presence of modern plumbing and electricity. The comfort room or CR (a term used for the toilet in the Philippines) was separated in the backyard with a modern loo and plenty of running water from the faucet. The house was very clean with some amenities such as wooden bed, wooden dining table, an old functioning television set and a gas stove. The Santoses purchased kitchen utensils and belongings for personal use. The kids, including Bart roamed around the surroundings. Bart heard giggles and laughter but when it was time to enter, he stared screaming and resisted the efforts of everybody who were trying to force him in the house. Mrs. Santos stayed with him on the porch for more than an hour. Mr. Santos tried tactics to convince Bart that it was safe to enter. He let Bart see him enter without any problems. He called Bart's name from the inside, holding a chocolate bar. Nothing worked until Bart could hardly open his eyes and tried to maintain his straight position. Mr. Santos put him to bed inside without any resistance. He usually squirms and screams when cutting his fingernails, but in that particular time, he allowed Mrs. Santos to do so without any problem.

"My boy! My boy! My dear boy!" Mrs. Santos said.

"I know that these are new to you."

"Hope you get used to it here because we will be staying here for a long time,"

She smiled and hugged him then let him have his sleep.

As the darkness of the night was getting near, Irene and Martin came home from exploring the outside with vegetables and wild edible greens.

"Where did you get these?" Mrs. Santos asked.

"We got it from the side of the creek," Irene said.

"Some old ladies helped us find some of the edible," Martin Added.

The vegetables were prepared and cooked as viand dishes always paired with rice as the staple food for most Asian countries. This was the start of the Santos children's exposure to the highland countryside of living.

The mayor and the municipal officials organized a town meeting for everybody to attend. It was held in the Kabayan Municipal Multi-purpose Hall to accommodate the expected number of attendees. It turned out to be a good idea for the venue was jam-packed. Such meeting was never done since the previous regime was in power. The mayor, vice-mayor, municipal councilors, Barangay (the lowest electoral unit of the Philippines) Chairmen, Barangay councilmen and the barangay policemen called "tanods", including Mr. Santos as the new chief of police, and other new positions such as municipal treasurer, health workers, school teachers and many newer government workers assigned in Kabayan were introduced. The main agenda of the meeting were non-exciting stuff. The treasure reported on the municipal's annual fund. Some simple reminders from officials and that was all about it. After the short meeting, everybody was eager to converse with Mr. Santos. The old folks present talked about his grandparents and his parents. Others were remembering some moments in his life. Some folks were asking about his siblings and how they were doing in their current lives. Mr. Santos was happy to converse with each one of them. He felt the welcome of coming back home.

While preparing for the first day of school, Martin was fidgeting with an unsettling look in his eyes, while Irene was the opposite. She had no signs of anxiety and could prepare without any assistance. Their teachers and classmates welcomed them. Martin tried to move his feet but he was fixed to the floor with his mother behind him smiling. All he could see was Chinese-looking people talking with pointed hats like those he saw in Vietnam War movies from the door. His teacher kept saying his name but he was unresponsive. The teacher then went closer to him and said his name again.

"Martin, Martin is anything alright?" (Martin, Martin okay ka lang ba?)

"I know you must be scared because you are new here but I assure you, you will be getting used to it" (Amok nga mabuteng ka ta damdamum ditoy ngem sigurado nga masanay kan ton.)

Then, she assisted him inside.

The students were free to choose wherever they wanted to sit. Martin sat on the available desk. The class became chaotic when everybody was racing to sit beside him.

"Hey! Hey! Hey! Keep quiet!" The teacher said with aloud resounding voice.

"What is that all about?" She added.

Then there was utter silence; some of the students stood in one corner while the others sat on the desk that they chose.

"Okay then. All of you come in front! Since you are all misbehaving, I will decide the sitting arrangement where nobody has a choice but to comply." The teacher said.

Martin had difficulty fitting in due to the language barrier in the first few days of his class. He spoke "Ilocano", the city dialect while the native residents of the town spoke "Nabaloi." He had some good days and some bad days. As many of his classmates were friendly, some believed he was just an arrogant city kid. Sometimes, he went home with school supplies missing. Other times, he was sinking with his own emotions.

"What's wrong my son?" Mrs. Santos asked.

"Nothing mom," Martin said.

"Mom, stop looking at me like that," he added.

"I know you, I know when something is wrong." Mrs. Santos said.

Martin went to his room to be alone. Mrs. Santos did not follow to give him some time for himself and maybe to think. After more than thirty minutes of silence, Mrs. Santos was about to knock when Martin burst out from his room as he screamed.

"Stupid! Stupid!" Martin screamed.

"Why? Why are you so angry?" Mrs. Santos said.

She was floored of discovering Bart's presence in the room with Martin. She felt worried of what Martin could have done with his brother.

"I was trying to play with Bart but I kept on telling him, stop being stupid, I told him many times, very easy to play the game but he is just being very stupid." Martin said.

"Hey, don't ever say those things to your brother. If you have any problem in school or anything you can talk to me. I'm your mother don't divert your anger or whatever is going on with you to your brother." Mrs. Santos said.

Martin got out of the house, baring the tiger look demeanor in his eyes. Mrs. Santos tried to talk him into staying until his anger transitioned into tranquility. Martin did not listen to his mother's appeal, instead; he ran straight into the woods without paying much attention to his surroundings. He didn't care if his actions would bring him in danger. He was in the state of uncontrolled jerking with loud beats of his heart as he went deeper into the unknown darkness of the forest. The trees' silhouettes were shaped like monsters with the branches as willow arms ready to snatch him up. He anxiously continued walking forward. He passed the forest arriving at a modest house surrounded by a vegetable garden, fruit-bearing trees, and some free-range farms and domesticated animals. He continued pacing towards the house when an enormous black pig was speeding towards him. He tried to take a step back or two but his entire body stiffened. An old man came out from the house driving the pig away when he saw Martin.

"Hey little boy. What are you doing here all alone?" (Ngaran ni muka pan deg-a chiyay ja man sak-sakey?) He asked.

"What is your name?" (Ngan ni ngaran mo?) He added.

Martin's eyes were blinking rapidly by the wrinkled face he saw and just stared because he still couldn't comprehend the "Nabaloi" dialect. Not sure of what the appropriate response was, he answered in Ilocano, "Please don't hurt me." (Pangaasim apo saan dak nga saktan). The old man understood a little of what was said but not enough to discern what Martin meant. The old man allowed Martin to enter his house for his own safety.

Martin was a bit hesitant at first but was forced to enter in fear of the animals. The old man gave him some sweet potatoes and a cup of spring water. The hesitation was still present, but because he was tired and hungry, he took a little bite and gulped some water. Rain poured as Martin was about to finish his snack. They waited indoors for the weather to clear before they went outside. The old man originally planned to accommodate Martin to the police but decided to bring him home when he learned who his father was.

The old man knocked at the Santos' door. A lady answered him. He had no idea that she was Martin's mother.

"Yes, may I help you?" Mrs. Santos asked.

She then saw Martin with the old man.

"That is my son Martin; I am very sorry if he bothered you or did something bad. Thank you very much for bringing him home," Mrs. Santos said.

"Oh, so Martin is his name. We did not understand each other when I tried to ask him for information and no worries. He did nothing terrible or something, I just saw him in the woods wondering around, uhm there, where my house is located," pointing towards the wooded area of the east. "That's the part where he went. I was supposed to surrender him to the police but he led me here," The Old man said.

"Sorry, but May I ask your name, sir?" Mrs. Santos asked.

"Tadaka Kibara is my name," the old man said.

"Again, how rude of me. We have been talking and I did not invite you in," Mrs. Santos said.

"It's alright, I'll be going then," Mr. Tadaka said.

"Martin, what have you done again? Instead of talking to me, you again got me worried." Mrs. Santos said.

Martin looked at Mrs. Santos straight in her eye apologetically. However he never uttered a single word.

Chapter III

Mr. Tadaka was on his way home when he came across a young man carrying "apay." (A type of tall grass used to cover the ground when preparing meat for an occasion.)

"Ambot, (general Ilocano term for young man.) where are you taking the apays?" He asked.

"Ama, (general Ilocano term for old man.) we are taking these to the municipal hall in preparation for the foundation day. Don't you know about it? It is always celebrated on the same date and it will start tomorrow," one of the young men said.

Mr. Tadaka smiled at them and nodded, then continued to move on his way home.

An intelligence report warned the citizens to be vigilant for terrorist activities all over the country. Kabayan was one of the hot spots for a terror attack because of its proximity to the alleged camp of the rebel group. The planned celebration had to be postponed as a safety measure for possible conflict any time soon. Government operations and classes were suspended. The citizens were advised to prepare for anything and limit themselves from going outside of their houses. Special curfews at night were strictly implemented and violators were detained until the next day or sent home. The entire municipality was in fear and in a state of panic. Everybody was hoarding food and water and other essentials for survival. Farmers were forced to harvest as many crops as possible, including those premature ones. Animal raisers kept their livestock in safe areas with feeds that could last long. Others butchered some of their animals and made the meat into "kinuday." (A preservation method where the meat is salted and smoked then preserved for weeks to months.) The local police immediately set checkpoints on the main roads to and from Kabayan. At dawn, trucks of the military from the national headquarters arrived as reinforcements. Men who had undergone the Reserved Training Officer Corps joined the military service without any refresher training due to time constraints.

The Santoses, led by Mrs. Santos, prayed for their current situation and for the safety of all involved. Bart went to the living room, turned on the lights, laid on the sofa and did whatever business he did unaware of the imminent danger. Mrs. Santos yanked Bart to the second floor bed room but he kept on getting out.

"Bart, why are you so hard headed?" Mrs. Santos asked.

"Come Bart stay. It is very dangerous out there," Irene said while he was being dragged back to the bedroom.

Mrs. Santos got some drinking water and crackers in the room; placed an "arinola" (a bowl-shaped vessel with an ear handle and lid used for urination.) in the corner in case they needed to take a leak or even take a dump. She then locked the door from the inside for everybody's safety, particularly Bart. Before they went to sleep, she reminded the children over and over again not to wander in the middle of the night due to their situation.

More than a month passed without any incident. The agreement for cease fire signed by both parties was one of the greatest news received.   Everybody went on with their normal lives with smiles in their hearts. The three main churches in town held abrupt services. There will be a more meaningful reason for celebration aside from the town's foundation day. Their celebration was shortly interrupted by the sudden broadcast of the number of casualties and injuries in the neighboring town. Everybody was in despair. Some prayed on their knees while others cried.

The foundation day celebration forged ahead despite what had happened. The festivities were compacted from a month-long celebration for only a week. The officials wanted to give the residents some time for fun and relaxation after the stress brought by the impending conflict. The official opening of the celebration started with a prayer for the casualties of the battle, for their loved ones and friends left behind, and for the safety and success of the festivities. The Philippine national anthem was played, and the Philippine flag rose simultaneously for all to respect by standing still and putting their right hand on their hearts. Inspirational speeches from respected elders and officials with intermissions of singing and dancing in between were the main bulk of the program.

Out of nowhere, Bart rushed to the stage as the program was on going with a marker pen in his hand. He went on scribbling on the stage backdrop made from the white cloth covering the plywood. The audiences were laughing as some of the members tried to get him off the stage. Mrs. Santos and the concerned members of the audience grabbed him and sent him home.

The sound of the traditional "Igorot" (indigenous people of the Cordillera Region of the Philippines) instruments such as the "gangzas" or gongs and "solibaos" (a bongo-drum like musical instrument) playing was heard as far as the Santos' residence about half a kilometer and beyond. "Ba-diw," the traditional Igorot chant telling the stories of the culture and tradition of the people were performed by the women elders led by the "mambunong" the "Igorot's" medicine man and high priest through the words of wisdom coming from his mouth. While the traditions were happening, meals composed of the staple rice, "batbat" (the large chunks of boiled pork), and "pancit" (the Filipino stir-fried noodle dish) on banana barks as plates where eaten using only bare hands. Irene and Martin got their share and were given extras for Mrs. Santos and Bart.

Later that evening, Martin saw some buttons and belts arranged in a straight line on his parents' room floor while his brother Bart was asleep right next to it. He pointed this out to his parents and sister to witness it themselves. Their eyes were wide open with amazement upon seeing what Bart did. Mr. Santos carried Bart gently to the bed without disturbing his sleep.

"What could this mean?" Martin asked.

"Yes, why did he do this?" Irene also asked.

"Your brother is learning something, maybe some form of art," Mrs. Santos said.

"Yes, that is definitely some sort of an art form," Mr. Santos said.

The festivities continued the following day. Many Filipino traditional games aimed at children were played. The "harang-taga" or block and catch; the "palosebo" (A game with an erected greasy bamboo pole that everybody tries to climb to get the prize on top.); the "pabitin" (A bamboo trellis with prizes is lowered then pulled up as everybody, mostly children, attempt to snatch goodies hanging from the bamboo contraption,) and the "pokpok palayok" that resembles a "piñata" except the paper mache shaped into figures filled with goodies is replaced by clay pots. Irene and Martin enjoyed the games they participated in. Martin got the most candies and goodies from the "pabitin" and "pokpok palayok." They went home after the games to share the prizes they won with Bart. The toys and school supplies presented were not enticing to him, and he grabbed the candies and junk foods instead.

The foundation day celebration ended with a benefit concert for the survivors' and the casualties' families. The event gained immense support both from the local and neighboring municipalities' residences. Bands and performers both local and from other parts of the country gave the performances of their lives despite not receiving any talent fees. The event even sparked part two in Baguio City.

The Philippine government launched a program for women's empowerment. In the local level of Kabayan, the program was titled "Empowering Women through Skills Enhancements." The program was intended for women, especially housewives and the unemployed, because it was observed that they lack skills in certain areas. Apart from the national government's funding, some of the proceeds from the part two benefit concert went towards the program. It was fitting for Mrs. Santos to head the "Skills and Training" programs, because she was a well-known highly skilled woman in dressmaking, crochet, knitting, baking and handicrafts. She was pleased to accept the offer with the condition that somebody must look after Bart while working. Bart needed such help because he could not perform daily activities of living without any assistance such as cleaning his bottom after taking a dump, taking a bath by himself, cooking his own food, doing his own laundry, doing some home chores, and others.

Bart was taken good care of, as was expected. The help had a satisfactory approval from the Santoses. As her stay progressed, the Santoses observed some minor injuries on Bart. Scratches and hematomas were present in some parts of his body. He had a strange vibe from her every time he and the help were close. There was an unexplainable tension. Mr. and Mrs. Santos did not think much about the situation. They assumed that Bart was still adjusting with the help. They never talked to the help and gave her more time with Bart. The situation wasn't improving. In fact, Bart became more aloof with the help.

"Enough is enough. The situation is not improving. We must replace the help," Mrs. Santos told herself.

"Leave our house. And never wonder why. You know the reason. You know what you did to Bart. I don't have to remind you. Just get out," Mrs. Santos said.

"Why, auntie? I don't know what you are talking about. I tried to wake Bart up but he refused," The help said.

"Just pack-up and get-out, I don't believe you. It is so obvious that you did something bad to Bart. We are not stupid to ignore the evidence. Get out," Mrs. Santos said.

She informed her husband about the incident as soon as she could. They requested their neighbor to watch over Bart temporarily until they could find a more permanent one. The neighbor was kind enough to oblige by sending her teenage daughter. Mr. Santos explained their situation to some of his relatives and pleaded if anyone was willing to stay with them to take care of Bart. He thought a relative would be better as Bart's caregiver because she would care for him more than a paid stranger.

Chapter IV

A teenage girl took over the household temporarily before a regular one came and stepped-up to the plate. Roxanne was the daughter of Mr. Santos' cousin. So far, nothing untoward has happened since she took care of Bart for a few days. She was closely monitored without her knowledge brought by the Santoses' previous experience.

The weekends were Roxanne's assigned day-offs, but it was not always the case. She sometimes stayed whenever she didn't have anything to do and no place to go. One Saturday, the Santoses decided to visit Mr. Tadaka. They were led by Martin who knew where they were supposed to go. Mr. Santos wanted to meet Mr. Tadaka and dig into his knowledge about their family lineage and genealogy. The Santoses emerged from the woods to the more open space where Mr. Tadaka lived. Mr. Santos knocked at the door but nobody answered.

"Hello. We are here." Mr. Santos said.

Mr. Tadaka did not notice the people at his doorstep. Martin saw him at the chicken coop just a few meters from the house. He told everybody the man he saw was Mr. Tadaka. Everybody was shouting and waving the moment they saw him. He rushed towards them as fast as he could. The wear and tear of his body throughout the years slowed him down. He was so worried about who they were. *Did their presence introduce potential harm or good vibes?* He recognized Martin and Mrs. Santos when he got closer.

"Sorry, I did not recognize any of you from afar," Mr. Tadaka said.

"No worries. Here we bought you some bread and noodles," Mr. Santos said.

"Thank you. I am really very sorry I don't know you that much but I guess you are the new chief of police if I am not mistaken," Mr. Tadaka said.

"Yes, you are correct," Mr. Santos said.

"Come to my humble house. Let me just unlock the door and open a few windows," He said.

The family introduced themselves and Mr. Santos introduced Bart as his son with special needs.

"Anyway, what brings your family here?" Mr. Tadaka asked.

"We just want to visit you and get to know you better, and how well you know my late father, God bless his soul and my mom. She is currently in Baguio with my sister," Mr. Santos said.

"Okay but before answering that, from where are you Mrs.?" Mr. Tadaka asked.

The adults went on with their conversation while the children were playing on the yard when it was abruptly interrupted.

"Be careful; don't forget to be mindful of each other's safety, especially Bart," Mrs. Santos said.

"Don't go too far. We might not be able to see you, You might all have accidents without us knowing. Be very careful," Mr. Tadaka added.

"Don't worry we will just play in this area where you can have a view of us," Irene said.

"Really, be very careful. We are serious." Mr. Santos said.

Mr. Tadaka became a storyteller similar to those written in books and portrayed in movies. Stories, not only about the clan but also the old Kabayan. He remembered the fine details of all the events and everyone he knew. He was also very candid about his experiences as a World War II soldier and how he was almost drafted to participate in the Korean War.   Mr. and Mrs. Santos were very attentive to every word Mr. Tadaka said without any interruptions. The only time they opened their mouths was for follow-up questions.   The stories went on until the day's brightness was almost overtaken by the dead of the night.

"I'm sorry uncle, Am I right? You are my uncle?" Mr. Santos asked.

"Yes, as I have told you. Your mother and I are first cousins, and since you mentioned she is still alive, I would love to see her again as soon as possible because I haven't seen her for ages. I don't know if we will be given the chance to see each other again due to our old age," Mr. Tadaka said.

"Don't say that. I am sure you and mother will have the chance to see each other very soon uncle, and again, sorry we must leave. It is almost dark. Nice talking to you, and we will visit again next time," Mr. Santos said.

The Santos kids were called inside to say their goodbyes before leaving. Mr. Tadaka gave them some ripe and unripe bananas.   The Santoses' initial visit triggered the start of a strong bond. As they were heading home, Mrs. Santos kept Irene and Martin close to her while Bart was with Mr. Santos and the bag of bananas. They were moving fast to avoid the darkness of the night, especially when going through the dense forest. Mr. Santos was pulling Bart when he stopped and attempted to remove his pants. Mr. Santos carried him on his back with the bag of bananas on his side preventing Bart from taking his pants off.

"Bart tried to remove his pants. Follow us and move faster," Mr. Santos said, while carrying Bart.

Mrs. Santos, with Martin and Irene sprinted to Mr. Santos' trail relying on the remaining dim light shining on their path. They heard Bart's loud screams and rushed towards it. They saw Mr. Santos wiping his bottom with some dry, coarse leaves. Everybody just laughed it out until they arrived home safe.

Roxanne woke early the next day as she always did to prepare breakfast. She noticed the banana peelings and other fruit scraps on the kitchen table and on the floor.   Bart came rushing to the CR (The term used for toilets in the Philippines) with a thunderous sound and the smell covering the entire ground floor. It's like poison gas was thrown in the house, preventing anyone from ever breathing. She then opened all the windows to alleviate the horrible odor. She wiped Bart's bottom, but the stench wouldn't disappear. She gave Bart an early morning bath and cleaned the toilet with detergent and water. The problem was Bart frequented the CR that indicated him having issues with his bowel movement.

Roxanne knocked on Mr. and Mrs. Santoses' room to inform them on what was going on with Bart.

"Oh, my boy! Oh, my boy! Go and buy diatabs or any anti-diarrheal drugs at any sari-sari stores (the Filipino version of a convenient store) available," Mr. Santos said.

It was about fifteen minutes since Roxanne went to buy the medicine. She scoured every store that she could. She even disturbed store owners who did not open yet. Mr. Santos was composed about the situation, while Mrs. Santos was the opposite and took turns wiping Bart. Roxanne arrived with two pieces of medicine.

"Thank God. I was able to get those because I went from one sari-sari store to the other and all of them ran out of medicine. Those were not even for sale. It was for personal use. I persuaded a store owner to sell it," Roxanne said.

"Hurry and give it to Bart," Mrs. Santos said.

She tried to give one but his mouth was sealed.

"Bart, open your mouth. That is medicine, my son. Please it will make you better," Mr. Santos said.

Bart's mouth was still closed and ran to his room upstairs, laid on his bed and covered himself up with a blanket. Mr. Santos took the medication with a glass of water and followed him.

"Bart, my son, please take the medicine for your own good!" Mr. Santos said.

Bart did not cooperate despite Mr. Santos' repeated requests. With a hard-hitting slap of Mr. Santos' palm hitting Bart's cheek, everyone was jolted.

"I gave him the medicine. I had to slap him because he refused to take it. I forced to open his mouth and shove the medicine in his throat! Leave him and let him rest," Mr. Santos said.

Mr. and Mrs. Santos were late for work due to the delay brought by Bart's situation. Mr. Santos' tardiness was not an issue, but he was still prompted to explain the reason. Everybody's heart seemed to melt when it came to Bart. Mr. Santos assured the station that Bart was okay. Mrs. Santos also apologized and explained why she was late for her class. Her students asked so many questions about Bart's welfare. They even suggested that the class be suspended if Mrs. Santos needed to attend to her son despite having the help. She was thankful for her students' concerns and reiterated that Bart was okay.

A bus that was new in the municipality was parked in the municipal hall parking area. Mr. Santos and the on-duty police officers saw the vehicle from the nearby police station but thought of nothing about it. They assumed that it was owned by a brand new Kabayan resident or municipal employee visitor. *Why would they allow it to park within the vicinity of the municipal hall in the first place if neither of the two assumptions were true?* Unknown to their knowledge, it was actually a charismatic group who believed that they were the chosen few instruments of God by bestowing them with the ability to heal all types of physical and spiritual disorders. Besides, they proclaimed that they were the only vessel to salvation. The group was traveling around the nation to spread their doctrines, heal, and convince the people to join them and explore God's gift in their personal lives. According to them, nothing was more powerful than God. Not cancer; not diabetes; not evil spirit; not life's problems; not failures; and they meant business. God is the ultimate answer to all.

They went to every household, near and far, crossing rivers and climbing mountains. They were there spreading the "truth" that they believed in. They were very persistent.

Sundays were allotted for church. Roxanne and the Santoses took turns taking care of Bart. Roxanne attended the early morning Catholic Mass and the Santoses attended the later United Church of Christ In the Philippines (One of the protestant Churches within Kabayan.) service in turn. As they were preparing, two ladies and a gentleman in a nice suit and dresses were in the Santos' property peeping through the window in search of somebody home.

"Who is it?" Mrs. Santos asked.

Then a knock on the door was heard.

"Who is it? I said!" Mrs. Santos said.

"Who could this be on a Sunday morning? Nobody comes to visit this early on Sundays," she mumbled as she trudged to open the door. She saw the three individuals she never saw before in her entire life. *Who could they be? What is their purpose of being here?* Those were the questions rumbling in her head.

"Hello madam, sorry to disturb you, but we are the "Chosen People of God " and we are traveling the country to proclaim the good news and to help our fellow men as God had ordered. We heard you have a son named Bart. We want to help him with his condition through the power of the almighty," the man spoke that looked like the spokesperson of the three.

Deep inside, Mrs. Santos wanted to drive the three away from their property but she did not want to be rude.

"Sorry I don't know. May I get my husband?" she said instead.

"Why are you here? What are you here for?" Mr. Santos asked.

The spokesperson just repeated what he said to Mrs. Santos.

"We are preparing for Church. If you want to preach your religion, then go to the pagans," Mr. Santos said sarcastically.

"Sir, we just want to help your son. God will help him through us," the man said.

"As I said, we are preparing for church and who told you about my son?" Mr. Santos said.

"The Mayor recommended us to visit your family, especially Bart, to offer our help," the man said.

Bart ran outside when he saw the door was accessible and took some chocolates from the store.

"Look. You let him escape. We always lock the door because of him and you let him escape." Mr. Santos said with his cherry face.

The three apologized simultaneously.

"Hey, what are you still doing here? Get away from us! This is not a good time and besides we are already late for church!" Mr. Santos said.

The three tried to convince Mr. Santos without any success before they left.

Mr. and Mrs. Santos were glad they did not miss the preaching section of the church service. They noticed that almost half of the congregation was absent. One of the parishioners caught their expressions and informed them that most of those absent went to the healing crusade of the charismatic group, the same group they encountered earlier. Mr. Santos was calm and participated in church rituals but deep inside of his being wanted to explode; not because of the charismatic group but the parishioners who were convinced of their advocacy. Nobody presumed that something was going on with Mr. Santos because he looked like having a positive demeanor like he always did every Sunday. He tried paying attention to the preacher delivering his sermons but his mind was on his worries about the absent members being indoctrinated by the charismatic group.

Some members of the charismatic group returned to the Santos residence with their leader that very same afternoon. The leader tried to convince them to let Bart be subjected to their healing ritual.

The leader was confident about his convincing power. The God given power of making Mr. Santos agree with the procedure.

Nothing but a false assumption, Mr. Santos agreed, for he wanted to get the procedure over with. He thought that if he kept refusing, they would keep on insisting and wasting their time. He only agreed if every ritual and procedure were executed in their presence. The group ordered Bart to sit, laid their hands on him and chanted in an unintelligible form of speaking. It was like they were speaking in tongues mentioned in the Bible. More rituals were done with something that resembled an exorcism. The leader told the Santoses that Bart's condition was caused by evil spirits wrapped around him that they were able to eliminate. They handed Mr. Santos a pamphlet with a prayer written in Latin with Filipino translations that were required to recite in Bart's presence before the sun rises every single day for forty days. Besides, the ritual needed some other procedures done by the Santoses without their presence regularly. The family could not wait for them to leave, and they pretended to agree with the group's advice. The group left and never bothered them again.

Chapter V

A few days had passed since the charismatic group left Kabayan. The dispensary was full of patients with various complaints. Some were simple aches and pains while others needed immediate medical interventions. The medical staff consisted of only a doctor, two nurses, a midwife and one available ambulance driver. The traveling dentist was not available that time. The situation was in dire need of additional medical personnel. Residents with medical training and those who practice traditional healing were requested as skeletal work forces. A few tourists who had EMT and Red Cross life support training volunteered to help. Many of the patients were given over-the-counter medications. Others were checked and sent home with home remedy advice. The health workers were swearing in frustration at the patients because their health issues could have been prevented or treated if they had gone to the medical facility sooner. The patients' history pointed to one aggravating cause, they all attended the charismatic group's healing sessions.

A seventy-seven-year-old man, Lakay, the genealogist of the municipality went to the dispensary for his swollen gums after the unsuccessful treatment by the charismatic group. The only remedy the doctor could administer was to prescribe him with generic painkillers and advise him to gargle with salinized lukewarm water. She also advised him to seek further medical attention at a more advanced medical facility as soon as possible. Sadly, he died the very same night. It was a great loss for the entire municipality because of his remarkable memory of the town's rich history and most of the lineage of the people. The people were always sad every time his passing surfaced in their conversations and questioned why nobody thought of recording his expertise on the town's genealogy. The doctor suspected that

Lakay died of meningitis which could have been addressed if treated earlier.

Mr. Santos wanted to take action when he learned about what happened to his town-mates. He did not have any legal authority to prosecute the Charismatic group but still felt it was his duty to warn other communities for the prevention of suffering from similar fate. The Mayor, who was a firm believer and advocate of alternative medicine and a heavy user of herbal medication himself, refused to admit that what happened to the patients was the charismatic group's fault or had to do with them. He speculated that there must be other explanations for the incident in the dispensary. Mr. Santos decided to pursue his plan with or without the mayor's support.

Mr. Santos went home to avoid the town's mess and to ponder on his next plan of action. He was seated on the sofa reading the newspaper while the kids watched their favorite television program.

"Kindly turn off the television, for I will tell you something," Mr. Santos said.

"I will go to Baguio City tomorrow, and who would like to come with me?" He asked.

"Dad, me," Martin said.

"No, me, please dad, let it be me, the one who will accompany you," Irene said.

"I can only bring one," Mr. Santos said.

Mrs. Santos heard their conversation from the kitchen and wondered why all of a sudden, her husband became spontaneous with the kids.

"Did I hear it right? What did you just say to the kids? That you will go to Baguio, and will bring one of them with you?" Mrs. Santos asked.

"Yes dear, you are correct. You heard it right," Mr. Santos said.

"And why is that?" Mrs. Santos asked.

"Did you hear of what happened at the dispensary?" All the people who got sick? Lakay passed away." Mr. Santos said.

"Yes dad, it is all over town, nobody could miss what happened and what has Baguio got to do with it?" Mrs. Santos asked.

"I will go with a police officer to let the entire country know what those no-good-so, called-healers did to us. To warn others, since our good mayor refused to do something about it. I will warn the people through the radio and TV media, If possible." Mr. Santos said.

"Okay, but be careful, take Martin with you, then." Mr. Santos said.

"Please take me instead." Irene said.

"Sorry Irene, you can't come. This trip is only for boys. You can't fit in with us," Mrs. Santos Said.

Irene stomped her feet with deafening screams. She and her brother Martin were competing about who will go to the city with their father. They wanted to tell their peers exaggerated tales about their city experience. For unknown reasons, kids who visit the city tend to gain popularity and be welcomed as if they were someone special among their peers when they return home.

Mr. Santos was satisfied with the outcome of his mission in the city. The warning was broadcasted on radio and television. It even sparked nationwide attention, not only to the people's awareness, but with the national government. Actions were taken to determine if the charismatic group was violating any provisions of the law. They were even featured and given chances to express their side on the issues thrown at them by the mainstream media. It was both an advantage and a disadvantage of the group. People were warned about them. On the other hand, they became popular due to the exposure they were gaining. A media personality invited Mr. Santos because he wanted to get the exclusive scope on how the controversy came about. He refused the invitation because he wanted to preserve his anonymity. He was even wondering how the media personality came to know about him and what he did when nobody knew about his mission except for his wife and children who could not understand the situation.

Mr. Santos expected a reprimand from the Mayor but nothing, not a word from his office. He had no idea that Mr. Santos was the one who exposed the activities of the Charismatic group in the media.

Did the mayor know I was responsible for exposing the Charismatic group and did nothing or he really didn't have a clue about it? Mr. Santos pondered.

Oh, Well, I will just keep quiet about it and wait. I don't want to risk reminding him or telling him if he didn't really know anything about it. He added.

He wasn't much worried about the charismatic group seeking revenge on him and his family. Kabayan was a tight rural community where anything unusual would be easily detected. He requested the police officers to be vigilant on anything out of place and strictly implement the registrations of tourists coming.

Lord please let everybody be safe, was Mr. Santos' prayer every day in his head.

Everybody was glued to the news. The headline was about the Charismatic group. The government made an intensive investigation of the group. It was discovered that the group had prominent members from all walks of life. The law enforcers raided the supreme leader's residence in the capital city of Manila. It was a massive three-story building with sturdy fences of concrete with barbed wire on top and armed men surrounding it. They resisted but it was a triumph for the government. Hundreds of unlicensed firearms, ammunitions, several bombs and knives were uncovered. Many forms of abuses such as the sexual kind, the physical kind and the emotional kind towards members were discovered. The supreme leader with the group's high officials were arrested and charged with such offenses.

Days turned to weeks then months and nothing happened except for the regular activities of the municipal government and the town's people. Mr. Santos was relieved that nobody in the media was relentless in trying to get an interview with him. Even more thankful that nobody from the Charismatic group wanted to pursue him and his family.

Chapter VI

The Philippine school system, specifically the elementary and high school, had the tradition of ending each school year with "closing programs." Every grade or year level had to prepare production numbers in any forms similar to talent shows. Award presentations for student achievers were also part of the program. Irene and Martin were consistent on the honor roll list. Their necks and collars never missed the medals and ribbons.   In that year, Irene got the 1st honors in the third grade while Martin got the honorable mention in the second grade. Mr. and Mrs. Santos attended the program without Roxanne looking after Bart. Everybody had their eyes on Bart as if they were in the presence of a celebrity or a VIP. Bart's presence constantly stirred some topics for conversations.

"You know why Bart turned out to be like that?" An old man asked.

"No, why?" Another old man responded.

"His father is intelligent, his mother is also intelligent, he must have inherited the overflowing genes of intelligence that's why. If a person is too intelligent, he will turn into a lunatic."

"Is that so? I see."

On the other corner, two mothers were conversing.

"I bet Bart had his condition because maybe his mother was taking some sort of medication when she was pregnant with him?"

"I don't know but maybe Bart inherited it from his bloodline."

"That's possible."

A man saw them from a distance thinking.

Maybe his family is cursed, that's why Bart is not normal. Maybe his parents or ancestors did something wrong to others and they had their revenge by putting a curse on them.

Young guys had something to say about Bart also.

"Bart is just mute. He will eventually grow out of it and talk when he becomes a man. Look at Richard, according to his mother, he did not talk when he was young but his brother taught him how to talk and now he talks so well."

"Really?"

The unending speculations went on.

The student achievers' parents were privileged to present their children's awards on stage. Mr. and Mrs. Santos asked some audience members whom they could trust to attend after Bart each time they were needed on stage. He was focused on the presentations with easy sounding music and colorful costumes. Others did not affect him and had his attention on his surroundings. The sounds of a soft drinks opening or the pop of a bag of chips being opened, the sound of a sip through a straw drew his attention. Right after the program, many people gave him chocolates, chips, fruit flavored drinks, cash and many more. Mr. and Mrs. Santos were deeply touched by the gestures everybody demonstrated and thanked as many as they could.

The Santoses went to the only restaurant in town to celebrate Irene and Martin's achievements. Due to the limited selection of dishes offered, Mr. Santos had to reserve menus earlier that day. Everybody enjoyed the meal with Bart.

"Bart, slow down. You will get choked. Chew your food first before swallowing," Mrs. Santos said.

Bart concentrated on his food and kept doing what he did.

"Hey, Bart! You will choke!" Mr. Santos said and got the dishes out of Bart's reach until he completely chewed his food. Bart was screaming and biting his right arm. They finished-up their food, paid the bill, and rapidly got out of the restaurant before things escalated.

"Hey! Hey! Shut-up! Hey. Bart. It was for your own good!" Mr. Santos said.

Bart ran far and back, still screaming and biting his arm. Mr. Santos' head was so red; it was ready to burst at any moment.

He grabbed Bart's arm and dragged him home straight to his room. Mrs. Santos and the kids could hear Bart's scream from the roadway as they were catching up on them. Mr. Santos locked Bart in his room. The deafening screams suddenly stopped and transformed into laughter.

"Can I open the door now dad? I must get something." Martin said.

"It seems that your brother is okay now. Open the lock. Anyway, I want to check on him," Mr. Santos said.

The father and son saw Bart restless and giggling on the bed.

"Dad, what should I do? Or should I ever do something?" Martin asked.

"Just leave him alone," Mr. Santos said.

Bart emerged laughing from the room to take a dump. Martin, who was cleaning his brother's bottom, noticed some blue markings on his nose. Martin checked on him after cleaning his bottom. He was caught sniffing the tip of a blue marker.

"Everybody, come look at Bart in the room!" Martin said.

Everybody was curious on what Martin called them for.

"Oh, my gosh! Bart is getting addicted to the scent of the marker because it is similar to the scent of "rugby," (a popular contact cement brand in the Philippines used as a cheap alternative to get high by sniffing its strong odor), Mrs. Santos said.

Mr. Santos snatched the marker from Bart while he continued laughing and searched the room for any other markers. All were collected and concealed from Bart.

The next few days were burdensome for the Kabayan people. The heat wave was felt earlier than expected. Earlier than the official summer season. Water supplies from faucets became scarcer until the dribble amounted to nothing. They were lucky to have nature's abundance, for it was expected for the river to dry-up, but the water was overflowing as ever. Mrs. Santos decided to wash the clothes with Roxanne and brought the kids with them for their baths. They passed by the privately-owned empty rice storage facility that served as the temporary shelter for the personnel of the engineering and architectural firm hired by the municipal government for a project they were implementing. The personnel had to go to the river because the facility had no water supply and the only utility available was the basic electric light and a few sockets on the wall.

The cool waters served as the heat reliever for many residences. Everybody was enjoying the benefits of the river. A portion of the population was taking a dip. Others were doing their laundry. Others were cleaning their dirty utensils. While fishing activities were seen in many parts of the river. The project personnel went to the river to take a bath and fetch water for household use. They kept on glancing at Bart while he was splashing on the water. Bart enjoyed himself on the shallow part when one of the personnel swam near him. He went screaming so loud the echo made the flock of birds from a nearby tree fly. Mrs. Santos finished her laundry and was about to take a bath when she decided to discontinue and got the washed clothes, then snatched Bart to be sent home, leaving Martin, Irene, and Roxanne.

The man swimming stared at Martin with a long face, wide eyes and an open mouth.

"Why did your brother scream? Is there something wrong?" He asked.

"I don't know but he is a special child," Martin said.

"Oh, I see. Sorry I didn't know," He said.

"Sorry we had no idea about your brother," One of his companions said.

"Yes, and again we apologize," The others told him.

"Kindly tell your mother we had no idea about your brother, and we did not intend to scare him," Another one said.

"No problem, I will tell my mother," Martin said.

Irene and Roxanne had no idea what happened because they were busy washing the rest of the clothes and taking a bath in a separate area of the river.

Veins popped-out from Mrs. Santos' arms and legs as she carried the bucket of wet clothes in one hand while she cradled Bart in the other. She was so pissed; her body was oblivious to the stress of the heavy load she was carrying. She brought Bart inside and hung the clothes to dry. Martin raced home to tell his mother what the personnel told him.

"Mom, the man who swam near Bart did not know that he was a special child and he is sorry. Even his companions told me to inform you that they were so sorry," Martin said.

"I don't believe them. Anyone can see that Bart is a special child. There was something peculiar about him. I don't believe them. Why did the man swim where your brother was at? There were plenty of spaces on the other parts of the river. Stop defending them. I don't believe them. I just don't," Mrs. Santos said.

Bart had ceased screaming while Mrs. Santos and Martin were having a conversation. He shouted words such as "Ahhhh! Apipi! Apiya!" and many others that didn't make any sense at all. He just randomly blurted out words.

Chapter VII

It was Saturday; the day for the Santoses to visit Mr. Tadaka. They always found Mr. Tadaka without any companions on every visit. They were surprised when Mr. Tadaka's niece Matilda was always present on their more recent visits. On the other hand, they were glad somebody was available to take care of him. Mr. Santos felt indifferent to Matilda but never brought it up in conversations, not even to Mr. Tadaka. He observed that Matilda was always keen on what he and Mr. Tadaka discussed. She had no idea that Mr. Santos suspected her of trying to acquire Mr. Tadaka's properties, for he was single and didn't have any direct heirs.

Matilda didn't have the slightest idea that the words "Mr. Santos is the police and he has the power to twist the law," was unintentionally whispered by her during one of the Santoses' visits caught Mr. Santos' ears.

There was no drop of truth in the mistrust and accusations against Mr. Santos. He had the honest-to- goodness intention of helping Mr. Tadaka the best he could. Despite Mr. Tadaka's age and condition, he was able to sense the Santoses' sincerity. Besides, he knew about some of his nephews and nieces' true intentions. During one of the Santoses' visits, he slipped a piece of note in Mrs. Santos' purse when she had to go to the comfort room. It contained very sloppy writings that Mrs. Santos could hardly read. The content was later deciphered with the discovery of an actual will indicating the Santoses as the beneficiaries.

It so happened that Matilda was unavailable with one of the Santoses' visits. The old man pointed out in his letter that Mr. Santos could check the property opposite the public market. In one of his stories, he confessed that Mr. Santos' grandfather, Kibara, was one of the wealthiest men in Kabayan during the Pre-World War II era. He owned vast lands. He possessed most of the animals such as horses, water buffaloes, pigs, cattle, goats and poultry. It measured a man's economic and general status in the community. The wealthier a man was the higher regard he had among all the people. As a tradition, Mr. Santos' grandfather was automatically the "pangudo" or leader of half of Kabayan as a wealthy individual. Women in the era had little to no human rights, and were considered men's property. The poor worked their entire life as slaves for the rich. Mr. Kibara was different from the rest of the wealthy. He was kind and non-abusive to his wife and slaves. In fact, he donated many of his properties to poor relatives, close friends and most of his loyal slaves. Mr. Tadaka explained that he was just paying the kindness of Mr. Santos' grandfather as one of the property beneficiaries.

"I heard that you still don't have your own place. I want you and your family to have a property you can call your own. It is even ideal for the construction of your very own house if ever you decide to build one," Mr. Tadaka said.

"Thank you for the offer. And again, I'm really flattered for choosing me and my family to be the recipient of one of your properties," Mr. Santos said.

"You really deserve that lot because you are one of the direct descendants of Kibara," Mr. Tadaka said.

"Your grandfather was so selfless. He forgot to reserve some for his direct descendants and you are a deserving one," he added.

Mr. Santos was in a dilemma. He wanted to honor Mr. Takada's wishes as a sign of respect. On the other hand, he was worried about stirring the situation. *I want my family to have a place of their own, a roof above their head but if I will accept the offer. Mr. Tadaka's nieces and nephews will think they were right all along.* Mr. Santos told himself.

I also want my kids, especially Bart, to have an area wide enough to play at than where we are currently living in, he added.

Mr. Santos took his family to Baguio City since it was the kid's school vacation. He wanted them to enjoy the city and for him to visit his mother and sister before making the final decision on Mr. Tadaka's offer. Irene and Martin were very excited about it and informed as many of their peers as possible. Bart hadn't embarked on a long trip for more than nine years, which worried Mrs. Santos. He got so sick and vomited blood the last time he traveled a long distance.

Mrs. Santos prepared an emergency kit with tissues, plastic bags, drinking water and readily available extra clothes in case Bart got sick on the way. A single bus company and licensed "jeepneys" (Vehicles that originated from the World War 2 military willys jeep which were modified with longer body and roofing at the back.) were the public transport going to and from the city with some free rides mainly elf tracks and privately owned "jeepneys' ' utilized for delivering vegetable and fruit produce. Johnny, Mr. Santos' nephew, owned one of those licensed "jeepneys' ' for public transport. The Santoses were about to take the bus but decided to ride on Johnny's "jeepney" without any special favor and pay the regular fare rate just like regular passengers. They instinctively chose him because they wanted to help him with his source of income. They were also very optimistic that Johnny would be extra careful with his driving knowing Bart was one of his passengers. It was generally a safe trip with the usual stopovers in between. The trip only encountered an unexpected interruption when Bart had to go for a dump on the side of the road covered by the presence of the bushes.

The Santoses stayed in the hotel where Mr. Santos always checked in every time he went to the city. Almost every employee knew him, including the owner. On the same day of arrival, Mr. Santos had to leave his family to take care of some business. He went to the Government Insurance office to check on the status of his loan application. The loan was approved, but he was required to return the next day to complete the paperwork. He returned to the hotel to a sleeping family and joined in to rest.

The check was issued but he found out that the only approved amount was half of what he requested. It was not enough for a down payment for the lot and to start the house construction.   He borrowed from his business people and government contractors friends to augment his loan. His friend never applied the regular interest rate because they had "utang na loob." (A Filipino tradition when a person did a favor to someone, then that someone is obliged to return the favor at any time and any form he could.)

"Let's go. Everybody wake-up and prepare. We will visit your Aunt Fecora and your cousins. She will come to fetch us to their apartment," Mr. Santos said.

"Dad, but we still did not have our breakfast yet," Irene said.

"Don't worry. There is a bakery near the hotel. We could buy "pandesal", (A Filipino bun that is usually consumed with butter or margarine for breakfast.) I also ordered some pancit from the hotel's restaurant ready for pick-up on our way out," Mr. Santos said.

Irene and Martin were so excited that they raced to the C.R. Mrs. Fecora was waiting at the front desk area when the Santoses were going down the stairs. Smiles were painted on their face when they saw each other for the first time in a long time. Irene and Martin could hardly recognize their Aunt Fecora and just stared at her face. Mr. Santos introduced their Aunt to them for that very reason. Mr. Santos assumed they had to ride public transport but Mrs. Fecora told him that their apartment was just a few blocks from the hotel. She led them to their apartment where her husband, Francesco, and children, Thea and Norman were present. Thea was about six years old and Norman was five. Bart stared at his cousins without saying a single word. They were staring back at him with expressions that could not be described on their faces.

"Hello, cousins. You tell them," Aunt Fecora said.

"Hello, Thea. Hello Norman," she added while smiling at Bart.

Mr. Santos handed over the food to Roxanne and prepared the dining table for breakfast.

"How's Kabayan?" Aunt Fecora said while everybody was enjoying their meal.

"Well, it's great. It is a relaxing rural way of living if you are into that sort of thing and most of the people there are related to us," Mr. Santos said.

"How are the kids holding on?" Aunt Fecora said.

"They enjoy the fresh air and calm environment. Plus, our expenses are low because many of our relatives shared their produce with us. We learned how to fish and gather wild edible plants and gather some snails, freshwater shrimps and crabs. What we have to buy are just rice, cooking oil, sugar, and salt only. Besides, the only bill we pay is the electricity because water is free of charge," Mr. Santos said.

"Oh, rural life must be great. Unlike here in the city, almost all the needs are with price tags. Only the air that we breathe is free, and yet, it is full of pollution," Mrs. Fecora said.

"We recently visited a nice beach with clean, and clear water and with few people visiting the area. Maybe the kids would enjoy swimming," Mr. Francesco said.

"That's a great idea because the kids have never been to the beach". Mr. Santos said.

"Me also, I never experienced the beach." Mrs. Santos said.

"Really? I thought you have seen the beach in your lifetime, Mommy," Mr. Santos said.

"I've seen several before from afar but I never swam on the actual water," Mrs. Santos said.

"Okay, since you are all here in the city, why won't we plan it now and go tomorrow if possible or the day after tomorrow," Mr. Francesco said.

"You can check-out anytime and stay here for the rest of your vacation. Anyway, we have a space in the second room. The kids can sleep with us. That way, you can pay less for the hotel fees and save," Mrs. Fecora said.

"That's a great Idea," Mr. Francesco said.

All of a sudden, the apartment smelled like a dump site that prompted everybody to open the door and windows.

"Bart is taking a dump," Roxanne said.

"It's like toxic gas, chemical weapon of mass destruction he! He! He!" Mrs. Fecora said.

"Sorry for this. Are you still sure you want us to stay? Because this could happen again," Mrs. Santos said.

Mr. Francesco smiled and said, "No problem. Don't ever worry about it. We understand."

After taking a dump, Bart was running back and forth to the living room and the kitchen uttering unintelligible words being his usual self. Then he kissed his uncle and aunt. He again ran towards the kitchen and stopped when his cousin Thea came out from the master bedroom. He stared at her and gave her a kiss. Everybody smiled in awe when they saw Bart's action.

The hotel measured the guest's stay through the twelve-p.m. mark. If the guest checks out past twelve then an additional day will be credited to his or her bill. Mr. and Mrs. Santos sprinted to the hotel to avoid any possible additional charge that would be incurred for checking out past the twelve-p.m. mark. They were in the hotel at ten-minute past twelve. They were so glad the hotel only considered a single day of stay.

Chapter VIII

Some relatives in the city were invited to join the excursion. They started from the cool weather of the highlands going, downhill to the warm lowlands where beautiful beaches can be found.

They hired a "jeepney", which was ill-equipped for warm weather since it did not have an air conditioning system.   Bart was screaming with obvious discomfort as his shirt was soaked with his own sweat.

"Bart! Bart! We are now near. Don't worry; you will quench the heat you are feeling in the water. There will be unlimited cool waters," Mrs. Santos said.

Roxanne and some relatives stripped him leaving only his underwear and a towel nearby to constantly wipe his sweat. They had to make a stopover at the "Bauang" Public Market. It was the market near their destination where they bought supplies such as Seafood, lowland vegetables, lowland fruits, rice cakes, and species. Bart was still uneasy and the ones left in the vehicle gave him plenty of ice-cold water and restrained him from going out naked.

They were finally welcomed by endless water, and a cool breeze brought from waves hitting the sand. They rented a shed where they could put their belongings and a place to cook. Everybody was busy with the kids enjoying the water. Bart went straight to the water from the "jeepney" without any company. Irene and Martin tried to pull him out of the water but with his massive size and brute strength, he brushed them away.

"Go after Bart. Accompany him please," Mrs. Santos said.

"Go Roxanne. Anybody go," Aunt Fecora said.

Bart was submerged in water faster than the blink of an eye. It was due to his sumo wrestler-like size and weight aggravated by his lack of swimming skills. Roxanne had difficulty bringing him out of the water; instead, it was Bart dragging them into the depths. Mr. Santos and a relative bolted the second they saw them. They pulled Bart and Roxanne, but Bart insisted on returning to the water.

A man going around the beach holding a "salbabida" (A recycled car wheel's interior used as a floating device.) shouting: "Salbabida" for rent! Get your "salbabida" here!"

Mr. Santos rented three of the "salbabidas" in different sizes. He allowed Bart to go to the water provided he had the largest "salbabida" with him. One or two of them took turns looking after him while floating. He enjoyed it so much that he had to be forced out of the water during meal time. His loud laughter, refusal to get out of the water, and enjoyment of the waves caught the attention of other beach-goers. Most of them had their attention on Bart, while a few enjoyed the beach without being bothered by his presence. It was an unforgettable experience for Irene and Martin, for it was their first time experiencing the beach. They took the opportunity to enjoy the moment the best they could.

Nobody expected what would happen when it was time to return to Baguio. Everybody was busy; some were taking showers in the public C.R. while others kept the left-overs and used utensils. Roxanne bathed Bart, dressed him up, and led him into the "jeepney" for her to take a shower. Suddenly, a commotion was heard.

"Bart! Where is Bart?" The driver yelled.

Roxanne heard the driver and went looking for him. She saw him in the water with his clothes still on.

"Bart, come! Bart, Come! We will go home, Come!" She said.

Bart was enjoying the water as he did a few minutes prior. Roxanne asked for help from the driver to pull Bart out of the water. There were no available dry clothes for Bart to wear. The only option was the bath towel wrapped around his waist to cover his private parts. Everybody was trying to spot a store where they could buy clothes that fit Bart on their way to Baguio. They saw a souvenir shop selling t-shirts, shorts, swimming trunks, and bathing suits. The only available that could fit Bart was a sleeveless shirt, and a swimming trunk. He resembled a child opening a present for the first time while wearing his new outfit. He was also giggling and shouting during the trip. Later, he fell asleep but woke up again when they had to stop for fuel. He charged like a raging bull to the gas station convenience store to avoid being blocked when getting some chocolates. He ate like a bear and never paid attention to those trying to slow him down. Some of the chocolates were hidden because it was too much for him. He was so full he fell asleep throughout the rest of the trip.

The following day was haircut day. Mr. and Mrs. Santos decided to have their haircut done in a hair salon and barbershop with their kids. The kids were getting their haircuts from friends and relatives using combs and pairs of scissors only in Kabayan. Mr. and Mrs. Santos wanted their kids to experience being attended to by professional hairdressers and barbers.

"Ahhhhh! Ahhhh!" Bart was shouting as the electric clipper was touching the back of his head.

"Sorry. This son of mine is a special one. How can I help?" Mr. Santos asked.

"Sir, kindly hold your son's head like this so I can finish cutting his hair and get over with it," the barber said.

Bart went on screaming and moving in his chair that other employees had to restrain him. The Barber did not continue with the straight razor anymore for fear of cutting him. Bart was still shouting after his haircut. He only stopped when he was given chocolate. Mrs. Santos and Irene had to wait a while for the chemical to set in their hairs for a few minutes. The men were done earlier than Mrs. Santos and Irene. They had to leave ahead because of Bart. Besides, they badly needed baths due to the accumulated hair fibers that irritated their skins.

Mr. Santos and his sons were getting out of the taxi cab when a man with grayish hair wearing glasses was staring at them.

Mr. Santos saw him but didn't pay much attention. He let his sons move along the apartment and anticipated what the man would do next.

"Hello brother," he said.

"Hi? I guess?" Mr. Santos said.

"Sorry for staring at you and your kids. I was just reserving a bus ticket when I saw one of your sons, the chubby one. His behavior picked my interest, and that's when I realized he must be a person with special needs. You know what I mean. And was he ever seen by a specialist?" The man said.

"We tried but there were no specialists for his condition," Mr. Santos said.

Mrs. Santos and Irene were on foot as they approached Mr. Santos with the man he was talking to. Irene went to the apartment while Mrs. Santos was curious enough to join in with their conversation.

"Dad, who is he?" Mrs. Santos asked

"Just a man who approached me and I am finding it out myself," Mr. Santos said.

"Sorry, I did not introduce myself first. I am Father Bert of the Brotherhood of St. Bernard. We are a Catholic charitable institution that helps underprivileged children and those with special needs. We have training facilities with competent trainers, teachers, and staff that can help your boy. Here is the address and number that you can contact. Hope to see you soon.

Sorry, I must go, and God Bless," he said as he walked away.

Chapter IX

On the Saturday morning of the following week, Mr. Santos was sipping his coffee in their front yard, having second thoughts on whether to accept Mr. Tadakas's offer. He imagined any possible scenario. Maybe those after his possessions would bring the issue to court? *Or would they will seek revenge on him and his family? What will happen to his career as the police chief? There must be a better way to resolve the matter.*

He tried to find other properties available for sale within the town center of Kabayan. It was so difficult for him to purchase a property at a fair price. All of the sellers asked for an overpriced selling rate, assuming that he was "Bill Gates rich" for being the police chief. He even tried to negotiate but none of them budged. With his desire for his family to have a place of their own, he finally decided to focus on the property offered by Mr. Tadaka and started the transfer process. He tried to approach the other claimants for a fair settlement, but they refused. A few close relatives of Mr. Tadaka did not contest Mr. Santos' property acquisition. They even expressed their shame of not taking good care of Mr. Tadaka. They only have limited amounts of time to visit him and usually left him to fend for himself.

"Who the hell do you think you are meddling with our family business?" A nephew claimant asked.

"You think you can just outsmart us because you are the Chief and we are just nobodies?" A niece claimant asked.

They kept berating Mr. Santos with such words without listening to his explanations. Mr. Santos was sick and tired of their persistent attitude on the matter. He disregarded them and went on with the finalization of the transfer. He planted in his mind that the property was not free and had to pay for it in due time.

Mr. Santos made a request to the Engineering and Architectural firm hired by the municipal government if they could take a side project. One requirement of the government for the issuance of a building permit was the approved building plan by a licensed architect. Some of the firm's personnel were scheduled to inspect both the project and the actual site. He started the construction with the help of the firm and friends from the municipality's permit division.

Everybody was eager to work for the Santoses. Several of them were expecting higher pay than the standard rate of a construction worker due to their irreparable notion that the Santos Family was made out of money. The surprising part was their close relatives were willing to work with less to no pay at all. They were the ones who cared for the completion of the Santoses' house. Mrs. Santos' father Baltimore used to work in the construction industry. He appealed to his friends who had construction businesses to grant his son-in-law some discount. Mr. Santos selected the workers according to their skills and willingness to do overtime if needed. He treated them all as regular workers with the standard rate of wages applied. No exception, even those who were willing to work for free were included. The lot was cleared, and the workers dug some holes for the foundation. Trucks of construction supplies were coming in. Mr. Baltimore pulled some strings for a permit from the Department of Natural Resources to transport the lumbers needed for the construction.

The construction became the center of attention. Many speculations were rising. The entire municipality was divided. One side believed that the property was systematically taken from Mr. Tadaka. The opposite side believed that the property was acquired with Mr. Tadaka's blessing.

Bart suddenly appeared on the construction site without any warning. Everybody was puzzled by his mere presence. They expected any of the Santoses to follow while one worker was watching over him. They opted to bring him home when nobody came after a few minutes had passed. Bart and his companion met Roxanne on their way.

"Thank you! Thank you!" Roxanne said.

"No problem," the worker who accompanied Bart said, coupled with a nice smile.

"Anyway, I am Mark," he added.

"Roxanne, that's my name, I'm Roxanne," she said.

"Nice meeting you," Mark said.

"Me too. Nice to see you," Roxanne said.

"I must go back to work," Mark said.

The two went the opposite direction with Roxanne holding Bart's hand. She glanced a bit on Mark's way, and her cheeks turned rosy red when Mark glanced back at her. She almost lost Bart again but she was lucky he ran straight to the house and nowhere else.

The Santoses heard noises within the vicinity of their residence that very same night. Mrs. Santos turned the lights on to see what was going on but Mr. Santos woke, turned-off the lights and prevented her from turning it on again. Instead, he peeked through the window without giving away their presence.

"Go and check on the kids without making any sound. Make sure they are asleep. Let's all pretend that nobody is awakened by the noise," Mr. Santos Said.

"Bullshit! God damn it! You land grabber! Pete (Mr. Santos), who do you think you are? We are not afraid of you. No police officer to us. We are ready to face you anytime!" It was heard from somebody who sounded like he was intoxicated.

Mr. Santos peeked again to identify who they were but it was dark. In his subsequent attempt, he saw two drunken men. He saw the pastel-colored jacket worn by one of them as he moved towards the moonlight. He tried to check on his companion but he was masked by the darkness of the night as they faded to the distance.

"Oh, you're here honey, you're already here. Who are they?" Mrs. Santos asked.

"Nobody, they are just a bunch of drunken men," Mr. Santos said.

"Okay then. Are you sure they are not a threat?" Mrs. Santos asked.

"I am sure. It was nothing. They are gone, and let's go back to bed," Mr. Santos said.

The Santoses eventually had their peace, and quiet and went back to sleep.

Roxanne woke early for her usual work routine. She fried "piskaw" (salted dried fish) and some hard-boiled eggs for breakfast.

"Uncle, who were those rowdy guys last night?" Roxanne asked.

"I have no idea. Maybe some random guys who didn't know how to drink? Putting alcohol to their heads instead of their stomachs. That's the extent of what I know," Mr. Santos said.

"Thank God, they went away because I was worried about our safety," Roxanne said.

"Yes, thank God. I am also thankful that nobody was hurt not only on our side, but them while they were in our vicinity," Mr. Santos said.

Mr. Santos confessed to Mrs. Santos that he had a glimpse of the guys. He recognized the jacket and the partial facial features of one of them. Unfortunately, he didn't have a clear identification of the other guy.

"I strongly believe that the guys yesterday are Mr. Tadaka's nephews and if someone asked about what happened last night, tell them they were just random drunk guys whom you didn't know about," Mr. Santos said.

"Why what's the problem?" Mrs. Santos said.

"Just say what I instructed you to answer, until I am positive," Mr. Santos said.

"Okay, I understand," Mrs. Santos said.

The old Filipino saying stating, "May pakpak ang balita at may tainga ang lupa", which literally translates to "The news has wings, and the land has ears," was true for everybody who knew about the incident about the two guys being rowdy during a night in the Santos' frontage. The Santoses were constantly asked about it. Untrue rumors about it were circulating. The kids weren't aware but became curious when they heard the unending questions and rumors being thrown around. Mr. and Mrs. Santos gave the same answers over and over again in an attempt to shut the relentless mouths up, but it was the opposite. They became the topic of the municipality's gossip mills.

The progress of the house construction moved smoothly with only minor problems encountered. The people blocked any attempts by the opposition to stop the construction. It did not matter which side of the rumor they believed in. They respected Mr. Santos' authority as the police chief. Their care for Bart amplified their support for the Santoses. The Santoses' busy schedule was never a hindrance from visiting Mr. Tadaka.

"I received the information that you have already started the house construction and I am happy for you," Mr. Tadaka said.

Yes, uncle. And again, thank you for the lot! Maria is here," Mr. Santos said.

"I just came to check on my uncle. I wish I could stay but I am sorry I won't be long. Its harvest season and it's the only time I can work on anybody's vegetable garden. We have to work to eat," Maria said.

"I understand, Maria. You have to do what must be done. And anyway, take this small amount for your kids," Mr. Santos said.

"No sir, I can't possibly accept that. It is shameful on my part," Maria Said.

"Just take it. I insist," Mr. Santos said.

"Okay, thanks again, sir," Maria said.

"Uncle, here is a down payment for the property," Mr. Santos said.

"And Maria, before you leave, kindly sign this paper as a witness," He added.

"You don't have to do this. I am awarding you the lot for free. It is your right," Mr. Tadaka said.

"Uncle, I already have the receipt I signed. I even let Maria sign as a witness. Here I am showing the payment, and give it to you through Maria if you refuse to receive it. Besides, you need it for your basic needs and for your check-up. I will arrange for the dispensary to schedule you for the full check-up," Mr. Santos said.

"After all, you still thought of my welfare. Okay then but the down payment is enough. You don't have to add any more," Mr. Tadaka said.

 "Sorry I have to go and give the workers their week's salary. Goodbye for now," Mr. Santos said as he saw Mr. Tadaka affixing his signature on the receipt.

Chapter X

The house construction was completed in more than two months. Friends and relatives from near and far were welcomed to attend the house blessing without formal invitations. It was a custom not only in Kabayan but the entire archipelago of the Philippines to welcome everybody on special occasions without formal invitations. The combination of Christian and "Igorot" styles of blessing was applied. The United Church of the Philippines pastor facilitated the service and house blessing. The "mambunong" (The "Igorot" medicine man or high priest) did his ritual. The Santoses were Christians but also respected the tradition of their "Igorot" heritage. Pigs were mostly butchered in typical "Igorot" occasions. The animal was killed by directly stabbing its heart with a pointed wooden stick. It was animal cruelty for other cultures, but it was how the "Igorots" butchered animals since the dawn of time. Loud squeals were heard all over the place of celebration when the pointed part of the stick was trusted directly to the heart creating a deep puncture wound until the animal stopped squealing. The animal carcass was burned and the skin scraped to remove the hairs then the belly was cut open to reveal the internal organs as the "mambunong" inspected the liver that determined whether the butchered animal brought a good or bad omen. The blood and viscera were collected as essential ingredients for the "dinardaraan" dish (blood stew). The rest was cut into large chunks and boiled without any spices, not even salt. The simple dish called "Bat-bat" in the "Igorot" tradition was ceremoniously distributed to individuals in attendance as a sign of abundance.

The Christian service inside the house started after the pig's noise was over. Prayers were performed. Christian songs and hymns were sung. The pastor preached with the theme related to house blessings, and the physical splashing of holy water in every corner of the house was performed. Bart woke from his sleep in one of the rooms on the second floor when he felt the splashing of the holy water.

"Sorry, my boy. Go back to sleep," the pastor said.

The Santoses persuaded Bart to go back to sleep, but he woke and went to the kitchen in search of something to eat. He had his meal first before the pastor gave his blessing on the food. He then went and sat among the men who were having their drinking sessions.

"Hey! Why are you here? Do you want a drink?" One of the drunken men said.

"Shot!" The other one said.

Bart just looked at them and did nothing. The drinking men laughed. Roxanne came out to bring him inside and sent him to the room where he slept.

Mr. Tadaka went to the celebration later that afternoon accompanied by Maria. Everybody invited him inside and served them a hearty meal in the kitchen. He stayed and chatted with Mrs. Fecora whom he met for the first time. Mrs. Fecora introduced her family and Mr. Tadaka was glad to meet them. He also had conversations with other relatives and friends.

The celebration continued until dark. Maybe, it should have ended earlier. Maybe, the enjoyment was too much. Maybe, everybody should have gone home. A loud thud was heard from the group of drunken men outside. The people inside were so relieved that the fallen one did not incur any serious injury since he fell on the soft part of the ground.

His companions tried to carry him inside but their strength and balance were affected by too much drinking. The fallen one was dragged inside and slept on the living room floor.

Mark spent his days in the Santos residence even after the house construction and blessing. The Santoses were not bothered by his frequent stay because he was a relative. They speculated that he just liked hanging out there during his free time. They had no idea about Mark and Roxanne's secret affair.

Mark and Roxanne did a great job of hiding it. Nobody was suspicious enough to see the signs right in front of them. It was months later until their secret was unraveled.

"Let me ask you straight and I want an honest answer," Mr. Santos said.

"Yes, Uncle," Roxanne said.

"You and Mark?" Mr. Santos asked.

"What do you mean uncle?" Roxanne asked.

"Yes, you and Mark, you two have a relationship," Don't deny. Everybody knows," Mr. Santos Said.

"Yes, Uncle. And it's been going on for months now," Roxanne said.

"Why did the two of you hide your relationship from us?" Mr. Santos asked.

"We feared that you and Auntie would get angry. Me being Auntie's niece and Mark being your cousin," Roxanne said.

"Why would we? Why do we have to get angry in a normal healthy relationship? For as long as the two of you are single. It's no problem with us," Mr. Santos said.

"You must also tell your Aunt," he added.

"Yes, Uncle, thank you very much," Roxanne said.

Roxanne and Mark wanted to separate and build their family life. Mrs. Santos appealed to them if they could stay more until they could locate Roxanne's substitute. Besides, the couple's finances were not ready for family life yet.

The frustrations of the claimants grew when they found out that they didn't have any legal authority to acquire the property. They wanted to seek revenge one way or the other. They could not apply intimidation to the Santoses because of Mr. Santos' position in the community. They tried to spread false negative rumors, but nobody believed them. They tried to brainwash the children and took their frustrations on Bart, but it backfired on them. The people's hatred of them deepened especially when they involved the children in their clash with Mr. Santos. They were the ones who became the town's topic in a very bad light. In fact, their ancestry was not purely from Kabayan. One of their parents was originally from other municipality or province. Several of them opted to migrate to one of their parents' place of origin. Mr. Santos kept his promise and paid the rest of what he owed to Mr. Tadaka through Maria.

The claimants who stayed refused to reconcile with the Santoses even the fact that they were willing to compromise. The claimants insisted that they were on the right side of the issue. They avoided the Santoses and everyone who was associated with them. The ever-insistent claimants never attended any occasions where the Santoses were present.

One of the claimant's daughters suffered a debilitating illness. The dispensary had no equipment and specialists capable of addressing the problem. She had to be rushed to the city for complete treatment. Mr. Santos risked his position as the chief of police and asked a politician whom he knew from the city to give the family any help they needed. He even pleaded with a doctor friend to accept the patient with a discount. The mother, as one of the claimants, refused Mr. Santos' help even though they could not afford to send their daughter for treatment without Mr. Santos' influence. Her pride was more important than her daughter's life. Her husband was the opposite. He gladly accepted Mr. Santos' help for his daughter's sake ignoring his wife's decision.

The treatment was successful without any complications. Friends and relatives of the patient were very thankful for what Mr. Santos did for them. Despite what happened, the hardheaded mother still did not consider reconciling with the Santoses.

Chapter XI

Everything was moving. The disturbance was all around. People were losing their minds. The air was filled with echoes of screams and cries. Mr. Santos rushed home, concerned about his family's safety. Roxanne scrambled to the room Bart was sleeping in. She could not open the door instantly, for it was locked from the inside. She banged the door, but was masked by the shaking of the surroundings. She tried to fit the right key from the bunch, but continues ground tremors attacked her attempts. The door was finally unlocked after several tries. She saw Bart asleep and didn't seem to be bothered as he was swayed on the bed like a baby on a cradle. Roxanne was about to get him out when Mr. Santos came to check on them. Bart was carried on the street where the whole town gathered. Mr. Santos tried to wake Bart and forced him to stand if he could. Bart was awake but still groggy unaware of what was happening. The tremors eventually stopped.

"Dear Lord, I pray that you make our town safe."

"Please Lord, don't allow us to die in vain."

"Lord please let this be the one and only earthquake that we ever feel."

"Amazing grace how sweet thy sound..."

"Oh! My! This is the end of the world."

"This is the time."

"We will all die."

Words, cries, prayers and worries of impending doom were spoken with the humming of some gospel and Christian songs.

Bart was still oblivious to his surroundings. He ran to the store to get some of his beloved chocolates when he had the chance. The store owner never charged him as Mr. Santos grabbed the megaphone and went to the center of the crowd.

"As your police chief, I am requesting every single one of you, so please don't take advantage of the situation. For the business owners, don't increase your prices especially on the basic commodities. I took it upon myself to tell my men to arrest anyone who will violate my order. If anyone is still hard headed and doesn't want to cooperate, then I will lock them up. I don't care who. Hope you all understand and hope I will not be forced to imprison anyone for the reason mentioned," Mr. Santos announced without the Mayor's permission.

"And please. Let's put our differences aside and start helping one another as a society in this time of crisis," he added.

The town's component system with enormous speakers was brought out and blasted. The crowd calmed down in silence as they listened to what was happening on the news. The Mayor requested abled men to prepare the school ground, and the multi-purpose hall to be the evacuation centers. The police were ordered to check each household if they needed any assistance. There was no official fire department, and rescue groups, so the police department, some elected officials, and volunteers were assigned to the rescue and rehabilitation activities. Health workers, some municipal employees, and volunteers helped with the daily operations of the evacuation center.

The municipal hall had a radio room equipped with the only existing radio communicator in Kabayan. Mr. Santos requested the sole operator to keep the radio communication open and connected to other radio communicators as much as possible. He wanted to relay to whoever was on the other line what their real situation was.

Mrs. Santos was in the city when the earth was shaken. She attended a seminar held in a hotel complete with accommodation for those like her who were from faraway places. She was in the hotel's function hall listening to the lecture when the trembling of the surroundings came. The lecturer went under the table which was one of the ideal actions done during earthquakes. The participants were racing towards the exit which was a terrible idea. Many were injured not because of the earth's shaking but by the chaotic exit.   Mrs. Santos was never injured thanks to her refusal to join the swarm of people headed for the exit. She was kin on listening to the announcements but did not comprehend the message due to the rowdy crowd. Mrs. Santos went to Mrs. Fecora's place right after the first shock.

"Hello, is everybody home?" Mrs. Santos asked.

Nobody seems to be home? Where could they be? I hope they are okay. She wondered.

A young man was rushing towards the apartment asking if she had seen the family living there.

"No I didn't. I am also searching for them, and anyway who are you? I am Mrs. Santos Fecora's sister-in-law. I am married to her older brother," She said.

"Auntie, I am Relly, I am Uncle Francesco's nephew, and where could they be?"

"They didn't even lock the door. What if somebody would come in, and steal something?" Mrs. Santos said.

"Auntie, you are right," Relly said.

They were startled when Mr. Francesco suddenly appeared catching his breaths.

"Where have you been, Uncle? And where is everybody?" Relly said.

"They evacuated us to the convention center while others were in the school beside it. I came here just to get some clothes, food and to check the apartment because I might have forgotten to lock it," Mr. Francesco said.

"Yes, Uncle. It was open when we arrived," Relly said.

"It is good we are here before anything would be stolen," Mrs. Santos said.

They helped Mr. Francesco packed and brought essentials to the evacuation center. Mrs. Santos was determined to go home to Kabayan even with the threats of aftershocks. She wanted to be with her family. She wanted to be with her son Bart, to ensure that he was okay. She went to the Kabayan bus station to inquire if the road was passable by means of land transportation. It was unfortunate for the bus company to receive a warning from the government that it was risky to be traveling because of the possibility of aftershocks and landslides that could trigger falling rocks. Besides, there were portions of the road that were impassable by vehicle. Few spectators were also desperate to go home. One of them was Mr. Tadaka's nephew, one of the claimants.

"I will not let this stop me. I will go home whatever it takes. I want to be with Bart," Mrs. Santos said.

"Hey listen, if any of you are also going home, then we must travel by foot. We have no choice as the bus company said; the road condition is not good for any transportation. It is better for us to travel as a group than to travel individually. Join me if any of you are willing," she added.

Two ladies and a middle-aged guy expressed their interest in going home. Mr. Tadaka's nephew was reluctant to join in. Time did not repair his animosity towards the Santoses. He attempted to form another traveling group but nobody was willing to travel with him. He was forced later to travel with Mrs. Santos' group than to be traveling alone. They agreed to meet at the bus station that afternoon. Mrs. Santos went back to the hotel to get ready and packed her things and some necessities such as food and water. She left some of her luggage in her hotel room and got what she could only carry. She accelerated thinking of anybody waiting but she was the first one to arrive in the meeting place. She waited in an open eatery next to the bus company's ticketing both. The group was completed as all of those who agreed with the arrangement arrived individually. An elderly man who appeared to be the eatery's owner showed up and approached Mrs. Santos then started a conversation.

"Hello, are you here to eat? Because we are not actually open. I came to assess the building if there are any damages," the elderly man said.

"I am sorry sir, I am just waiting for my companions to come and I have no place to sit," Mrs. Santos said.

"I will leave if you want me to," she added.

"No, it's okay. No problem," the elderly man said.

"Where are you heading? Because I believe there are no public transportations available for now. In this situation," he added.

"We are hiking to Kabayan," Mrs. Santos said.

"Kabayan you say? I have a son in the police force that had a classmate in the academy who is actually from Kabayan. What was his name uhhh... Pete, yes, I remember him because he used to sleep in our place during their breaks from the academy. Anyway, I am Richard Lee. The son I was talking about is Adam Lee."

"Really? Pete is my husband. I am Mrs. Trisha Santos. Nice to meet you."

"Nice to meet you too and you were saying that you are going home on foot? I believe Kabayan is far from here. The last time I was there was in 1969 doing business," Mr. Lee said.

I have to go home because I have to be with my family in these times of crisis. Besides, I can't stay in the city any longer. Kabayan is my home," Mrs. Santos said.

Mrs. Santos and the group were ready for the long journey when Mr. Lee gave them cookies and tetra packed fruit juices. They tried to refuse politely, but he insisted on his offer. He also offered to let them stay for a bit longer because he had leftover rice and instant noodles that he could cook for a few minutes but the group declined and explained to him that they must really be going. He told Mrs. Santos to give his regards to her husband. They all thanked him, said their goodbyes and started walking. Along their journey, the sky became gloomy and a loud thud was heard. The group assumed that a roaring thunder produced the loud sound. They looked at the skies but nothing. They pressed on, and boulders came tumbling down from the mountain slopes. Tadaka's nephew was ahead but returned to help their companion, who was trying to move fast but was slowed down by the attack of gouty arthritis on his left ankle. They were inches away from being crushed by the boulders, but they moved to safety thanks to the quickness of Takada's nephew who pulled the gouty man from danger. They moved on for a few kilometers when they reached the portion that was closed for both vehicles and by foot. They had to pass through the high mountain without the presence of recognizable trails. They crossed a river and encountered another impassable portion of the road. They came across the kindness of some residents who welcomed them. They rested their feet and had their refreshments in a resident's place for a few minutes to an hour or so before carrying on. They had their goodnight's rest at some of Mrs. Santos' relatives and friends along the way. The trip lasted for about three days before finally arriving home in Kabayan.

Chapter XII

The affected municipalities had begun the road reconstructions when there were fewer aftershocks. Mrs. Santos and her companions were thrilled to arrive in their respective houses when they could already see the town center. Their excitement gave them boosts of energy to move faster as if their bodies were still fresh after days of hiking. They didn't mind passing through a landslide prone area of the road. Their only focus was about going home. The clearance team with heavy equipment was their temporary hindrance. Everybody could not wait and risked their safety passing through the site. Some of them went ahead through the rice fields below. Mrs. Santos and the gouty guy waited for the personnel to clear the road before passing.

As a mother, Mrs. Santos' instinct was to check on her children, especially Bart. The first thing she did was to give Bart a tight hug with tears wetting her face. He escaped her grasp and rushed to the CR expelling loud chunks of solid gasses.

Mrs. Santos burst out with laughter with the words, "What a great timing!"

A long cool bath washed away Mrs. Santos' exhaustion and worries. She became relaxed while embracing her two-other children with motherly love.

Mr. Santos was not available to welcome her back home for he was the "eyes, ears and mouth" of the entire crisis operation. He was very particular with the "ins and outs" of the supplies. He ordered the personnel in charge of the supplies never to allow anybody to access the supply room without her supervision. They can't afford another "headache" to branch-out in times of uncertainty. Unfortunately, some rotten volunteers were blended with the well-intended ones. It was discovered that the record did not match the actual number of the supplies. Mr.

Santos made an unexpected announcement in the distribution area. When the records were confirmed, and perpetrators confessed, he divulged the information to the public of what happened and was not deterred from mentioning the suspected participants of the anomaly. The people were rumbling screamed with passion that the perpetrators must be punished. He invited the perpetrators to the precinct but due to the circumstance, he released them with the condition of signing promissory notes and was disallowed from participating in any activities of the evacuation center. He was ready for any retaliation but no actions were executed by the perpetrators.

There was still no electricity for weeks after the initial onset of the earthquake. Mrs. Santos asked Roxanne to buy a box of matches. She returned with a different kind from what they used. It was a different brand with inferior quality. Mrs. Santos had to buy another box of matches when she passed a store in the market. The seller was so busy with his customers that it slipped his mind to hide the "Not for Sale for Relief Purposes Only" and "Donated by U.S. AID" label on the main box of the matches he was selling. Many had already noticed the labeled product for sale when the owner tried to cover it after realizing his mistake.

"Why are you selling relief goods?" Mrs. Santos asked.

"No madam, I am not selling relief items. Those are just boxes for recycling. It is made of a strong material," the salesman said.

"I swear you are selling relief goods. I saw you trying to hide it. It's too late to hide your wrongdoing," Mrs. Santos said.

"You can't deny it. I saw it too. Those should have been distributed to the people for free," Another customer said.

Mrs. Santos did not argue further and left. She later told her husband what she discovered. They both were against the store owner's actions.

"Imagine what they are willing to do for profit?" Mrs. Santos said.

"Yes, I totally agree. I wish I could do something or execute them right away but we must focus on the more important things that must be done to rehabilitate the community," Mr. Santos said.

"Let God reign upon them. They will reap what they sow someday. I am sure about it," Mrs. Santos Said.

Help from allied countries such as the United States continued to flow in. Relief goods and other essentials were transported through military helicopters. A handful of Kabayan locals took advantage of the presence of the air transport for traveling to the city of Baguio that did not ring well to others including Mr. Santos.

"Announcement! Announcement! People!" Mr. Santos said through the megaphone.

"It came to my attention that we are taking advantage of the helicopters."

"Listen! The helicopters are not for public transportation, but for the delivery of relief goods and people with severe medical conditions or emergencies."

"I noticed that since you people are so stubborn. I required you to list your names in a logbook. But there were still those who did not follow the instructions."

I am humiliated because the American pilot and his companion were questioning me about their extra passengers. Don't wait for their refusal to help, if this continues. If any of you don't have any important business in the city or if it can wait, then don't go. Wait for the roads' rehabilitation to be completed.

The crowd was silent and listened intently. Someone was running, hopping and screaming in laughter in the corner. Everybody's attention was shifted to him. It turned out to be Bart. He became the ice breaker of the tension present in the air. Laughter replaced the silence. There were concerns from the crowd that he might slip or injure himself. Irene and Roxanne chased him with the help of others to bring him home. Mr. Santos dropped what he was doing briefly to give some cash to buy chocolates for his son Bart.

"Don't mind my son. Please listen and don't forget. Please let us not abuse the kindness of the American Military. They might refuse to help us the next time around," Mr. Santos said.

The crowd returned to being silent. A few were nodding in agreement to the announcement while others just stared at Mr. Santos as if nothing important was announced.

An old lady was carried to the evacuation center right after the announcement. The young man who carried her claimed that a tree in her yard fell over her. She sustained major fractures on the right side of her body and minor bruises on the other parts. The medical personnel administered first aid measures to alleviate her condition. Splints were applied to her arm and leg. Bandages were wrapped over her ribs, given pain reliever medications and applied antibacterial ointment on her bruises. They waited for the helicopter to arrive to transport her to the city for a more advanced medical intervention that she very much needed. A double propelled helicopter landed. The pilot and its companion assumed that the residents who got closer to them were there to help carry the relief goods but they were wrong.

Mr. Santos apologized to the pilot and crew on the town's behalf. Those who attempted to get in were ordered to help with the unloading of supplies instead. He asked permission and explained the condition of the old woman that needed to be transported to the city for more advanced medical attention.

"Bullshit! Stubborn people! I warned them about this!" Mr. Santos uttered while kicking the ground with a bull face ready to attack.

The following relief delivery barely landed on a rice field a few meters away from the school ground where they dropped the supplies. The volunteers had to run towards the supplies to transfer them to the evacuation area. The chopper did not bother about anything else. They were there to deliver what was needed. They never even talked to a single soul. They missed the man with a swollen mouth who needed transportation to the city for medical reasons.

On the megaphone, "Listen. People Listen. I warned you. You stubborn people. I told you. They landed on the field because of your stubbornness. The choppers are not shuttle services. It's for our supply and emergency only. To transport any injured or sick patients. I warned you. It is your fault if his condition worsens," he said, pointing to the man with the swollen mouth sitting beside him.

The evacuation center was expecting helicopters to arrive with the relief goods but no helicopters for the entire day of waiting. Mr. Santos suspected that his fear came from an apparition that the U.S. aid operation halted due to the stubbornness of the people. There were no helicopters landing either for the next few days until they received the information that the road was 90-95% passable. All types of vehicles could use the road going to Baguio and vice versa.

Chapter XIII

A large part of the Kabayan people had assumed that the Santos family belonged to the upper class. It came about by what they witnessed in the everyday life of the Santoses. The house was regarded as a "mansion house" when it was an average-sized house for a middle-class family in reality. The contents of the house such as cabinets, beds, television set, radio component system, blender, Betamax player, washing machine, and many others which in their lack of knowledge were actually the cheaper alternative brands. Food items such as corned beef, peanut butter and jelly, pizza, cake, hamburger, biscuits, and the like that are usually eaten in western countries, and even their simple nuances such as reading books in public or wearing clothes similar to the latest fads of the west or the children having unique toys intensified their notion that the Santos family were really an affluent member of town. The greatest factor was their willingness to help others the best they could. In reality the Santos family had low household income compared to the farmers, animal raisers, gold prospectors, business people, and many other people that are considered blue-collar-workers.

A family was in dire need of treating their son who had leukemia. A bone marrow and blood transplant were needed. The procedure had to be performed in a hospital in Baguio City, which could accommodate such treatment, for the municipality of Kabayan didn't have a hospital but merely a dispensary only equipped for basic and simple ailments and diseases. Their main problem was the lack of funds required for the payment of the treatment and operation, plus the rent for the family for they didn't have any relatives or friends to stay in the city. The parents were scrambling to raise the amount needed for their son. One of the sources of help that they thought of was the Santos Family.

"Hello! Knock! Knock! Hello! Is anybody home," the mother said.

"Somebody is at the door. Would you kindly get it, Martin?" Mrs. Santos said.

"Who is it?" Martin asked.

"I need to talk to your parents. Are they around?" The mother asked.

"My mom is here. Kindly wait for a second, and I will get her for you," Martin said.

"What is it?" Mrs. Santos said.

"I need to talk to you," the mother said.

"Okay, come in," Mrs. Santos said.

The mother was almost in tears before saying her first world.

"I! uh! I! My son is suffering from leukemia and the doctor in the dispensary advised us to bring him to Baguio Hospital for treatment as soon as possible or he could not possibly make it. I am begging you to please lend me 70,000 pesos for the expenses needed for the treatment. I know you and Sir could provide that amount for us," the mother said.

Mrs. Santos took a back, and her eyes were wide open saying "Of all the well-to-do people in Kabayan, we are the ones you approach. Where in the world would we get that kind of money? We don't even have a single centavo, and yet that large amount. Yet that large sum you are asking for."

Please! We need it for our son. Please, have a heart! It is all for my son!" The mother said.

I understand your situation, and I sympathize with you. I would also do everything for my loved ones if I was in your shoes, but the reality is, we don't have that amount of money," Mrs. Santos said.

"No, I believe you can. Your husband is the chief of police, and you must have money to spare," the mother said.

Mrs. Santos' senses flared up but didn't want to be rude and still tried to talk with the mother in a calm manner.

"You know my husband's salary is not that much. It is only enough for us, his family, and Bart. You know Bart, our special child. Don't you think it is easy for us? I hope you also understand our side. Approach the Mayor, approach the officials, your cousin the vegetable trader. Approach him. He is even far richer than us. I am sure he can help your son," Mrs. Santos said.

The stubborn mother was tearing up and still pleading and refusing to leave the Santos residence. Mrs. Santos left her alone in the living room and went upstairs. She didn't care whatever the mother did for as long as she left their house. After a few minutes of shedding tears, she left. Mr. Santos arrived home, shaking incessantly and mumbling like he had a bad day in the office.

"Dad, what's the matter?" Mrs. Santos asked.

He took a deep breath and said, "One of those who thought we are rich tried to borrow 70,000 pesos for his sick son!"

"What? A mother was also here asking for the same amount for her sick son! They must be husband and wife!" Mrs. Santos said.

"Yeah, I know them and my question is why they chose to borrow from us when they have wealthy relatives. That's what pisses me off," Mr. Santos said.

"What did you do with him?" Mrs. Santos asked.

"He was so stubborn but I forced him to go to the mayor's office," Mr. Santos said.

"You did the right thing. I left the mother here in our living room crying until she finally left," Mrs. Santos said.

"Thank God Bart was asleep in his room and never woke during the confrontation or he might have escaped," She added.

"This is the problem with wrong assumptions. The people think we are rich people. They don't realize that they are wrong. That we are just a middle-class family who also has needs. And they tend to forget about Bart, who has special needs," Mr. Santos said.

Mrs. Santos agreed with disgrace and they both did their best to let the situation pass.

The problem was the situation spread all over town like butter on bread. There were people who believed in the rumor and others who knew better, mostly were Mr. Santos' fellow police officers, ordinary government workers and professionals. Those who knew the Santoses well agreed with what they did as true and justified. Irene and Martin were at school when the incident occurred. They only learned bits and pieces about it from gossip they heard outside.

A group of school children were passing the Santos' residence. One of them screamed while others were throwing small pebbles, dirt and whatever they could grab from the ground. Nobody noticed what was going on outside because they were busy preparing for work and school. A neighbor saw what the school children were doing and drove them away.

Bart went outside with the rest of the Santoses when they were exiting the premises. He pushed Martin aside and dashed towards the public market across the road. Martin had minor bruises on his palm and knees from what Bart did.

"Shit! Why did Bart do this to me?" Martin screamed.

"Hey shut-up! You know your brother Bart! You know he did not mean to do it!" Mr. Santos said.

"But still, he should not have done it in the first place!" Martin said.

"Go back inside and your "Manang" Roxanne will clean your wound instead of complaining there!" Mrs. Santos said.

Mark followed Bart. He went to the clusters of sari-sari stores on the opposite of the public market.

"You went the wrong way. Bart went inside the market," one of the bystanders said.

He moved fast towards the market to witness a store owner who was screaming and trying to drag Bart out of his store.

"Let him be," another store owner said.

"He means no harm. Just let him choose what he wants and I am sure the Santoses will pay for it." Another store owner said.

"No, get the hell out of my store! You are disarranging the items!" The store owner said.

"Please, just let him get what he wants and we will be on our way," Mark said.

The store owner had an unpleasant attitude and stared at Mark with a devilish look.

"Get him out of my store! He is not wanted here!" The store owner said.

A concerned bystander held a chocolate bar in his hand and showed it to Bart. He was moving away from the store while making sure that the chocolate bar was visible for Bart to see. It worked. Bart followed him until they were out of the market building. He handed the chocolate to Martin and went on his way.

"Thank you," Martin said.

"No problem," the bystander said.

Martin was thinking of paying for the chocolate bar but because of the circumstances he was not able to do so. He gave the chocolate bar to Bart and they went back home.

Later, it was discovered that the outrage of the store owner was rooted in Mr. and Mrs. Santos refusing to lend money to his cousin and her husband for the treatment of his nephew.

Chapter XIV

Kabayan is a relatively small populated community. A new face can be easily spotted. A tall, fair skinned man with a nose line that resembled an eagle's beak caught the town's attention. Everybody was curious. *Who is this man? Where is he from? Is he a foreigner?* And the locals were asking similar questions.

The "Igorot" love affair is always shrouded in mystery. Details about love affairs are never public. Couples don't celebrate special occasions such as anniversaries, Valentine's Day, and others. In fact, public display of affection is never present. An "in-echab" (a Nabaloi term for a single mother) was kissing, holding hands, hugging, and even being frisky with the new guy in public for everybody to see. Jaw lines were dropping; eyes were widening and faces resembling somebody in fear of their lives as onlookers were witnessing such acts. The children and teenagers were giggling as if they were witnessing something exciting.

Mr. Santos was dedicated to his duty. Kabayan always had a home in his heart. The new guy picked his interest because he appeared out of nowhere as somebody's love interest. It was bothering him, and he wanted to keep a close eye on the guy.

The Mayor's birthday celebration became a town event. Native black pigs were butchered. The "mambunong" did his rituals, and the people were in attendance. Mr. Santos was called to the second floor of the Mayor's house. There he saw the municipal officials and employees enjoying the prime cut of the pigs, such as the innards and grilled meat with the premium "tapuy" or rice wine. The new guy was present, with the Mayor taking much interest on him. His concern for the new guy got stronger as he wondered how he weaseled his way into the Mayor's radar.

"May I know the gentleman?" Mr. Santos asked.

"Sir, I am Spencer Reyes."

"Okay, where are you from?" Mr. Santos asked.

"I am from La Trinidad sir," Spencer said.

"You probably know who I am," Mr. Santos said.

"Yes, sir, I do," Spencer said.

"Well welcome to Kabayan and nice to meet you," Mr. Santos said.

"Thank you, sir. Nice meeting you also," Spencer said.

Mr. Santos did not ask more personal questions to avoid revealing his true intentions. Everybody had a great time. They enjoyed each other's company. They talked, ate, drank a little and had somebody take their pictures. Mr. Santos requested a copy of the film to be sent to the city to be developed. A copy with Spencer in it was sent to Mr. Santos' city cop friend to check him out. Computer systems and the internet were not readily available during those times. The investigation was done manually with the use of Spencer's photo. Mr. Santos was skeptical if it was the new guy's real name. For over a month of searching and follow-up, the truth was unraveled. A certain Sandro Garcia's mugshot had a strong resemblance to the photo submitted. The difference was the hair color. The mugshot photo had grayish hair while Spencer's hair was as dark as the coal. He had a pending case of murder from Mt. Province that made him a wanted felon hiding in Kabayan.

I must do something. I must make certain he is not a threat to Kabayan, Mr. Santos told himself.

I must set my eyes on his every move without creating any suspicion from him, he added.

He did not immediately arrest Spencer when he learned the truth about him. He asked his colleagues from Mt. Province to wait for his signal before coming to Kabayan for Spencer's turnover. He wanted to take him into custody by surprise to prevent him from ever fleeing.

Spencer was permitted to open the second restaurant in town. It was actually his lover who was registered as the business owner. The restaurant was full of customers eager to try what they had to offer. There were wide varieties of dishes that were unfamiliar to the people. It had become the primary choice of both locals and tourists to eat at since it opened. He and his lover were present in the everyday operation of the restaurant. Spencer was the cook, and his lover was the cashier, with a single employee as the waiter, and errand boy. Spencer and his lover sometimes acted as the waiter and waitresses especially when the restaurant was full. The Santoses were one of the regular customers. They even brought Bart with them on weekends or holidays as his special days. His palate came to love several dishes that he seldom tasted before such as buttered fried chicken, special "lechon kawali" (deep-fried pork belly) and other meat dishes. The best seller of the restaurant that Mr. Santos came to love was the "lomi" (a noodle dish with thick broth, shredded chicken, carrots, highland beans, green peas and a hard-boiled egg.) The owner of the original eatery was furious and blamed Spencer for the decline of his business, his source of income.

The owner confronted Spencer and his lover. He claimed that since he was the original and only existing restaurant for years, he had the sole right to operate and demanded that the second restaurant be closed. Spencer never gave up, telling the original owner to his face that they did nothing wrong. They had the right to own a business whenever they wanted. He also shoved it in the original owner's presence of mind that it was his own fault for his restaurant's failure because he never updated his menu. The customers were tired of the limited choices. In addition, most of his relatives called him "communist" for his unpleasant attitude that did not fit the mold of a restaurant business owner.

The original owner went to the Santos' residence to complain and perhaps gain sympathy.

"Hello chief. I can't take it anymore. I am an original son of Kabayan and I own the original eatery! Why did an outsider do this to me? Get him out of our place!" The owner said.

"No, I can't. He is not violating any laws! I can't arrest him and kick him out of here for that reason! No, I can't!" Mr. Santos replied.

"Why? Even you, you don't give a damn about your fellow son of Kabayan!" The owner said.

"Hey! Drill this in your coconut! We can't discriminate against anybody from doing business just because he is not originally from Kabayan! The point is I am basing my actions in accordance with the law! You even have the nerve to order me around!" Mr. Santos said.

"Get out of my face if you have nothing good to say!" He added.

The original owner was mumbling as he was heading to the front door. Bart was lying on the couch like nothing was going on. The owner gazed at Bart with a bird of prey's vision ready to devour its victim. He was about to do something but with Mr. Santos' intimidation, he left instead. From there on, the Santoses were not welcome in his place of business.

Aside from the restaurant, the owner was also the proprietor of a sari-sari store adjacent to a restaurant operating without a permit. The restaurant was forced to shut down, but the sari-sari store was still operational. There were many sari-sari stores near the Santos' residence, but it was a mystery as to why Bart ran towards the original owner's store.

"What the hell? They let their pet escape! They didn't put a leash on him!" The owner said as he saw Bart running towards them.

Roxanne followed him, paid for the chocolates, and forced Bart home. The original owner was still running his mouth, but Roxanne had no time to argue with him and just left.

Mr. Santos learned about the status of the original owner's sari-sari store. He threatened to disallow the sari-sari store's operation if the original owner did not apply for a permit. The original owner took it as a form of revenge for hating Bart's presence in his business. Mr. Santos didn't care about their relationship with the owner if they were on good terms or not. What's important was his compliance with the permit to operate the business.

Spencer was busy in his restaurant when Mr. Santos came to arrest him. Spencer knew that there would be a time when the skeletons in his closet would be unraveled. He knew it was his time when he saw Mr. Santos moving in his direction. He dropped what he was doing and asked his lover to take over the business and went outside to meet Mr. Santos.

"I know, but please, don't put handcuffs on me. You don't even have to state my rights. I have nowhere else to go," Spencer said.

"Come, let's go for a stroll," Mr. Santos said.

They both walked to the police station as if nothing was going on. He was detained while waiting for the police escort from Mt. Province to pick him up. The mother and Aunt of Spencer's lover knocked at the Santoses, interrupting their dinner.

"Sir, please don't do this to Spencer. Please don't do this to my daughter. He is a good man. He is good to my daughter's son. Please, sir, I beg you," the mother said with tears in her eyes.

The Aunt said nothing, but it was evident that she was tearing-up and sympathizing with her sister.

"Your plea is useless. He is a suspected murderer. He must face the law. Besides, a police escort will come to get him tomorrow," Mr. Santos said, feeling uncomfortable talking to them.

"But Sir, please. He is a good man. I swear. Let him go," the mother said.

"What do you want? Do you want me to charge all of you for harboring a criminal? Get out of my house! You are desrupting our peace and quiet!" Mr. Santos said.

The two eventually left in tears.
The police escort arrived the next day. Mr. Santos and the Kabayan police force prepared a meal for them before they turned Spencer over to them.

Chapter XV

Mark had to leave to take care of his aging mother. He and Roxanne decided to move to Mark's hometown. Mark was the only one available among the sibling to take care of their mother. His younger sister was in Baguio, and her work did not allow her to move. His mother's companion graduated high school and moved to Baguio to further her studies in college as a working student.

They explained their situation and their plan to leave. Mr. and Mrs. Santos understood and did not protest their next move. The timing couldn't be better for Mrs. Santos was unemployed at that point. The government cut off the funding of the program she was heading. She had ample time for Bart. Right after Roxanne told her intentions to leave, the vacancy of municipal clerk was officially announced. Mrs. Santos was interested in filling-up the position.

Mrs. Santos was the most qualified candidate among the four applicants. The other unselected applicants were so mad about what happened. They assumed that Mrs. Santos got the position because of Mr. Santos' power and influence. One of the applicants charged the Santoses with her husband.

"Why are you not considerate? Just because you belong to a powerful family then you can just get what you want," she said.

"What are you talking about? And what gave you the right to disturb us?" Mr. Santos asked.

"You don't need the job. You have a well-to-do family," she said sobbing while her husband was silent on the side.

"Hey, honey. Why aren't you doing something?" She told her husband.

"What I am so pissed-off about is your notion that we are "Bill Gates rich" with an influential power. But you are all wrong because my husband found out about my new job just at the last minute. I applied by myself without my husband's knowledge. Get out of our house you shameless fool! Get out!" Mrs. Santos said.

"Get away from our house! There is no use of you barking in front of my family!" Mr. Santos added.

"Let's just get out of here honey and let it be," the Husband said.

"What do you mean? Why are you doing this to me? Why are you taking their side over me?" She said.

"It's not like that, honey. Let's just go home. I don't want any scandals. It is humiliating if anybody would see us like this," the husband said, dragging her wife outside.

The other unselected applicants heard what happened to one of them. They sympathized with her and spread false accusations of the Santoses putting weight on the selection bodies in order for Mr. Santos to be selected. The town was again divided with the issue with a few believing in the rumors and the others having the opposite beliefs.

Roxanne highly recommended Bell. She did a great job, not much different to Roxanne. She and Bart got along for a in an instant without any problems.

"Crazy boy! Crazy boy! Family of Crazy!" Young guys were shouting on the streets, passing through the Santos' residence in one gloomy afternoon. Bell got the broom-stick and drove the young guys away. Her shaky hands were wiping her tears as she returned to the house. She was like a devastated mother protecting her young. The incident unlocked the door without supervisions. Bart took the opportunity to grab his favorite chocolate from the sari-sari store.

Not again! Why don't these people lock their pet in chains if they have to? Now, he is littering around my business!" the store owner said; the same guy who had a grudge against Mr. Santos.

"Shut up.! You piece of nothing! You know damn well that Bart has a condition. He can't help what he is doing! Normal people like us should be the ones to be understanding and be willing to adjust to the situation!" Bell shouted in front of the store owner as the other customers jolted.

The store owner did not answer back but gave her a piercing look. Bell grabbed Bart, paid for the item he got, and went home. She made sure that the store owner could sense that she was not a friend if he messed with Bart while they were getting away from his store. She was a bit overwhelmed by everything but it did not deter her from staying with the Santoses, staying with Bart.

Mr. Santos was the first to arrive home. Bell's lips were so eager to move in his presence.

"Uncle, the store three houses from here is pure evil. I argued with him because he was screaming, uhm, referring to Bart like he was not human. He was a pet that we didn't put his leash on."

"Ah, never mind him for as long as he wasn't physical with the both of you. Just avoid him. I am sorry if Bart chose to go to his store that you had to deal with, do your best to be civil. We don't want any trouble even if he is wrong," Mr. Santos said.

"You know, he is known around to be a communist, as his own nieces and nephews claimed. But if he becomes physical with either one of you, tell me, and I will take care of it," he added.

"Yes, Uncle, I will, and thank you very much," Bell said.

The house was spotlessly clean every time Mr. and Mrs. Santos were home. Not that Bell was better than Roxanne, but there was something about her that was pleasant and how she did things that Mr. and Mrs. Santos could not put their finger on. The inside of the house was clear, the aura was fresh, and the front yard was well tended. The Santos family had great vibes almost every day with her presence.

Bell was shutting her eyes a bit on the living room couch after cleaning when Irene stood in front of her trying to sway her body.

"What are you doing?" She asked.

"Manang, I am trying to dance," Irene said.

"I see dancing. Come and sit for a while and let me tell you something. You too Martin," Bell said

"How about Bart? Martin asked.

 Forget him. He is scribbling in the kitchen. The important thing is the doors are locked," Bell said.

"Let me tell the two of you this, dancing is one of Satan's instruments to spread evil," she added.

"Really?" Martin asked.

"Is this true?" Irene asked.

"Yes, dancing is the purest evil in all activities that Satan made. Look at "tayaw" (the traditional Igorot dance). It is being practiced in paganism worshiping the devil. And in hell Satan and his devils dance in celebration when human souls commit sins or enter hell," Bell said.

The Santos kid was all ears as Bell went on with her explanation as to why dance was an evil activity. The siblings nodded and agreed with what Bell had narrated to them. The siblings then refused to participate in school or community activities that involved dancing. They truly believed what Bell told them about dancing. Many of their peers were attentive every time Bart and Irene's beliefs in dance were discussed. The majority of their friends, acquaintances, and even those they didn't know, were persuaded to believe the siblings due to their family's popularity throughout town.

The school principal and the teachers became weary of the sibling's blatant opposition to any forms of dancing. The matter was brought to the attention of Mr. and Mrs. Santos. The school wanted to resolve the issue because it interrupted some of the school's activities. A grievance concerning Irene and Martin was brought to the PTA meeting. Mrs. Santos who attended the meeting learned about the extent of trouble caused by Irene and Martin.

"What are these complaints that we received from the school about the two of you spreading the idea of dancing as an evil activity?" Mrs. Santos asked.

"Mom, dancing is evil. Bell told us about it," Irene said.

"That's true mother," Martin Added.

"No, dancing is not evil, No! No! No!" Mrs. Santos said.

"Stop telling everyone that dancing is evil. Promise," Mr. Santos said.

"Yes Mother," Irene said.

"Okay and you Martin," Mrs. Santos said.

"Yes mom, never again," Martin responded.

Mrs. Santos explained why dance is not evil in detail. Mr. and Mrs. Santos learned that Bell's religious affiliation was the reason why she believed that dancing was pure evil. Mr. and Mr. Santos respected religious freedom and belief, but they kept on reminding Irene and Martin that dancing was okay and not evil until the negative idea about dancing was erased from their consciousness.

Chapter XVI

Mr. Santos' parents Agapito and Maxim were some of the early Christian Protestant converts during the American occupation of the Philippines. They were pioneers of the religious faith that they were introduced to, specifically the United Church of Christ in the Philippines. They played crucial roles for spreading the faith throughout the northern part of the Philippines. Mr. Agapito was ordained as a full pledge minister, and Mrs. Maxim was given the task of the children's Sunday school teacher. The Santos family was all over the place; each sibling was born in different territory of the mission. The family settled in the Municipality of "Potia" in the Province of "Ifugao" when their parents could no longer take the pressure of traveling so much due to their aging bodies. It was the town where Mrs. Maxim and the daughter Alexia had been living ever since Mr. Agapito passed several years ago.

A bus conductor handed Martin a letter addressed to Mr. Santos form his sister Mrs. Fecora. The letter contained the details of their mother who had a stroke that made her paralyzed from the waist down. Their mother needed a caregiver for the rest of her life to assist her activities of daily living as per advice of the doctor. Besides, it would be better for their mother to be in a clean, fresh and stress free environment. The letter also revealed that their mother wanted to go home to Kabayan for she already missed her hometown and people rather than staying with them in Baguio or returning to Potia with Alexia through the lengthy and stressful trip her condition could not endure.

Kabayan was anticipating the arrival of Mrs. Maxim. It was like a special homecoming of a living legend. Everybody, mainly old-timers, were eager to visit her. The municipal government loaned one of the ambulances for her safe trip. The abundance of people welcomed Mrs. Maxim. There was one familiar face that stood out. She did not recognize him at first but tears came rolling when she realized who he was. Mrs. Maxim and Mr. Tadaka were delighted to see each other again which rejuvenated the bond they had with each other. Mr. Santos had no idea how close of a family they were. They reminisce about the past that could go on for eternity. None of the other visitors complained of not having their turns to speak. They were seated and listened intently to their conversations. A bit of sadness was painted on their faces when it was time for Mr. Tadaka to go.

The Santoses' home became a public place for the influx of visitors. Bell had her work cut out for her. Instead of focusing primarily on Bart and the households, her additional load were the people going in and out of the house. Many were eager to spend time with Mrs. Maxim, while others used her as an excuse to have free food. Mrs. Maxim's old age did not prevent her from identifying who were genuine from the freeloaders. She never confronted them about it. She only gave excuses for her inability to face them when a freeloader or somebody that irritated her awareness of the real world intended to visit her the second time around.

The hectic schedule forced the Santoses to neglect some regular activities such as quality time for Bart and the regular visits to Mr. Tadaka. On one of the busy days, Bart ran up and down the steps screaming, biting his arms and couldn't stay in one place. Mrs. Maxim's room was full to its maximum capacity that overflowed to the living room like patients waiting for their turn in a doctor's clinic or an audience in line for a show or something.

"I know all of you wanted to visit my mother-in-law but, please, be considerate enough to leave, and you can return for some other time because of my son Bart. You saw what was going on. Please," Mrs. Santos said.

A few of the visitors really heard what she said and left. The problem was most of them were still in the house expecting to be served with some kind of edible treats.

"Please go home. I don't have a choice. You have seen my special son Bart. Please understand. Those who are already in the room are exceptions. We won't accept any more visitors at this moment. They are the last," Mrs. Santos said.

They all went out but not without leaving any bad taste in the air. Words were flailing around. "What a selfish lady." "Bad, bad, attitude." "Selfish fool," As if Mrs. Santos was the enemy.

Mr. Santos witnessed part of what happened and encouraged his wife not to talk back and let them be.

"Honey, just let them be. It will be worse if you talk back. I am sure that sooner or later those no-good people will realize they need attitude adjustments."

Sure enough. The house was silent without any signs of Bart's outcries.

Mr. Tadaka succumbed to death a few weeks after he and Mrs. Maxim reunited. Mr. Santos became the unofficial manager of the wake because nobody was willing to take the role of a lifetime. Only a few of Mr. Tanaka's loved ones were willing to help during the wake and funeral process. The worst was the claimants. None of them helped in any forms or kinds during the wake but were eager to acquire Mr. Tadaka's remaining properties.

Elders insisted on practicing the "Igorot" tradition of wake and funeral for the deceased who have lived in the past, the more traditional way of living. The primary practice was every decision-making must go through the "mambunong's" approval. One was the butchering of black native pigs which was very expensive if they could find even one due to its rarity. The number of pigs to be butchered must also be considered in accordance to the reading of the "mambunong" of the animals' innards. "If the innards were bad and could possibly bring bad omen then the entire pig's carcass must be burned, another pig must be butchered until several good ones was found for the consumption of the attendees." The corpse was usually in a sitting position while rotting. Most of all, the wake could last for one to two months, and even after the funeral, butchering was still required that could last for several weeks after. All of the rituals must be implemented with precision. Modern funeral services were absent in town that included embalming. Some of the elders overheard Mr. Tadaka's plans.

"No, no, embalming. No impurities in his body. Mr. Tadaka was one of the people from the past. Traditions must be followed," one of the elders said.

"As we said, traditions must be followed because he is a child of the past," another elder said.

"I have nothing against tradition, but you all know it is expensive. The family has limited resources. If all of you are insisting on adhering to tradition, then you can apply it. If tradition is a must then do it. But all of you must be responsible to shoulder the expenses for the requirements needed for the rituals of the tradition you are all calling for. If we need to kill ten pigs no problem. I'll allow it, for as long as all of you who want to implement tradition must be the ones who will buy the pigs and you all know how expensive a pig is, especially the native ones. But, it is very obvious that all of you who require such tradition are not willing to empty your pockets and pay for it. And, and I don't give a damn at this point, I already contacted an embalmer from the city. I don't want a rotting corpse," Mr. Santos announced on the wake with the intention that everybody listening would understand his point of view.

Mr. Santos gathered the loved ones and the elders including the "mambunong" for a meeting in hopes of getting into a compromise. The meeting was held at the forest where the sunlight could penetrate. The participants of the meeting felt a large man running through the forest, but they did not recognize who it was. Bell came running later.

"Who were those running?" An elder said.

"No idea, I guess one of those who want to attend the wake," one of Mr. Tadaka's relatives said.

"I also felt them passing. But let's focus on why we are here," Mr. Tadaka said.

The elders and some of Mr. Tadaka's relatives present had a clash of beliefs. The elders insisted on implementing the traditional "Igorot " ways while some of the relatives were Christian purists. They believed that all native traditions were evil. Mr. Santos could not get into a mutual agreement. He had no choice but to get into a decision that he must implement. Both sides did not agree but he made it upon himself that if a decision was not made, then the disagreement would last for eternity. He didn't care less if the participants of the meeting would agree or hate him because of his decisions.

They went back to the wake only to be surprised by Bart eating a mountain of food on his plate. The people assured he was well taken care of during his absence.

How in the world did Bart know about the wake? Maybe his radar detected the abundance of meat here. Mr. Santos told himself.

After Bart finished his food, he pulled the old ladies from the sofa facing the coffin in the living room. Some of the old ladies were confused while others smiled and understood what he was doing.

"Sorry, just let him be. He means no harm. He wants to lie down and relax," one of the old ladies said.

Bart was just lying alert and quiet. He ran home again after a few moments. Bell went after him again with a bag of meat and "pancit".

Mrs. Maxim felt the arrival of Bart and Bell from her room. She expressed her eagerness to attend Mr. Tadaka's wake when Bell went to check on her.

"Take me to my cousin Tadaka. I want to see him for the last time before they bury him," she said.

"I am sorry I can't attend to you and Bart at the same time. Bart has to be here and I can't magically divide myself into two for Bart and you. We will ask manong's permission first if he allows you to go," Bell said as she was leaving the room.

Mrs. Maxim did not react. Maybe her aging eardrum did not hear what Bell was saying. She again insisted that Bell must take her to Tadaka's wake the moment she returned. That evening, Mr. Santos came home to take a shower and change his dirty clothes to fresh new one. Mrs. Maxim complained to him that Bell did not allow her to attend the wake. Mr. Santos heard what Mrs. Maxim was saying but did not respond. He returned to the wake after he had taken his shower and changed his clothes. It was the following day when Mrs. Maxim attended Mr. Tadaka's funeral. Mr. Martin allowed the mambunong to perform his rituals before taking Mr. Tadaka's body to the UCCP church for a Christian burial ritual. Few who still opposed his decision, but the majority agreed with the funeral rites. Mr. Tadaka was finally put to rest at the back of his house. Mr. Santos was just glad it was over.

Chapter XVII

Bell felt the strain of having to do three jobs in one household. She had to complete the house chores and take good care of both Bart and Mrs. Maxim. It was clear that another set of hands was needed. The only willing in the entire town at those times was Gina. Her father was known as a scam artist and was good at it. Not only good, but excel from avoiding apprehensions from the authorities. His illegal ways of living dragged the name and reputation of his family. The Santoses were skeptical about hiring her at first, but believed in second chances. Besides, it was not her who did the scams but his father. Mrs. Maxim was different. She could not understand certain things in life. Maybe her old age, or maybe it was just the way she was.

"Dishonest! Dishonest!" Mrs. Maxim was uttering while Gina was cleaning her and even after she left.

Mr. Santos overheard what his mother was saying.

"Mama, what are you saying?" Mr. Santos asked.

"That Gina! Her father was a dishonest thief! She is dishonest!" Mrs. Maxim said.

"So, if her father is dishonest. It doesn't mean that Gina herself is dishonest too. Give her a chance. She could be the best companion you had for all we know. If you just give her a chance," Mr. Santos said.

"Dishonest! Family of dishonest!" The words were still coming from Mrs. Maxim's mouth.

Don't you damn get it mama? Gina is not her father. And it isn't easy to find someone to take care of you. You are so lucky someone is willing to do so. Don't you know that your attitude is the reason why nobody wants to stay with you? People are pretending to visit you because of the free food. Don't you ever get it?" Mr. Santos' blunted out as he was getting fed up with his mom's relentless bantering.

Mrs. Maxim kept quiet with the assumption of understanding what Mr. Santos wanted to imbed in her head. It was not near the truth. She acted worse than her actual condition every time Gina came to assist her. Gina was there doing an excellent job without complaints not because she was in dire need of the job but because of the Santoses' kindness towards her.

The people of Kabayan ostracized Gina's family because of her father's past. Mr. Santos hated the idea of someone being treated unfairly in life. He believed everybody had a fair shot in life no matter what their creed, religion or tribe were for as long as they were also fair to others and law-abiding citizens. He did his best to explain to the people that the act of one family member did not reflect the entire family's character. He even protected some of the family members from bullies and criticisms.

"No, they are very evil! His father is dishonest! They are not children of God! They don't have the right to enjoy life!" Mrs. Maxim said.

Mr. Santos did not say a word when her mother said such hurtful words again. Instead, he suggested to Gina and Bell to switch places. Gina will focus on Bart while Bell will take care of Mrs. Maxim. The arrangement was effective for only a short period of time. Mrs. Maxim could not avoid seeing Gina the fact that they lived under the same roof. Gina would ignore the situation if Mrs. Maxim shouted at her with blatant hurtful words, and as much as possible, she would avoid cleaning in Mrs. Maxim's presence.

The Santoses' front yard was full of fruit bearing trees that the late Mr. Tadaka cultivated. It had one of the unique varieties of natural edible fruit-bearing trees, from the more well-known "kape" or coffee and "tambuyog" or pomelo to some rarer ones like "kaymito" or star apple, "mabolo" or velvet fruit and loquat fruits. The warmth of the summer was the perfect weather for bearing fruits. Bart's palate could not wait to taste the sweet flavor of the star apple. The house had a shaded walkway connected from the front door to the patio that also served as the parking lot. The roof was accessible through Irene's room front window as the pathway to the fruit bearing trees. Bart went to the window through the roof of the walk way to gather some star apples.

"Bart, where is Bart?" Gina asked.

"Why? Bart is not in any rooms?" Bell asked.

"Yes, not even in the living room nor the kitchen and the CR," Gina said.

They checked the front and back doors but it was locked. *Where would Bart be? How could this be possible?* Both wondered.

Blog! Blog! Blog! Were the noises from the walkway roof. Bell sprinted to Irene's room and there was Bart caught picking random star apple fruits.

Bell breathed a sigh of relief.

"Yeah, Bart, you made us so nervous," Gina said as she was pulling Bart into the room.

"Sorry, Bart, but no picking of fruits for now we are busy. Later we will get you some. Maybe what you picked is still unripe," Gina added.

Later that afternoon, Gina climbed the trees through the same passageway while Bell was attending to Mrs. Santos. Bart, without warning, woke from his nap and attempted to join in the fruit gathering with a smirk on his face.

"Bart, it is dangerous. Wait for Gina to come," Bell shouted as she was pulling Bart in.

Bart slurped the entire harvest without leaving some for others. He does not share when it comes to food he really liked. He sprayed the CR after his consumption of the star apples, leaving a bad smell in the house. Gina opted to wash his behind with soap and water rather than just wiping with toilet paper. Bell went on to open all the windows to alleviate the bad smell. They forcefully let Bart drink "oresol" or oral rehydration solution from Mrs. Maxim's medication box to remedy his overactive bowel movements.

Gina had observed Bart wearing his long untidy hair for quite some time and wanted to do something about it. She had no idea she would have a difficult task on hand. Bart had an illogical fear of scissors. She let Bart sit on the backyard stool and was about to do the first cut when he began moving his head and screamed.

Bell heard the screams and dropped what she was doing to check on it. She found Gina struggling to cut Bart's hair. She went and retrained Bart's head from moving.

"Bart, keep your head still or your ear will be cut," Bell said.

Bart continued on moving which forced Gina to hold his neck with all of her might. He might have been hurting from it but the important thing was the prevention of more devastating injury.

Mrs. Santos saw Bart peeping through the window when she was arriving home from the day's work.

"Uy, Bart. Nice haircut hah! Wow, you look handsome," Mrs. Santos said.

Bart wore a big smile while staring at his mother. He also saw the bag his mother was carrying. He had to inspect what was inside like what he normally does with similar situations. Mrs. Santos let him see what was inside and specified the chocolates. Bart got the goodies and consumed it right on the spot.

Mrs. Santos noticed that his fingernails and toenail were long and dirty.

"Your "manangs" gave you a haircut but neglected to cut your nails. Hehehe!" Mrs. Santos said.

"Come let me cut your long nails," she added.
Mrs. Santos held Bart screaming from his nails being cut and cleaned.

Chapter XVIII

I t was like any other day. The buses and jeepneys usually stop on the Santoses' frontage every evening because of their proximity to the town's public market. The Santoses did not expect any visitor that particular day but somebody got off the bus with companions looking for Mr. Santos. It was in the nature of Mr. Santos of not showing any emotions but tears rolled when he got an unexpected visit from his brother.

"Hey brother, surprise," Jewel said.

"Wow brother, you are here," Mr. Santos said.

The brothers gave each other hugs with tears flowing from their eyes. Mrs. Santos handed them tissue papers. She too was in tears as she witnessed the brother's reunion.

"Yes, and you know my wife, Brea," Jewel said.

She smiled at everybody with tears in her eyes.

"Yes, the last time we saw each other was a long time, during your wedding, right?" Mr. Santos said.

"Yes, "Manong" (older brother or elder man)," Mrs. Brea said.

"Anyway, my wife Trisha." Mr. Santos said.

"Yes, I recognize you "manong" and "adding" (younger man and woman)," Mrs. Santos said as she shook both of their hands.

"Here are our three daughters: Lady our first, she is eight years old; Queen, seven and Princes five," Mrs. Brea said.

"Children go and bless (In English bless and the Filipino translation is "mano" as a sign of respect to elders. The back of the hand of the younger person is rubbed on the forehead of the elder saying "mano po".) to your Aunt Trisha," Mrs. Brea told her daughters.

"Bless all of you too. All of you are cute and pretty," Mrs. Santos said with a smile on her face.

The Santos kids were not around to greet their relatives. Gina was preparing a room for Mr. Jewel and his family. Bell was in the kitchen preparing snacks and refreshments. The kids had their snacks while waiting for their room to be ready. After a long and bumpy ride, the kids took the rest they needed when the room was ready.

"How's my brother?" Mr. Santos said.

"I am doing great, and it's been seven years now since we saw each other," Jewel said.

"Brother, I still can't believe you are here and I am very glad to see you," Mr. Santos said.

"Same here Brother, Same here. Anyway, I am an assistant to the bank manager in San Juan La Union where my wife is from. They have their ancestral house in a more rural part, but we are renting an apartment in the city center because it is near the bank where I work," Mr. Jewel said.

"Okay, great and your wife, what does she do?" Mr. Santos said.

"She is the barangay (the smallest political unit in the Philippines) secretary…. and I am happy for you. I heard you are the Chief of Police here," Mr. Jewel said.

"Yeah, thanks I am happy for you too," Mr. Santos said.

Bart came and pulled Mr. Jewel from the sofa he was sitting on and laid there. "Oh, you know Bart. The special one of the family, your nephew," Mr. Santos added.

Mr. Jewel looked at Bart and gave him a hug and said hello. Bart wasn't into it and wanted his uncle to get out of the sofa for his comfort. His uncle smiled at Bart and transferred to an empty chair beside Mr. Santos.

Queen woke and went to her father as he put her on his lap while conversing with his brother. She saw Bart blubbering some words that did not make any sense, clapping, and rolling his eyeballs. She was so mesmerized by Bart that her eyes were focused on him.

"Daddy, what is he doing?" Queen asked.

"Darling you know that's your cousin and he is kind of special. That's how God made him unique," Mr. Jewel said.

"Still, but why?" Queen asked.

"You know, darling, he is just enjoying himself and we must let him be," Mr. Jewel said.

Mr. Santos looked at Queen and smiled.

"Queen is too young to understand," Mr. Santos said.

Jewel responded with a smile.

Queen stopped asking questions but her eyes were still glued on Bart. Mr. Santos and Mr. Jewel continued with their conversations. Mrs. Brea and the rest of the kids did not wake up until dinner time. The Santoses and Jewel's family resumed their bonding over dinner and went to Mrs. Maxim's room after finishing their meals.

Everybody was asleep for the night except for Mr. Jewel and Brea, who spent more time with Mrs. Maxim. Mr. Jewel did not waste time the next day. He woke early, eager to visit relatives and childhood friends. They went to as many relatives and friends' households as they could.

"Dad, please. Can we just rest and relax and spend some time with your brother and his family? I am tired from all this hiking," Mrs. Brea said.

"Okay, Mama. We will not be roaming tomorrow. We will be having some guests at Mr. Santos' residence. They will come to visit us." Mr. Jewel said.

They resumed their visitation with the rest of the relatives and friends within the town center and other adjacent barangays.

"Why do we have to visit all of your relatives and friends now? Don't we have time to visit them some other time?" Mrs. Brea said.

"My employer gave me the opportunity to spend my accumulated mandatory vacation leave that I never used before. I opted to spend it with my family and friends, whom I never saw for years. I don't want to waste it just staying at home or going to expensive vacation places," Mr. Jewel said.

Gifts flowed to the Santoses' residence since the people knew of Mr. Jewel and his family's visit. Most were from their products such as fruits, vegetables, "Kintoman" (native red rice variety) Tapuy, "bunog"(a variety of freshwater fish), "ka-dang"(freshwater crab), and many others. Mr. Jewel and his family were almost in tears and could not express their appreciation enough every time people presented them with gifts. Relatives and friends that reside from far areas were visited when the municipal mayor authorized the use of one of the municipal vehicles through the request of Mr. Santos for his brother's travels for a couple of days only. There were no signs of sadness when Jewel and his Family left Kabayan. The Santoses were very calm with the absence of tears when they expressed their goodbyes. They knew that they would see each other again very soon. They were ready to leave when Bart ran and touched each one of them. He stared at Mr. Jewel for a few seconds after going back inside which was very peculiar of him.

Jewel and Family finally entered the bus with the Santoses waving and shouting "Happy Trip."

Mr. Santos received the sad news through a letter from Mrs. Brea that his brother, Jewel, died due to the complication of congenital heart failure weeks after his hometown visit. His last request to his wife was to bury him in Kabayan when his time was finally up. Mr. Santos went to Family and Friends that he could reach to break the bad news. He also requested for them to spread the information. Many speculated that Mr. Jewel's recent visit was his way of saying goodbye. Mr. Santos borrowed a municipal vehicle to transport his brother to Kabayan from the city. It was a "jeepney" because it was the logical vehicle large enough to accommodate the coffin. Two male relatives and an employed municipal driver went with Mr. Santos to retrieve his brother's body.

Mr. Santos and his companions went straight to Mrs. Fecora's apartment, but the door was locked and nobody was home. A neighbor told them that they were in a funeral home located along Naguilian Road. When they finally arrived there, Mr. Santos and his companions were greeted by the cries of his sister, Fecora, his brother, Jewel's wife Brea, and the other mourners. They had been there for two days before Mr. Santos and the company arrived. Mr. Santos went beside the coffin in front of the people to make the announcement that they would bring his brother to Kabayan the very next day.

Mr. Santos had no problem preparing their house for the wake because it was always customary for everybody in town to voluntarily help whenever there were events like funerals, weddings, birthdays and others. Everything was already prepared ready for the wake when Mr. Santos and others who came from the city arrived.

"Oh, my God. Please!" One of the mourners said.

"He left his very young daughters! What a sad ending!" Another one said.

Mrs. Maxim cried her heart out as she tried to get up to see his son's dead body. Everybody was concerned and helped her out.

"Why? Oh. God, why? Why did you take my son? He is so young! Why not me instead?" Mrs. Maxim cried.

Out of the blue, Bart came busting screaming and crying.

"Look at Bart. He knows that his uncle has passed away," one of the mourners said.

"Yes, poor Bart. He must love his uncle," another mourner said.

The planned week-long wake was extended for a few more days. The relative from Australia made her routinary call to her relative in Baguio, City. A telegram was sent to Mr. Santos expressing her intention to attend Jewel's wake and funeral. She had to finalize a deadline in her job which delayed her trip to the Philippines. Her traveling time from the capital city Manila to Baguio City and to Kabayan was also considered.

A speeding vehicle that could hardly be seen due to the disrupted dust in the air suddenly stopped. There emerged a fair, towering lady running towards the wake and immediately embraced Mrs. Fecora and Alexia while crying out loud. Mrs. Fecora introduced her to everybody.

"Brea, this is our cousin, Rhoda, from Australia. And Rhoda this is Brea Jewel's wife," Mrs. Fecora said.

"So, you are my cousin Jewel's wife. I am sorry. I wish I could have spent more time with him. I wish, oh I wish," Ms. Rhoda cried while giving Mrs. Brea a hug.

The Santoses decided not to practice and allow any traditional rituals during the wake. Many religious groups conducted services for the wake. The United Church of Christ was the home church of the Santoses which was not surprising. The Baptist and The Catholic churches were also given chances to conduct their services for being parts of the main churches in Kabayan. But the puzzling of all were the presence of groups from faraway places that the Santoses were unfamiliar with. The door was opened for the visitors but nobody expected Bart to escape at any given time.

Mrs. Santos went to the room where Bart was lying. "Bart I know it must be difficult for you to understand but please Bart, Be a good boy. Please Bart. Please stop running out. Don't be a burden in this time of sorrow. Please, be a good boy," she got the bag of chocolates given by his Aunt Rhoda from the drawer and showed it close to Bart's face. "Look, Bart. Look, Just look at this bag of chocolates. Don't wander your eyes and concentrate on what I am holding. You have too much supply of chocolates that you don't need to go to the store anymore. Please Bart. Be a good boy."

After a few minutes, Bart went downstairs and ran to the store for a bar of chocolate. Mrs. Santos stamped her way of chasing after Bart. She grabbed him and yanked him from the store back to their house.

"What are you doing my son? I told you earlier that you have ample supplies of chocolate from your Aunt Rhoda. Here, I even showed them very close to your face. Please, I beg you, don't repeat this foolishness please," Mrs. Santos said as she sent Bart to the master bedroom.

The eulogy service took place at the UCCP church. The three church leaders of Kabayan the UCCP, Baptist Church, and The Catholic Church were invited to conduct different parts of the service. Those who wished to talk were given chances. The remains were brought to the public cemetery for his final rest. Several of the relatives and friends from faraway places left right after the funnel. Others such as Rhoda, Jewel's family and in-laws including Mrs. Fecora and her family and Mrs. Santos' sister stayed for a couple more days before leaving.

Chapter XIX

Bart was in his room arranging some buttons and scribbling on the walls with crayons.

"What did you do to our walls?" Mrs. Santos asked.

Mrs. Santos felt her blood boiling when he saw what Bart had done. She smiled when Bart stared at her with a smile on his face. She squinted and saw the scribbles on the wall in detail and recognized shapes that resembled everyday objects such as trees, a wheel, a chain, circles, squares, triangles, lines and other.

"My son, my son, my talented son. I hope that God will take you first before us when he decides to take any of us," Mrs. Santos said.

Someone surprised the Santos household with a knock on the door. Gina peeped through the window to check if anyone was around. Gina saw a tall, muscular, and beautiful Chinese looking lady in front of the house.

Who could she be? Gina said to herself as she was opening the door.

"Hello, Miss, Is Auntie home?" The lady asked.

"Yes, she is," Gina answered.

"Kindly tell her Liza Knoepe, the son of her cousin Mathew, is here," the lady said.

"Okay, come in, and I will tell her you are here," Gina said.

Gina went to Mrs. Santos and told her about the visitor.

"Hello, so you are Mathew's daughter? Am I right?" Mrs. Santos said.

"Yes Auntie," Liza said.

"Come in please and how is your dad? And everybody back home?" Mrs. Santos asked.

"They are all good and my dad makes furniture for a living," Liza said.

"Okay, good for him." Mrs. Santos said.

The conversation continued. Mrs. Santos learned that her niece was part of the recent hiking team to Mt. Pulag. It was opened for tourism despite being guarded by the Kabayan people as a sacred place. "Mt Pulag" was considered the home of the "Ibaloi" gods by the town's forefathers. The hiking team lost a male member during the hike. The authorities, including Mr. Santos, went to the site where they last saw him. The villages around the mountain also helped with the search, but none were successful. Three days had passed, and several search and rescue groups made some attempts, but again with no success. The search was only done by land due to the unavailability of resources to launch an aerial search. A "mambunong" from the nearest barangay claimed that he sensed the presence of the lost hiker within "Mt. Pulag." He claimed that the missing hiker was brought by the unseen to the dimension of the spirit world due to the inconsiderate actions of hikers and tourists. The indiscriminate throwing of trash, the over-harvesting of orchids, the hunting of "buwet" (cloud rats), the recent forest fires and the disturbance brought by the over-population of tourists every single day destroyed the sanctity of the mountain. The "mambunong" suggested to the authorities that he must perform a ritual to bring the hiker back to the world of people. He led the officials present and the rescue team to the spot where he believed the hiker was lost. He sacrificed a native chicken by cutting its neck upside down and letting it bleed to the ground while performing a prayer chant. A vague figure was moving from a distance towards the people. The closer it got, the more defined it became until it took the shape of a naked enchanting woman. All eyes were on her when the missing hiker cropped-up from nowhere, tired, confused, and with scrapes all over his body, and the woman just faded. The group accompanied the rescued man to the town center with questions on their mind regarding what they had witnessed.

The survivor was sent to the dispensary for a general check-up. The hikers were accommodated at the old house where the Santoses used to stay. They were free to do whatever they pleased in town with the condition that they would not cause any troubles and disturbances to the residents.   After they were given ample time to rest, Mr. Santos and a police officer interviewed the survivor.

"Hello, I am Mr. Santos, the police chief, and this is just a routine interview. Don't worry, nothing will be held against you. We are just doing this for our record. Kindly state everything you remember about what happened to you at Mt. Pulag."

"Okay sir, we were hiking up the mountain and I was the last behind the porters, and suddenly, I could not take another step on the same spot where I was found. I shouted so hard hoping that those who were in front of me would notice but they kept going without glancing back at me," the survivor said.

"I could see and hear them, but it seemed like there was a force field or something that became a barrier between my companions and me. They could not see nor hear me back. I cannot even believe until now that I was missing for three days. I thought it was only for a couple of hours or so. Oh, The same phenomenon happened with different groups who were looking for me. I was there standing in front of them but they could not hear nor see me at all," he added.

"Okay, no further questions," Mr. Santos said.

"I almost forgot, what is your name and when will you plan to leave?" Mr. Santos said.

"Sir, I am Samuel and not certain about the day we are leaving. I must ask my companions," the hiker said.

"If you will stay a bit longer, you are all welcome to attend my son Bart's simple birthday celebration on Saturday. That will be the day after tomorrow," Mr. Santos said.

"Thank you, sir. I will inform the others," the hiker said.

There was one missed detail, the time of the birthday celebration. The hiking group went to the Santos residence in the morning. Gina saw them approaching and welcomed them in. Mr. and Mrs. Santos walked to the living room and conversed with them. They asked each of their names and where they are originally from. They also informed the hikers that Bart's birthday was a dinner gathering. The hikers asked to see the birthday boy. Bart showed up and the hikers greeted him with a happy birthday with smiles on their faces but Bart had no reaction and just looked at them individually.   He went back upstairs and everybody laughed. The hikers returned to their quarters with the promise of returning later to help with the preparation. Visitors came late that afternoon with gifts or with dishes they cooked themselves. Some of the hikers were already there helping with the preparation while the other members were searching for Bart's gift. When everything was set, the pastor started the celebration with a short devotion and a prayer for the birthday boy and for the blessing of the food, followed by the traditional birthday song.

"Hapi birtdi tono," Bart tried to sing with them.

 They all laughed with great happiness and then enjoyed the food served. The other hiker came with a large pack of "Milo" (an Australian powdered chocolate drink brand that is popular in different parts of the world, including the Philippines.) Bart appeared to be enjoying his food when he was distracted by the Milo. Mrs. Santos opened the package and made Bart a mug. Most of the visitors left after the meal except for a few that included the hikers. Mr. Santos brought out two bottles of Fundador. (a brand of Spanish brandy.) The ladies went ahead after they were done helping with the dishes while the men stayed and had a drinking session with Mr. Santos. They laughed at Bart as he mistakenly drank a cocktail of coke and brandy like a non-alcoholic drink. The drinking men again laughed when Bart shook his head and shrugged his shoulders after swallowing the drink. They gave him some of the leftover food which he feasted on and went to bed.

Chapter XX

Bart was going down the stairs with his face coated with his own blood. Mrs. Santos cleaned his face with a clean towel. She inspected the other parts of his body for injuries but nothing was found.

"What happened to your face? Please be careful my boy," Mrs. Santos said.

Bart's face was smeared with blood again just a few hours after it was wiped clean. Bell saw what was going on and washed Bart's bloody face. She applied antibiotic cream on the affected area to prevent infection.

"Bart, why? What the damn? What are you doing with your face? You are destroying your handsome face. Please quit what you are doing. Please," Mrs. Santos said.

Every time the wound was healing, Bart removed the scab making it fresh. The Santoses could not express how mad they were and let Bart understand that his actions were wrong. Blood stopped oozing from his face when he tasted some ass-whooping.

Irene was about to pee when she noticed a foul smell. She searched the source and saw dark- colored liquid on the toilet bowl. Bart rushed and shoved Irene to the side to pee. He was screaming with only dribbles coming out. Bell and Gina heard the noise and rushed to check it out. They asked Martin to inspect Bart's organ to see if there were visible problems, but it looked fine to him. The only unusual thing was the foul smell. Mrs. Santos came home from work, witnessing what was happening. She again inspected Bart's private parts closer and saw nothing wrong. She thoroughly washed it with soap and water to alleviate the smell.

"Bart ceased the scratching of his wound, and now this. He really needs to consume more pure clean water. This must be the effect of drinking Milo, soft drinks and sweet drinks throughout these years. He really needs water to help cleanse his urinary system from now on. Get some drinking water and let's force it into his system. Martin, open his mouth while I pour the water little by little. You, Bell and Gina hold the rest of his body to prevent him from ever escaping," Mrs. Santos said.

Swallows replaced Bart's attempt to scream. It looked like a ruthless torture scene, like a prisoner being forced to drink something for not confessing. The only difference here was the participants were doing the act for Bart's sake.

Water was still being given to Bart in the subsequent days. His complaints were lesser as he consumed water more frequently. It was until one day, he drank water on his own. His pee also became less painful and odorous. He also drinks water most of the time when he consumes sweets. Maybe he realized he needed water in his life after all.

Mr. Santos took Bart with him walking outside as a form of exercise that Saturday morning. He requested Gina to unlock the door. Right away, he sprinted to the store to have his chocolates. Mr. Santos followed him to pay the store owner. He grabbed Bart's arm to direct him when they were strolling around, to encourage perspirations in order to wake their sleeping chunky bodies into physical activity. They did not go far from the house when Bart began screaming and limping on his left foot. As Mr. Santos inspected the deal with Bart, he saw blood oozing from the sole of his foot. He swept away to carry Bart home.

"Gina, anybody. Please open the door," Mr. Santos said.

"Uncle, what happened to Bart?" Gina said as she opened the door.

"He was wounded on his left foot. And clean it up, please," Mr. Santos said.

"Oh my, yes. Does the wound need some stitches?" Mrs. Santos asked as she went to check on Bart.

"I believe not, I will just clean it and put on some band-aid," Gina said

After the treatment, they carried him to his room so he could take a rest.

He was his usual self when he woke-up. The affected foot was colored red. Stains were on the blanket, on the stairs, and on the CR. The band-aid was removed.

"Blood again? Maybe it's Bart?" Irene asked.

"Mommy, mommy. Bart is bleeding again," she added.

"Why? Why are you so hard headed? Why do you always love bleeding? Instead of being cured, you go do that," Mrs. Santos said.

"Bell, go to Dr. Reagan's residence, and tell him about Bart's bleeding foot. Go quickly. Run like the wind if you must," Mrs. Santos said.

"Look at your foot, Bart. It was already okay, and doesn't need any more treatment. Now that it got worse, maybe it will need stitching," Mrs. Santos said.

Mrs. Santos kept wiping Bart's foot with a piece of cloth. The doctor inspected the foot the minute he arrived. The wound really needed some stitching. He requested Mrs. Santos for her assistance with the minor operation. The wound needed to be stitched up to prevent further bleeding. Bart was strained by others present while the operation was going on. The doctor wanted to administer an Anti-tetanus shot after the operation, but there were none available. He only prescribed an antibiotic and painkiller medication hoping there will be no complications.

"Someday, you Martin, and Irene will be dealing with this by yourselves. I hope your future partners will be understanding enough to be with you in all of this," Mrs. Santos said after the doctor had left.

Everybody relaxed after and had their afternoon nap. Mumbles and screams were heard from Mrs. Maxim's room. Bell went to check her out, and as she opened the door, the smell of fecal matter hit her face. She went inside to open all the windows to help alleviate the odor. She glanced at Mrs. Maxim, talking with her eyes closed. She escaped from the unpleasant odor for some fresh air outside. She went back later to see her conscious and cleaned her behind. The "lampin"(a piece of cloth big enough as a diaper substitute) because adult diapers were still unavailable during those times.

It was time for Bart's medication. Mr. Santos tried to give the medication but he refused to take it. He refused to open his mouth and faced the opposite side away from the pill.

"Take the damn pill," Mr. Santos said.

"Swallow the pill," he said. As he was trying to put the pill into his son's mouth.

"Let him be, Daddy," Mrs. Santos said.

"The medicines are in capsule form anyway. The outer covering can be removed and the contents can be mixed with the milo that I am making," Mrs. Santos added.

It worked. Bart never detected the presence of the medications that were mixed in his drink.

The bandage of the feet was again removed later. The wounded area was still intact due to the presence of the suture despite the presence of scratch marks.

Chapter XXI

The family car was a 79 Mitsubishi Galant unsuitable for the rugged terrain of Kabayan. It had to be sold or traded for a more appropriate vehicle. Mr. Santos, with a mechanic relative, went to the city to trade the vehicle. The seven-hour drive took them ten hours because they had to travel at a slow, careful pace. They ended up with a second-hand two-door Volkswagen Beetle that was built for the toughest roads ever. Their return was interrupted by a powerful sound. They both checked, but they found no damage at all. They wondered throughout the rest of the trip what caused the sound. They arrived home safe and unscathed. The kids were very excited to get in the new family car. Irene opened a door and saw an elongated piece of metal. Upon Mr. Santos' inspection, it was a bullet from a "paltic" gun. (The Philippine version of a 38-caliber handgun.)

Mr. Santos took the bullet from Irene's hand, saying "My God, the loud sound we heard on our way home made us think of a flat tire or something wrong with the car. Thank God none of us was hit."

They all inspected the car for damages or bullet holes but nothing was found. The mystery was never solved, but the important thing was Mr. Santos and his companion were not hurt. The Santoses planned for a simple car blessing inviting only those who were closest to them. Nothing can be kept secret in town. News can easily circulate on everybody's senses. It was exceptional with the Santoses because they were always in the public eye. The original plan was to prepare a simple dish of "pinikpikan" (Igorot chicken dish), "pancit" and macaroni salad but it ended up adding dog and goat dishes to the menu.

The version of macaroni salad in the northern part of the Philippines has the main ingredients of elbow macaroni pasta, condensed milk, mayonnaise, cheese, fruit cocktail and raisins. Other ingredients are optional such as all-purpose cream, cubed gelatin, sweet corn, fresh or candied fruits. Bart loved macaroni salad, with the exception of fruit cocktails and raisins. Bart saw the macaroni salad stored in the fridge and consumed a portion of it. He felt the preserved fruits when he took a bite and pieces kept sticking on his teeth. He went screaming and biting his right arm like he had a severe problem.

"What's wrong?" One of the guests asked.

"What's wrong, my son?" Mrs. Santos asked.

"Sorry my son, we forgot. We should have separated a mixture exclusively for you. A mixture without fruit cocktail and raisins," Mrs. Santos said.

Bart kept on screaming and biting his arm.

"Hey, stop being noisy! We will remove the raisins fruit cocktail from the macaroni salad, you finicky one!" Mrs. Santos said.

"And look, you are injuring yourself! Your right arm is injured so badly!" She added.

"Stop it! You are very noisy! This is no big deal!" She added.

Bart refused the macaroni salad that Mrs. Santos fixed and persisted in what he was doing. She then sent him to his room to cool down and not disturb the entire occasion. He lay on his bed and gradually eased from crying. He went back to the kitchen to have a full meal prepared by Gina. He returned to bed after he was satisfied with his meal. He never again woke throughout the night except for several visits to the CR.

Bart woke the next morning without any signs of distress. Nobody detected the red spot on his head that was covered with hair. They went on with their normal day. It was only exposed when Bell was about to rub shampoo on his head during a bath. She could see what looked like blood mixed in with the shampoo on his head. She informed Mrs. Santos about what she had detected.

"Bart, Bart, why again?" Mrs. Santos said.

"Why is that? His head is bleeding," Irene said.

Mrs. Santos immediately cleaned the wound and applied bandage on Bart's head.

"Go to the dispensary, and ask for the doctor," she told Gina.

Gina ran as fast as she could but nobody was around. She then went to the nearest house of a health worker, the school nurse and explained what was going on with Bart's head. The nurse responded immediately at the Santoses' residence.

"Why don't you quit your habit of scratching? See, you could die from this thing!" Mrs. Santos said.

The nurse made a thorough check-up on Bart's head. She discovered a single spot that was the source of bleeding. She also saw some crust and redness in other areas. She carefully removed Bart's hair, making him bald. She cleaned the wound and applied medicated cream on the entire head before covering it with a clean cloth. Mr. Santos was in the station and had no idea what was going on with Bart. He rushed home the second he heard about it. Nobody expected that Bart's condition was worse than the simple bleeding of his head.

"What had he been eating?" The nurse asked.

"I don't know? We just had the car blessing yesterday with goat meat, dog meat, "pancit", "pinikpikan", and salad," Mr. Santos said.

"The Doctor is not here, so I have to use some remedies and observe if his condition worsens, then he must be rushed to the nearest hospital," the nurse said.

"I remember there was "balut" (a partially fertilized duck's egg with a developed chick that is a delicacy in the Philippines and other Southeast Asian Countries) brought by our neighbor Mrs. Garcia and I believe he ate some," Gina said.

I will assume that he has an allergic reaction to food, maybe the "balut" and "pinikpikan" because of his symptoms," the nurse said.

She advised the Santoses to avoid feeding him with poultry products and wash his head with boiled guava leaves before letting it dry and applying the medicated ointment she recommended. In addition, she recommended Bart to be seen by the doctor as soon as possible.

A visitor noticed what appeared to be a turban on Bart's head sealed with tapes. He asked what the purpose of the cloth on his head was. Bell told the visitor the details of what happened to Bart's head.

It so happened that the visitor was a "mambunong." He had his attention on Bart and forgot he was there to visit Mrs. Maxim. He instructed Bell to gather some materials for the healing ritual.

The "mambunong" entered Bart's room, with Bart taking a nap. Nobody was allowed in the room while he was performing the healing rituals. He closed all possible entrances and exits of air and went on burning some plant materials while chanting a prayer. After the room was filled with smoke, the "mambunong" went out and instructed Bell not to let anybody enter for an hour or more. He also instructed her on what to do later on. It was not certain if it was the nurse's interventions or the "mambunong's" ways of healing that cured Bart. Nobody cared, what mattered was Bart's recovery.

Mrs. Maxim was against what the "mambunong" did. She claimed that what happened was the work of pure evilness direct from the power of Satan himself. "You devil worshiper. You devil's children," were even her accusations to Bell for allowing Bart to go through the "mambunong's" healing rituals. The household members kept on diverting the discussion whenever she expressed her strong opposition about the matter. The strange thing was despite of her opposition to the supernatural and the unchristian ways, she was seeing dead people. She was able to describe every person she had seen in details. Her perception dictated false presumptions that whoever she could see were still living. It gave her confidence to argue with her housemates about weather what she saw was dead or still alive.

Chapter XXII

The members of the clan could not wait to attend the reunion that Mrs. Maxim tried to initiate. Unfortunately, the fast-approaching reunion was converted into Mrs. Maxim's wake. Several relatives received the news while others came to the venue, Kabayan expecting a family reunion but were welcomed with a funeral instead. A few stayed long enough to give their condolences to the Santoses while others stayed until the funeral. Mrs. Maxim lived in the past, and "Igorot" rituals were expected to be applied during the wake and funeral but because she was a devoted Christian, such rituals were prohibited. Gambling and alcohol were also banned. A neighbor relative opened his doors to relatives who wished to drink and gamble.

A group of unfamiliar faces surprised the Santoses and relatives present during the wake. They were supposed to attend the family reunion but ended up attending Mrs. Maxim's wake.

"We are here for the family reunion, but we can see that it is the death of a relative, if I am not mistaken," The elder of the group said.

"Yes, it is Mrs. Maxim's wake," one of the present relatives said.

The group approached the coffin to pay their respects and expressed their condolences to the Santoses. They each introduced themselves and the elder explained their family lineage and how they believed they were related to the deceased and the rest of the relatives who were also attending the wake.

"So, your grandmother is the "in-eshab" of our grandfather? And if that is true then welcome to the clan," Mr. Santos said.

"Yes, what you heard is right," the elder said.

"Okay, we must allot a time to talk before you leave. We have more reason for the reunion to materialize," Mr. Santos said.

Bart ran to the store when the opportunity presented itself. He went to grab the chocolates he loved. Most of the new acquaintances looked at the situation with big bright eyes and rounded lips like someone yawning.

"That's my special son, Bart," Mr. Santos said.

"Bear with him. He is just like that," Mrs. Santos said.

"It's okay with us. We were just stunned with the way he ran but other than that, we understand," one of them said.

"Yes, no problem with us," one of them added.

Mr. Santos gathered the remaining relatives for a short meeting. Temporary officers and committees were assigned with the tentative date of the reunion. Everybody wanted Kabayan to be the initial venue for the respect and memory of Mrs. Maxim for being the initiator.

Mrs. Maxim's room was locked and unused for more than a year. It was just an extra room in the house. Prior to locking, Gina and Bell did general cleaning in the house. Gina was tired from the cleaning and was unaware that she had fallen asleep in Mrs. Maxim's room. In the darkness of the night, she dreamed about Mrs. Maxim then felt a heavy crushing pain on her chest impeding her breathing that woke her. She couldn't remember the entirety of the dream, but she remembered Mrs. Maxim sitting on her face. She never told anybody of the incident in the room. Gina and Bell knew that one of them would be released anytime. Gina pre-empted the Santoses' decision and informed Mr. and Mrs. Santos about her plan of renting a vacant space in the market to start her own business. The Santoses were very supportive. Mr. Santos helped her acquire the necessary permits and a fraction of the capital she needed to start the business.

Mrs. Maxim's room was utilized as a storage room in the meantime. Many junk and unused things that took up space were stored in the room. The bed was relatively maintained. Bart was drawn into the room day after day and just laid on the bed which was Mrs. Maxim's final resting place. All members of the family, including Bell, noticed some peculiarity with Bart every time he was in the room. One was the moment when he was laughing so hard like someone was tickling him. Goosebumps and shivers all over the body were felt by anyone who had heard him. There was another moment when Mrs. Santos heard Bart in the room as if he was talking with a clear diction to a live person. Irene witnessed a time when Bart was laughing by himself in their late grandmother's room. She had the strange feeling of an actual being invisible to the naked eye that gave her chills through her spine.

Paranormal happenings were not new at Kabayan. There was a time when teenage high school girls were transformed into different creatures. Their timid normal-self became violent with a deep voice, bloodshot eyes and the strength of a thousand men. Their fellow students, teachers and men could hardly restrain them. It required as many as ten people to restrain a single student. The municipal government didn't want to take any chances and got all the help they could. They summoned the church leaders, health workers and even the available "mambunong" to help with the crises. The priest sprayed holy water coupled with prayers that agitated the affected students until they were transformed to their normal selves. The "mambunong" chanted a prayer while scattering salt around the affected student. The student was irritated every time her skin touched the salt until her behavior improved.

"What is all this? Salt? What's happening? Why so many people?" The young girl asked.

"You were in a "suknog" (possessed by evil spirits) state and acted violently. So, I had to cure you and cast what was causing your behaviors away," the "mambunong" said.

"Oh, really? I thought I was just asleep, having a weird dream," the young girl said.

"Well you didn't! So, tell us what was the dream all about?" The "mambunong" said.

"There was this group of "ampasit" (the "Igorot" version of leprechaun or elf) that dressed me in a white gown and they tried to feed me with uncooked flesh that tasted awful. I asked for salt to mask the taste but they were angry at me and tried to hurt me. That was when I woke up to this salt all over me," she said.

The girl looked fine until she returned to her previous state, and the "mambunong" was not able to prevent it from happening again, and called the priest who was busy with the other girls. He prayed, splashed some holy water, and said the holy word, "In the name of the Almighty Got I cast thy demons. Leave this child of God alone." Then the young girl was okay again.

"A lady in a white gown without a face is floating towards me. Please don't let her get me, please." The young lady was saying in a loud voice as she was crying.

The other affected girls were faced with similar situations. The school system suspended all levels of classes from kindergarten through high school until they could sort things out. People were in fear of the phenomenon spreading and claiming more victims. The crisis was all over the nationwide news. Available religious leaders were requested to have services on the school grounds. The 'mambunong" was also encouraged to perform rituals to make the situation better. A vacant lot in between the multi-purpose hall and the school ground was being developed as an additional building for classrooms. When the bulldozer was digging, piles after piles of human bones were uncovered. Before continuing with the construction, the authorities and volunteers carefully dug all the bones that they could and requested the "mambunong" to shed light on whose bones were discovered. The "mambunong" did his ritual and was in a trance with the vision of who they really were.

"The piles of bones were those of World War II Japanese soldiers, and they were telling me that their souls are lost in this physical realm. They just wanted to find their way to the other side, to the next life," the "mambunong" said.

The bones were transferred to another vacant lot and given a proper Christian burial. That was when the mysterious occurrences stopped. After what happened, the Santoses were a bit worried about what was going on with Bart recently. On the other hand, they were very confident that God wouldn't allow dreadful things to happen to him because he was his special son.

Chapter XXIII

The Santoses received an invitation to Johnny and Chaligto's wedding two months in advance. Johnny's father was Mrs. Santos' first cousin and Chaligto's family was from Kabayan. It is a wedding tradition in the Philippines that the venue is always at the bride's residence or hometown. A note was enclosed with the invitation asking the Santoses if they could accommodate several of Johnny's family and relatives during the wedding period.   The Santoses knew Chaligto's family, but they were not close with them even though they were a few blocks away from each other. Mrs. Santos wrote an approval letter and sent it to Johnny through the "bus conductor." (The helpers of the public transport bus or "jeepney" drivers who act as the fair collector and stewards/stewardess of the land.)

Mr. Santos has been eyeing any vacancies in the police force of Baguio City or any of the municipalities near the city for quite some time. A telegram addressed to him was received during the wedding preparation. The Santoses attended the wedding and bonded with the newlyweds' relatives and visitors. Mrs. Santos was enjoying her bonding with her relatives, for she had never seen most of them for a long time. The following day, Mr. Santos hitched with the visitor whose ride had enough space for him going to the city. Mr. Santos should have been qualified for the position. Besides, he was only requesting a lateral transfer, but more must be done. He had to seek help from some powerful political personalities or some high government officials for their influences. He needed to do such a thing because everything was all about politics. Powerful officials' influences were big factors in the employment selection process, especially for high-profile positions, thus, the saying "It is not what you know but whom you know." He was automatically guaranteed to be appointed for the position. For formality's sake, he had to go through the entire selection process just like the other applicants. Ideally, Mr. Santos was against the twisted system, he had no choice but to go with the flow in order to survive in the real world.

Mr. Santos shared the good news with his family. The children showed the opposite of eagerness despite being big fans of the city. They were fidgeting and could not keep still thinking about the adjustment they had to pull through from the peaceful life they were comfortable at, to the new bustling and hustling city life. He explained that the main reason for moving to the city was for Bart's sake.

"Why do we have to move?" Martin asked.

"Yah, why do we have to move? Isn't Bart the only one who needs to move?" Irene asked.

"Both of you must understand. Your father and I cannot take care of all of you when your brother is in the city, and the two of you are here. We must learn to understand and compromise," Mrs. Santos said.

"But I don't want to leave our home. My friends and my life are here," Irene said.

"We all have to go with Bart whether the two of you like it or not," Mrs. Santos said.

The Santoses were adjusting to city life. Irene and Martin were very shy rural kids that didn't have the confidence to talk with their city peers and the city folks. They were the new kids in school who were reluctant to interact with their classmates. They did not participate much in class activities. Martin saw the sign "Popsicle for sale" on a convenience store's window on his way home. He stopped and stood in front of the establishment for a few minutes. His mind was going back and forth on whether he would enter to buy the popsicle or just leave and continue walking. The person in the store noticed him and went out the door.

"Hi, there, young boy. How can I help you?" She said.

Martin looked at her without any expressions. He tried to answer but his throat became so dry that sounds never came out. He then ran as fast as he could and felt the beat of his heart while his body was trembling.

"Why? I am such a wheeze. Popsicle! Popsicle!" Those were the words he uttered so loud while hiding in an area where he thought nobody could see him.

It had been weeks since they moved, but Martin still felt like he didn't belong. He kept moving, feeling disappointed with himself, and almost cried, but he kept it all to himself.

"What is Bart doing in the living room all covered with a blanket on the sofa?" Martin said.

"There is not enough room to sit with him doing that," he added.

"Just let him be. He is still freaking-out and refuses to enter his new room," Bell said.

"Oh, well," Martin was saying while shrugging his shoulders.

A few months later, a stranger came to visit while Mr. Santos was preparing for work.

"Good morning sir, I am the man living at the house across the street, and I am just here bearing gifts for your son," the man said.

"Gifts? What for? Okay then, so kind of you. Just leave it there, and I am sorry I don't have time to entertain visitors right now as I am preparing for work," Mr. Santos said.

"It's okay, sir. Just make sure that your son enjoys it," the man said.

"Wait for a moment. Who are you referring to? I have two sons," Mr. Santos said.

"Your son. The chubby one, sir," the man said.

"I am sorry I will not disturb you anymore sir. I'll go ahead," he added.

"Okay thank you." Mr. Santos said knowing that the gift was for Bart.

Mr. Santos had his daily morning routine of reviewing arrests and case files. It was also his habit to know what was happening in the precinct and with each of the police officers. One of the files caught his interest. He saw a picture of someone he was familiar with. He could not remember where he saw the guy on file at first but something sparked his memory.

So, this guy was oiling me up huh, trying to get on my good side. That scumbag. Now I get it. Were playing on his thoughts while reading the file.

The same guy gave another surprise to Bart. The last time was a teddy bear, and the next was a battery-operated toy police car complete with sirens.

"Sorry again, Sir and Madam, but I really love your cute son. It just melts my heart each time I see him," the guy said.

"Okay, thank you. You can go now and never come back again. I know what you are trying to do. If you attempt to return, I will not think twice about putting you in the slammer," Mr. Santos said.

He bowed his head and left without saying another word.

"Who the hell was that?" Mrs. Santos asked.

"Somebody who has a record of fraud and a pending case trying to get on my good side through Bart. In fact, he lives just across the street," Mr. Santos said.

"I hate it when someone does that," he added.

The Santoses went on with their day; Mr. Santos with his job and the kids with school. Mrs. Santos had taken the opportunity to return to school for her master's degree while she was still free. The kids were becoming well-adjusted to the environment. They realized that they were not in Kabayan anymore, where they lived a quiet and peaceful life and where everybody knew each other. The city life was different; there was no time to be shy and weak. Everybody must be active and assertive about what they want in order to survive.

Bart was moving into the apartment, unlike before when he stayed on the living room couch. He also slept in his room at night or when he was sleepy. The Santoses were stricter in terms of his safety. They knew that the city wasn't as considerate as Kabayan. They knew that the outside world was full of bad things. Bell knew that she must have extra eyes when taking care of Bart.

Bell went to the store to buy something, making sure to lock the door from the outside when she left Bart. Bart managed to escape the apartment while she was away. He ran across the street without any regard for the ongoing traffic. He was lucky not to get hurt, but it created a stir.

"Bullshit! If you want to commit suicide, please don't involve us!" A driver on the street yelled.

Bart went on to a grocery store at the side of the road. The sales ladies were shouting. "Help, police! Call the Police! A shoplifter is here!"

Bell heard the commotion, ran towards it and saw Bart eating a tub of ice cream. "Please pay! If it's not paid, it will be deducted from my salary, please!" The sales lady was telling Bell as if she was ready to hit somebody.

"Yes, don't worry I will!" Bell said.

"Please pay for the Ice cream. Please pay!" The sales lady kept on saying.

"I told you not to worry! Can't you see that he is not well! Can't you see that he has a condition?" Bell screamed just inches away from the sales lady's face, catching everybody's attention.

"I must bring him home first and come back to pay for the ice cream he got!" Bell said.

"But, don't go. Pay first. Don't go," The saleslady was persistent.

Some shoppers and employees stared and did nothing because they didn't want to be involved.

"Don't you understand the situation? And didn't you hear what I said? Are you stupid? Bell said.

A middle-aged lady entered the grocery store and saw what was going on.

"What is the problem here?" She asked.

"This thief and his companion refused to pay for the ice cream!" The sales lady said.

"No, she should understand. Bart here is a special child, and I must accompany him home before he takes more items here. I promise. I will return to pay what we owe. She doesn't understand what I am telling her. She is so inconsiderate!" Bell said.

"Okay, I will pay for the item, if it needs to be paid now, to get over with," the lady said.

"Are you sure, madam?" Bell asked.

"No problem. Don't worry about it. Just take your son or nephew home," the lady said.

"Thank you very much," Bell said.

Bell held one of Bart's arms while returning to the apartment. Bell was still dumbfounded on how Bart managed to escape. She was also thinking about the kind lady who paid for Bart's item. She wanted to thanks her but the situation didn't let her. She inspected the door only to find out that the locked padlock was not correctly connected to the padlock bolt.

Chapter XXIV

The Santoses lived in a five-story apartment building with three dwelling units in each floor except for the fifth floor, where the landlord and his family were staying. They rented the three-bedroom dwelling at the center of the fourth floor. The unit right below them was vacant when they moved in. It was later occupied by an elementary teacher from Kabayan who was promoted as a principal in a public school in the city. The Santoses welcomed him with overwhelming excitement because he was from the same municipality as they were. Mr. Santos tested the contact number of the foundation given to him a couple of years ago to see if it was still active. A secretary answered his call and set an appointment.

Everybody had to go on their day. Mr. Santos had to attend the appointment first before going to work. Bart and Bell were left alone in the apartment. The downstairs neighbor gave them two slices of chocolate cake before he went to work. He turned out to be generous to Bart. He sometimes gave him chocolate bars, candies, and many other goodies. His daughter was about the same age as Martin. They were both in the fifth grade. Irene would usually tease them of being a cute couple which always ignited conflict with Martin.

Bart must be prepared for his school life. It was strongly recommended that if he must be exposed in a new environment gradually. The school had a shuttle bus for the students, but they must be in the waiting area at the right scheduled time. In the case of Bart, he must be accompanied at all times when going to and from school and during class for the first few days until he was ready to be alone in school. Mr. Santos drove Bart with Bell on the first day of class. Bart went on screaming and biting his arm when they were entering the school gate. They tried convincing him to get out the car and enter the school premises but he continued screaming that caught the attention of the school headmaster

"Okay, stop forcing him to enter if he doesn't want to," the school headmaster said.

"Don't leave yet and let him relax. Let him feel the environment from the car," he added.

Bart was left screaming until he became more relaxed and the school headmaster allowed him to peek at the school building and the school grounds. At that point, he wasn't forced to do what he refused to participate in.

"Sorry, but he is not yet prepared for class. Be patient with him. You can bring him home now and accompany him again tomorrow. It must be the two of you, not another set of people," the school headmaster said.

Bart became comfortable at school. He was able to ride the" jeepney" accompanied by Bell to and from the school service waiting area without any problem. A girl who was as massive and behaved similarly to Bart joined the class a bit later. The staff observed the similarities they had. Even some of the students noticed.

"What if they grow up and have children?" One of the students asked.

"They must be sweethearts. So sweet together," another one said.

The school headmaster relayed to the school driver and his helper that he needed to meet with either Mr. Santos or Mrs. Santos to discuss Bart's progress in a given schedule. Bell and Bart went home safe without any mishaps. Bell always kept in her mind to anticipate any possible scenario when they were in public. She also carried with her chocolate bars and soft drink or either of the two incase Bart will misbehave.

The meeting was on a Saturday morning but Mr. Santos was unavailable. Mrs. Santos wasn't busy that day and went.

"Oh, you are here, Mrs. Santos. Come in to my office," the School Headmaster said.

"Hello sir. Just tell me what I need to know and I will listen," Mrs. Santos said.

"Mrs. Santos, it is normal for Bart in his condition to have certain habits, but we need to control his eating habits. He just shoves food in his mouth like there is no tomorrow. I know it is difficult, but we must try," the school headmaster said.

"He must also be taught the concept of ownership. He must understand that "What yours is yours and what is mine is mine" He just grabs chocolates and sweets from his classmates. He should know it's not right to do such an act."

"Also, his drinking preferences must be considered. He does drink lots of fluids, but he should drink more water than sweet or artificially flavored drinks."

"His diet must also be controlled. We don't want someone like him especially in his current condition to suffer from debilitating illnesses, do we? We all know that food is one of his enjoyments in life but do we still need him to have heart problems, or diabetes, or stroke? It is very difficult for someone like him to have such conditions."

"Interact with him like talking to a normal person when catching his attention or calling him. Those sorts of things, no baby talk and get him outside, go to the park as a family, let him experience other people as much as possible."

"Other than that, he is fine here, making progress bit by bit."

"I must have talked so much. Do you have any questions?"

"Well, no problem, sir. I am glad you told me about these things, and I will remember them. I will   even tell everybody at home about it," Mrs. Santos said.

"Yes, we must work together. Don't just expect us to do everything. He must also be taught at home," the school headmaster said.

They both had some humble snacks and casual conversations before Mrs. Santos left. She bought a take-away pizza which Bart almost consumed if nobody interrupted him. Each one must have at least a slice.   In this kind of simple situation, Bart must be taught a lesson that not everything revolves around him and not everything goes his way, as was advised by the school headmaster. Aside from chocolates, Bart's palate came to love junk foods, processed meats, sodas, and many unhealthy foods. He became less and less interested in fruits and vegetables that used to be part of his diet when they were in Kabayan. He became taller, gained more weight, and with Chinese Chua eyes, he was like being built-up as a sumo wrestler.

Mrs. Santos and Bell took turns accompanying Bart to school. This was with the exception of Friday. The whole day was dedicated to her master's class. In one of her turns to fetch Bart, Mrs. Santos rushed to the school service waiting area and kept on looking at her wrist watch while looking around for the school service. She waited, but the school service was not around. She again waited for another few minutes before she decided to go straight to school. As she was about to flag a taxi, the school service arrived only to find out that her watch was ahead of the actual time. She soon discovered that she made a big mistake of forgetting to buy chocolates or sweets on her way. Mrs. Santos and Bart entered a "jeepney" ride with ease, but Bart tried to grab the chocolate the lady brought out from her bag.   Bart's action almost hurt the guy beside the lady. Mrs. Santos tried to restrain him but without success. He was subsequently subdued when another person assisted Mrs. Santos.

"Why do you have to eat your chocolate in front of everybody? Why can't you just wait until you arrive home?" Mrs. Santos said.

The lady did not utter any word and returned the chocolate back in her pocket. A few of the passengers were understanding and weren't affected with Bart's behavior. In fact, the driver just went on driving and was not bothered by the commotion.

A passenger, at the top of her lungs said such words. "What the hell is this chaos?"

Another passenger reacted, "Oh my God. Oh my God."

"Hey lady, can't you see? Can't you even understand the obvious? That kid has a condition and please be considerate enough to give-up your chocolate to him. Or sell it if you want your money's worth," another passenger said.

The lady with the chocolate refused to give-up her chocolate but was forced to due to the pressure from a few of the passengers. Several passengers were startled with what happened and left the "jeepney" as soon as they could. Others who understood Bart's condition went on with their trip like nothing major happened. He finally behaved when he enjoyed the chocolate bar.

"Hey, what did you just do? You were not a good boy. You made the passengers fear you. Never do that again, or else you will receive the beating of a lifetime," Mrs. Santos was saying while they were walking a few blocks to the apartment.

Chapter XXV

Mrs. Santos' father, Patrick, was admitted to the hospital due to stroke. A relative of hers relayed the information. It was surprising for everybody because he was as strong as a bull in spite of his advance age of 71. He could even do some manual work as a young man would do. He even went for general check-ups every time he was in the city. Mrs. Santos rushed to the hospital for a visit to find her mom Maria and a cousin with him. They have been Mr. Patrick's watchers. Mrs. Santos visited every free time she had. Mr. Patrick stayed at the Santoses' apartment to rest and to avoid any stress, as recommended by the doctor. It was also more accessible for Mr. Patrick's doctor appointments as opposed to the five-hour trip from their hometown of Duckland. Mrs. Maria, on the other hand, went home to tend for their crops, pets and livestock.

Bell had to multiply herself with the situation. She had to attend to Bart, the home chores and the addition of Mr. Patrick. Summer vacation was great for her. Irene and Martin got to help her with the work at home. Irene was alone with Bart and Mr. Patrick because everybody was busy. She was wiping Bart's behind and bell was hanging the wet clothes outside when Mr. Patrick unlocked the door and went outside. She didn't expect it to happen.

"Oh shit, oh Shit. Where would grandpa be?" Irene said.

"Excuse me. Did you see a bald old man who walks awkwardly with a pair of white pajamas?" she asked a man walking towards her.

"Miss, sorry, I have never seen someone with that description," the stranger said.

"I saw him. He was going towards the main highway. Move fast. You might catch him. Be careful. He might cross the highway," a lady who was sitting in front of her porch said.

There was Mr. Patrick, exactly as the lady said. He was about to cross the street with cars racing when Irene pulled him in the nick of time.

"Hey, grandpa. What were you thinking? Don't you know it is dangerous?" Irene asked.

"I...I...I was just going for a stroll and see my friend, Larry," Mr. Patrick said.

"Let's go back home and let this be a lesson for me, and I hope everybody at home will not find-out about it" Irene said.

That was a relief. Imagine grandpa surviving a stroke but dying because of me. Her mind was telling herself.

Bell entered their unit and saw Mr. Patrick seated on one of the living room chairs with Irene slumped on the couch breathing heavily.

"What happened to you? You look like you have run a marathon?" Bell asked.

"Nothing manang," Irene said.

"Are you sure you are okay?" Bell asked.

"Yes manang. I am fine, really fine," Irene said.

She never mentioned what happened to the rest of the family but she promised to be more careful next time. Mr. Patrick stayed with the Santos for a few more weeks without any more untoward incidents. He went home to their home-town when he was fit enough to travel with the doctor's seal of approval.

I am a bit glad that dad was never neglected in his time of need when he was with us. We, at least did what we could for him. Mrs. Santos told herself.

Summer vacation was over after Mr. Patrick left the apartment, and everybody was preparing for their weekday activities. Bell helped Bart with his shower, changing of clothes, and went on with the other chores thinking that everybody was watching over him. After she was done with the chores, she called for Bart, but nobody reacted. They searched for him in every room, but he couldn't be found. Irene and Martin went ahead to school while the rest were busy searching for him. They knocked on every door in the apartment building but nobody saw him.   Mr. Santos went looking for him in the nearby establishments before going to work. He never filed an official missing person report but he organized some of the available police officers to join him with the search. Mrs. Santos did not continue with the search and stayed in the apartment just in case he was found. Other apartment occupants also helped with the search. A couple of hours later, a pretty Chinese-looking teenage girl brought Bart to the apartment. Mrs. Santos was there to receive Bart and before she could express her appreciation, the girl rushed away. The girl looked familiar but Mrs. Santos wasn't sure where she had seen her before.

Mr. Santos surprised the rest of the Santoses with a more spacious apartment. It was a two-story duplex with an ample yard for parking, and playground. The inside had its living room, kitchen and dining room with separate CR and laundry room. The second floor had three-bedroom spaces. The Santoses were very excited for Bart, for they expected him to like the new place. They thought he would be more relaxed due to its spacious nature. Just like any other unfamiliar place, it was the opposite. He screamed and refused to get out of the vehicle the moment they tried to let him in the new place. The majority of the neighbors watched what was happening. The Santoses were ready for any reactions or even retaliations from them. They discovered that most of them were either Mrs. Santos' relatives or Mr. Santos' friends and acquaintances.

Martin immediately went outside and roamed around the vicinity and their neighbors once they were settled in. He discovered a mini-mart selling cheap made-in-China products just across the main road from the duplex. It was a private home converted into a place of business. The main store looked like a living room, and the garage was converted into a fruit stand. Bart ran into the mini-mart, the same mini-mart that Martin discovered. A middle-aged woman not taller than five feet smiled, looked at Martin and Bart and spoke with a soft sweet voice.

"Just let him be. Maybe he is still choosing what he wants."

Mr. Santos suddenly entered the store not so long after. He saw Martin and Bart then approached the lady on the counter, intending to apologize and explain Bart's situation. He was surprised by a very familiar face smiling at him. It was one of his very good friend's widows.

"How are you?" Mr. Santos said while smiling back at her.

"I am fine. I am the store owner," the lady said.

Few words were said, but it was meaningful. Mr. Santos tried to pay whatever Bart got but the lady refused. Mr. Santos insisted, but the lady wasn't still accepting the payment. Mr. Santos wasn't happy about it but he kept within himself.

Business is business; it shouldn't matter if the customers are friends, family or acquaintances. It is not a place for socialization and free stuff. It is the business owner's source of income. Was bothering his conscience.

I hope I can pay her someday. It is not easy to earn a living. He added.

Mr. and Mrs. Santos were still finding answers and treatment for Bart. They found a psychiatrist and it gave them hope that maybe he could shed light on Bart's condition. They had speculations about Bart based on the newspapers and T.V. documentaries that touched on the subject but they wanted clear and straight answers directly from experts. The doctor confirmed their speculations when they brought Bart for a check-up. What he recommended to them was a drug-based treatment. He prescribed certain medications that Bart had to take for his lifetime.

The Santoses were preparing for church on a Sunday, just like what they always did. But Mrs. Santos had to leave earlier to go somewhere first before joining them later. One of the daily routines was Bart taking his medications.

"Bart, be a good boy and take your medicine," Mr. Santos said.

Bart still wouldn't open his mouth and tried to back down from his dad.

"Bart, take the damn medicine, so that we can go now!" Mr. Santos said.

"Martin, help me with your brother to make him take his medicines," Mr. Santos added.

"Yes, daddy. I will try to hold Bart," Martin said.

Mr. Santos and Martin's attempts failed. Irene joined the force, but it did not make any difference. Bart was powerful enough to refuse the medications. Mr. Santos' emotion could be palpable throughout the apartment. He slapped Bart across the face in an attempt to make him comply with taking his medicines, but again it failed. They went on without Bart taking any medicine when they realized they were late.

Mr. Santos and the kids arrived at the church full of people. Mrs. Santos was already there waiting for their arrival. Mr. Santos had no idea the kids weren't behind him. Just as he was about to enter, he called for them, but nobody answered. He went to the CR, but he only saw Martin with his cousin Norman.

"Where is Bart?" Mr. Santos asked.

"I don't know, Dad. It is you who's supposed to look after him. I was in front of him facing the opposite direction while you and Bart were at my back," Martin answered.

"You were supposed to look after him. And now he is lost. You are distracted by your cousin." Mr. Santos said.

Martin insisted on his explanations, but his dad kept on blaming him which shut him up. Instead of attending church, it became a search party.

They searched the church vicinity, and he was not there. They also searched the neighboring park but he was nowhere to be found. Mr. Santos asked some of the church goers for some help. Mrs. Santos went to a radio station to announce Bart missing to the public. They tried to search the city but without any success. Mr. Francesco tried his luck and there he found Bart in the distance eating an ice candy beside an old lady vendor

within the city park. The park guard talked to the vendor and tried to accompany Bart to the nearest police station but Mr. Francisco intervened. He took Bart, smiling at him, to their apartment and waited for the Santoses to pick him up.
The Santoses bought some take-out food and had their lunch at Mr. Francesco and his family's apartment before going home. Neighbors, relatives, and some friends waited for them at their apartment. They cheered for joy as the Santoses arrived with Bart. Days had passed and people were still asking about Bart's condition and wear bouts.

Chapter XXVI

Mrs. Santos' Aunt Kasumay the younger sister of Mr. Patrick, demanded the Santoses' presence at her birthday through his son Mack, who visited Mr. Santos at the police station. He gave the date and time of the occasion. A rough sketch with a simple direction of the house's location was also given because it was the Santoses' first visit to the place. Martin and Irene had never met relatives on her side of the family and never been to their grandaunt's residence, the suburban part of the city which ignited their desire to attend the occasion. They were welcomed by relatives with smiles on their faces the moment they arrived. Their expressions and how they treated Mrs. Santos demonstrated how much they missed her. Most of the relatives present were eager to speak with Mrs. Santos. Irene and Martin felt some shyness and just ate in a corner. Bart immediately lay on the sofa while nibbling the pieces of bones with meat given to him. Mack took the liberty to change Bart's meat as it was almost consumed with a lean one without any fat and bones. Bart was looking for his meat and began screaming and kicking the armrest of the sofa.

"What is happening to him?" Mrs. Kasumay asked.

"He was so upset because somebody got his meat," Mr. Santos said.

"Sorry, I didn't know. I only removed the bones in exchange with the lean meat," Mack said.

Mr. Santos got the plate of lean meat from Mack and tried to offer it to Bart but he just continued with his actions.

"Martin, come and help me get your brother off the couch he might destroy the arm rest," Mr. Santos said.

The Santoses were so mad; dragged Bart out the best they could and drove home as the people were focused on them.

"What were you doing Bart? What the hell? We were just there for only a few minutes? We were not able to bond with our relatives," Mrs. Santos said.

Bart offered his hand for hi-fives from the backseat while his father was driving. Everybody was more infuriated with his action and prevented him from doing so on their way home. Bart went straight to his room and sobered like he was guilty or something the moment they arrived. The Santoses closed the door and left him alone in his room.

Mrs. Santos' younger brother Benjie suddenly came for a visit the following week. He was a towering man that almost reached six feet tall in height with a skinny build and a face that could brighten up a room.

"What brought you here, my brother?" Mrs. Santos asked.

"Well, somebody back home had informed me that there is an agency here in the city recruiting for a carpenter abroad, and I am interested in applying. They told me that the agency would help the applicants with all they need as long as they follow their instructions. The other applicants also informed me about their "Fly now Pay later" promo." Mr. Benjie said.

"Oh, great. But be very careful. There are lots of fakes out there," Mrs. Santos said.

"Yes, sis the main reason for coming is to check them out and if it turns out to be legit. By the way, can I stay here until my application is approved?" Mr. Benjie asked.

"No problem, anytime, you are family, and I will tell my husband but I am sure he will understand," Mrs. Santos said.

Benjie temporarily stayed with the Santoses while he was accomplishing and waiting for his application. He helped with some chores in the house, especially cooking, a skill he excelled in. He was also responsible for driving Bart to and from school. The children became more intimate with him and so with Bell that people often mistook them for a couple when the reality was they were relatives.

The longer Mr. Benjie stayed, the more he became hammered with breaths that could disinfect a room. There wasn't a moment that he was sober to the point of neglecting his application.

"Bro, I think you must go home already. You are wasting your time here. You are not being serious with your life. Take care of dad. He needs the best care he could get. It is even very shameful to my husband who doesn't say a damn word to scold you. You know him. How he gets mad. But he is kind to you," Mrs. Santos said.

"You are wasting all our time and life with that habit of yours," she added.

The next day, Mr. Benjie had already packed his clothes ready to go home. Mrs. Santos gave his brother some cash for the bus fare and meal. Mr. Santos never talked to him nor gave him any advice, for he wanted his wife to resolve their own family mishap. Mrs. Santos went to the agency to request for a refund because of the large number of expenses incurred for his brother's application. The agency representative present in the office explained to Mrs. Santos that she nor her brother were not entitled to a refund because the fees were used to pay the embassy, his paper works and the utility expenses in the office. She also emphasized that it was her brother's fault why his application was never finalized or he was discredited as compared to the other applicants who showed so much interest in their applications. Mrs. Santos soon realized the situation, then apologized and scooted away as fast as she could.

Mrs. Santos received a letter from her mother asking for the refund. Mrs. Santos responded with the explanation that it was her brother's negligence on why his application was canceled with the "no refund policy" of the agency when the applicant was at fault. Mrs. Maria was asking for the fees paid with the hopes of a refund because most of the money used was half her pension. Aside from the expenses in the agency, Mrs. Santos was also generous enough to give his brother for his personal use.

The Santoses noticed the frequent presence of Bart at the apartment in school days. They believed Benjie was the cause of it. They believe that Benjie was too lazy or too hangover to drive Bart to and from school. The truth was only revealed when Mr. Santos requested one of the police officers to drive Bart. The police officer saw the empty building with the sign "Lot and Building for sale or lease. If interested, contact National Bank. 4*2-*9*61" posted on the gate.

With nothing to do in the apartment, Bart stayed all day. He sometimes slept the day through with few conscious moments of visiting the CR or for a meal or snack. He became more of a slob, gaining more weight and becoming lazy.

Mr. and Mrs. Santos observed some changes with Bell. She became nauseous in certain situations; vomited every morning, and had some weird food combinations that she ate. Bart was also neglected at times and found Bell lying on bed in her room. They already suspected what her condition was due to the symptoms appearing.

"What's going on with you?" Mrs. Santos asked.

"What do you mean auntie?" Bell asked.

"You know what I mean, Pregnant?" Mrs. Santos asked.

"I...I...I...I am sorry auntie," Bell said.

"Do your parents know?" Mrs. Santos asked.

"Not yet, auntie," Bell said.

"Well, you better inform them about your condition as soon as possible." Mrs. Santos said.

"Yes auntie, I will do that. I am sorry again," Bell said.

"The father? Who is the father?" Mrs. Santos asked.

"Auntie, his name is Peter, I met him in the university, but we broke up before finding out that I was pregnant. The problem is, he went to Japan to be with his parents, and I don't know what to do, and I don't know any other relatives of his, I am really sorry auntie," Bell cried.

"Fine then, the only thing I can do is send you home after your first trimester, and give you some cash to start with your life.

It is difficult here in the city. At least in the barrio, the expenses are less and your family can help you. They may get angry with you at first, but they will accept you and your child eventually," Mrs. Santos said.

"I am sorry, auntie," Bell responded.
"Don't worry; everything will be okay. What's done is done," Mrs. Santos said.

Chapter XXVII

Mrs. Santos had to stop everything for the time being. She did not enroll for the next semester of her master's class and halted her work applications. She needed to take care of Bart since Bell had to go. A man with a familiar face was looking for something as she was about to hang the freshly washed clothes to dry on the clothesline outside.

"Hello, are you searching for something?" Mrs. Santos asked.

"Yes, "manang," I am actually looking for you," the man said.

"You look familiar and why are you looking for me?" Mrs. Santos asked.

"They relayed the bad news back home that I must tell you. Your father passed away last night," the man said.

Mrs. Santos was about to ask who the guy was but he was in a hurry and left. She stood, stared at the blank space, and did not move for a few minutes before she entered the apartment.

"Your grandfather is gone. He is not with us anymore," the words she was telling Bart as if he cared.

Tears flooded her face for a few minutes before she fixed herself up and resumed her activities. She broke the sad news when everybody was in. Bart cried or screamed in the middle of the night sometimes before but his cry the night Mr. Patrick died was something different. The whole night was filled with his cry as if somebody was mourning the loss of someone. The whole night was also chilling. The Santoses could not explain in words what happened. None of them were able to sleep. The Santoses were still baffled on what had transpired but they had to attend the wake and funeral.

Mrs. Santoses had the same feeling when they arrived at Mrs. Santoses' old house. The living room was full of smoke from the burning pinewood in between Mrs. Maria and Mr. Patrick's body. The body was not in a coffin like the dead would normally be in. He was wrapped with a traditional "Igorot" cloth on a woven mat. The close relatives such as wife, daughter, son, grandchildren, and in-laws were restricted from watching television shows, having fun, wearing something red, and taking a baths the entire wake until the dead was buried. Mr. Patrick had many animals such as pigs, cows, carabaos and even horses that he originally inherited from his parents were butchered with the specifications of the "mambunong".

"I am a modern woman. I am a practical lady," Mrs. Santos publicly declared as she saw her father's animal being slaughtered into extinction.

Bart ran while others were participating in the rituals. The majority of the mourners were concentrated on witnessing the ceremonies. There were only a few who went after Bart including Mrs. Santos.

"What in the world of nonsense? This is what I am talking about. Instead of watching over my son, I have to participate in these nonsense rituals," Mrs. Santos was saying with burning lips.

Mrs. Santos kept on searching for Bart but he was nowhere to be found. Martin joined in with the search, but he too was unsuccessful. They returned to the wake only to find Bart with his bar of chocolates. Since Mr. Benjie was the only man among the siblings, he was automatically considered the man of the house. He was required to be alert at all times to lead all the rituals the "mambunong" imposed. The problem was he and some relatives and friends were wasted from too much drinking. Mr. Santos had to take over for he was the eldest man among the son-in-laws.

Martin was seated among the crowd when an old lady came to attend the wake. She was searching for Mr. Patrick's loved ones because she wanted to express her condolences to them. The people directed her inside where Mrs. Maria and some of her children were present. Later that evening, she saw Mrs. Maria directing Martin to get her a cup of coffee.

Who is this little boy? She asked.

"He is one of Mrs. Santos' son," one of the present elders said.

The old lady sat beside Martin asking him a bunch of questions.

What is your name? She asked Martin directly.

"I am Martin "Lola" (Filipino term for grandmother or respect for any elder women.)" He responded.

"Where is your "nabung-og" (A Nabaloi term for a moron or an idiot.) brother?" The old lady asked.

"What are you talking about? I don't have a "nabung-og" brother!" Martin said with a loud voice.

"But, I thought your mother is Mrs. Santos?" The old lady asked with a confused look on her face.

"Yes, you are right but she has no "nabung-og" son. My brother has Autism. It is far different from being nabung-og!" Martin said in a loud voice at the old lady's face.

Everybody in the living room including Mrs. Maria heard their conversations. They smiled and giggled a little. Mrs. Maria called Martin's attention and specified that he must respect his elders no matter what the situation was.

"But she was wrong," Martin said.

"Even though, don't you know that she is your lola? My relative," Maria said.

Mrs. Santos was not present to witness the incident. She was asleep in one of the rooms on the second floor or she must have said something.

Everybody learned what Martin did. It popped-up in their conversations from time to time. They did not consider it a serious matter. They just laughed every time. Mr. and Mrs. Santos heard about it but did nothing. They just went on with the flow of the wake.

The "mambunong" with many relatives strongly demanded that the funeral rites must be held in the deceased residence with the traditional "Igorot" rituals. The immediate family objected to the idea and requested for the priest to conduct the funeral in the Catholic Church just a few blocks from the residence. Many were glad about the decision, especially to those who could only attend the funeral. They got some chances to give their piece during the eulogy, which was absent if the "Igorot" ritual was followed. Slaughtering of animals with other "Igorot" rituals was continued several days after the burial.

These people are leaving us dry without any more animals to raise as a source of livelihood. Mrs. Santos told herself.

The Santoses let everybody know about needing someone who would take care of Bart before leaving.

Everybody was back into the city, back to their hometowns, back to their normal lives. Mrs. Santos had to stay home for Bart. She was waiting and hoping for help to arrive. Martin went to school just like any school days. He passed a dirty homeless guy lying on the pavement on his way home, which was not an unusual scene in a developing country such as the Philippines. He didn't mind about him and went on. He saw a bunch of young men making fun of the homeless guy when he was just a few miles away. He was thinking twice about helping the homeless guy because he was thinking he might be harmed or even killed in the process, but he was able to fend his worries and got the courage to say something.

"Hey, what are your problems? Leave him alone!"

"Let him be! Get away from him!"

He could see that the bullies were not cool with him interrupting them because it created attention from the passers-by. They saw a guy running towards them to help Martin, but the bullies were already inflicting pain and injuries on him and the homeless guy. Punches and kicks were coming from every directions. Martin pushed the homeless guy away from the beating that prevented him from incurring more injuries. The other man managed to get a metal pipe lying on the street and swung towards the bullies, but they managed to disperse. The man hailed a taxi to rush Martin to the hospital. They found out later that the homeless guy was a former classmate of Bart in the closed school foundation. The identity of the Good Samaritan was never found out. Mr. Santos made a formal request to the City Welfare Department to take care of the homeless guy.

"Who were the guys who attacked you? I will make sure they will feel the wrath of justice. Yes, they will be imprisoned," Mr. Santos said.

Martin was conscious and just stared at his father from his hospital bed without any answers due to the pain throughout his body.

"Dad, dad. Calm down. Let him rest first for now and interview him later. I know you want to punish those who did this to your son. We all do but the best for him now is some peace and quiet," Mrs. Santos said.

They tried to pursue the culprits but they were never identified until the case faded away like the night.

Mrs. Santos had an experience of her own when she went to the market. She saw an unkempt pregnant lady from a distance. Mrs. Santos' route included the park near the market. She was supposed to pass by the pregnant lady when it caught her attention when their paths crossed. She recognized her as Bart's former classmate. Mrs. Santos was focus at her like she could not believe everything. She let the pregnant lady sit on the park bench and gave her some bananas.

"Hello, why are you alone? Where are your parents or guardians?" Mrs. Santos asked.

The young lady did not answer and just smiled with a look of innocence. Strangers were giving her food, from rice cake to banana cue (Filipino banana snack) to bread and many others. Mrs. Santos was heartbroken and wished to help the poor girl, but all she could do was report her to the City Social Welfare Department.

"Oh, my God, that poor girl. I hope the wrath of God will punish those who did her wrong," Mrs. Santos was thinking and praying with much intent.

Nobody knew what got into Bart. He welcomed Mrs. Santos with a devastating chop on her chest. Mrs. Santos dropped some of the items she bought from the market.

"Bart, stop it! Why are you doing such a thing to your own mother?" Mrs. Santos.

"Ahhhmmm! Chop! There! So, that you will know how it feels," Mrs. Santos added.

Martin saw what was happening, pulled Bart away, and locked him in his room as he cried the day away. He helped Mrs. Santos with the items she bought. They unlocked the door when the room was quiet. Bart ran to take a dump. Mrs. Santos followed to wipe his bottom. There again, another chop on the chest.

"Bart! Bart! I am cleaning your bottom! And you are being ungrateful! You are even lucky because we love, and care for you and this is the thanks that I get!" Mrs. Santos said.

"I saw one of your classmates as a homeless man. Bart, you are the luckiest man! We really love and care for you, but why are you doing such a thing to mother," Martin Said.

"Yes, that is true. I also saw your other former classmate and she was pregnant without anybody caring for her. You are very lucky, Bart. Why don't you give your mother a kiss instead of that painful chop? Mrs. Santos said.

She gave Bart the strongest chop that she could, and Bart felt every inch of it and cried like there was no tomorrow. Again, nobody knew why or how he quit giving his mother a difficult time. They did not pay much attention to it. They were glad it was over.

Chapter XXVIII

Martin blamed Bart for most of the negative incidence in his life. One time he discovered he had one of the lowest test results in class when their teacher handed him his paper. His eyes glared with disbelief and kept on mumbling as he returned to his sit.

"What the hell? This is all Bart's fault. He cried all night, I could not concentrate on my studies," Martin mumbled.

"Martin, what is that all about? I announced the test in class and you should have prepared for it." Martin's teacher said.

Martin apologized and concentrated on the lecture. He forgot about his feeling of outrage at his brother for a while but continued on ranting until he arrived home. He got his paper and shove it on Bart's face saying "Bullshit! You are the bad luck of the family! You always bring us bad luck!" Mr. Santos yanked Martin out of his brother and slammed him on the ground.

"What the hell are you doing with your brother? You know he don't know many things! You know very well he has a condition!" Mr. Santos said.

"But dad, I could not concentrate and did not sleep well last night. You know, you heard his screaming and crying last night. I am sure our sleep was all disturbed," Martin said.

"Don't blame it on your brother! You should have read your lessons every after class rather than cramming only in one night! I always see you watching television rather than studying! And it is not brotherly of you shoving your paper to his face!" Mr. Martin said.

Martin left his father and brother in the living room and locked himself in his room blaming his brother. He was thinking of how he wished his brother was not born or if killing other human beings is not a mortal sin then he could have done it or how he wished his brother never woke from his deep sleep. His deep thoughts about his brother were washed from his memory when nothing negative transpired in his life.

Martin's unresolved feelings about his brother resurfaced when he was completing his map poster for a school project. The drawing was half done; he kept it in the corner of Bart's bed then left for school. He caught Bart red handed scribbling on the poster when he arrived home from school. His body flared and discharge of hot sweat soaked his uniform.

"God Damn it! I kept on reminding you your entire life not to touch anything that does not belong to you!" Martin screamed.

His hand nearly touched Bart's check into a slap when Mr. Santos prevented him from doing so. Everybody rushed into the room and witnessed what was happening. Martin tried a second time but Mr. Santos dragged him out of the room.

"Bart shouldn't have done it in the first place! He is so nonsense!" Martin screamed.

Hey! Shut-up! You are making noises! The neighborhood might be disturbed! You are nonsense! Please stop it!" Mr. Santos said.

Bart did not react like nothing happened. He went to sleep while Martin was sent to his room to cool down. He had no other choice but to remedy the ruined poster for the following day was the last date of submission and stores were already closed in the dead of the night.

"That Bart, nothing good always comes from him." Martin was saying while repairing the poster.

On the day of the submission, they were required to present their projects individually when their names were announced. The teacher was not pleased with the quality of Martin's project. He humiliated him in front of the class and regarded his poster as trash. The error side was very visible to the proper side of the poster. The drawing on the proper side looked like it was done out of desperation. Martin returned to his seat with a heavy heart and never paid attention to the lecture for the rest of the class.

He was thinking of pummeling Bart when he saw him in his room upon his arrival from school; however, his emotion of compassion was fighting against him. It was literally similar to what was portrayed in movies and TV shows when a character is confused on choosing between the good side and the dark side where an angel on one side clashes with the devil on the other side. His consciousness went back to reality when he was called outside to help his mother and Sultana with some heavy lifting. The conflict was momentarily erased on his mind.

Martin had the tendencies to barge in Bart's room unannounced and perform random acts that Bart's reactions would indicate that he was not making sense at all. One time, he entered standing in front of Bart lying just staring at him straight at his eyes for a couple of minutes and left. Sometimes Martin would creep-up at Bart and tickle him all over. At times Martin would dance in front of Bart that would make him scream. The moment that would make a lot of sense was Martin making remarks about Bart in his face.

"My brother, what is going on in your mind?"

"I wish I could experience how your mind works and how you perceive the world we live in."

"How could people think they understand you when me, your brother who's been a part of your life, doesn't even understand you completely?"

Those are just a few questions or statements Martin had formulated.

There was a time when the help resigned and the Santoses were searching for a replacement. Martin at those times had finished with his studies and had time to spare. He became the all-around help temporarily. Bart was asleep in his room upstairs while Martin was mopping the ground floor. Martin unlocked the door and went outside to rinse the mop. Bart escaped and again dashed to the store. Martin followed him when a man was making disturbances at the store premises.

"What? Who the hell is that?" He asked with a resounding voice.

A young beautiful lady, who was the storekeeper went from being sweet and pretty to a lady with a grimace on his face ready to bite at any given time.

"Get the hell out of here! You don't have business disturbing all of us here! The lady said.

"Who does he think he is? He just goes behind the display stand and gets what he wants!" The drunken man said.

"I am far more handsome than he is!" He added.

"Bullshit! He is still a customer! Leave us alone as I have told you!" The lady said.

The drunken man wasn't aware of Martin's presence or saw him but did not have a clue he was with Bart. Martin never uttered a word and shoved the drunken man as far from the store as possible. The drunken man even fell on the dirt.

"God damn it!" The drunken man screamed until he walked away.

"I am sorry about that." Martin said.

"It's okay, he was a disturbance before your brother came," the lady said.

"You can pay later. You better follow him there. He ran just a few seconds before you entered." She added pointing to the direction of the Santoses' house.

"Martin rushed home to find Bart enjoying some sweets and a bottle of coke from the store.

He had the routine of going to a bar alone to have a couple of beers which is unusual in the country of the Philippines. A patron usually drinks in a group to bond and talk or enjoy karaoke. He just sits in a corner minding his own business sipping the drink. He sometimes talked with people he met in the bar or had little chats with someone he was familiar with who happened to cross paths with or join in with a group he also knew. He mostly drinks alone and reminisces about things in life. About what happens a week or months before. On what lessons could be learned from it or if there should be done differently to improve the situation. Also, with Bart; *what does he really think? What if I were in his shoes?* And the like.

Chapter XXVIX

" If we analyze, the total amount of rent we are paying would be enough to build a house of our own." Mr. Santos told everybody especially, the neighbors who were renting too.

The government awarded properties to the employees, right after gaining independence. It was hectares of a subdivided area where the beneficiaries could build their own houses. Mr. Santos had to find ways to fund house construction again. He filed for a government loan, but the approved amount wasn't enough as expected. He had to borrow from loan sharks; they gave him leeway because he was the police chief. Bank loans were also approved but with limited amounts. Relatives also volunteered to pitch in to help.

A police officer at work recommended a Psychologist expert with Autism, ADHD (Attention Deficit Hyperactivity Disorder) Asperger Syndrome, and many similar childhood disorders. The Santoses were tight on budget due to the house construction, but they were willing to do everything for Bart. Many improvements were recognizable. He was willing to brush his teeth with assistance, unlike before. He learned to wait his turn when getting food on his plate every meal. The Santoses continued with the sessions because of the improvements.

The house construction was completed in more than two months. The house blessing was conducted by the pastor of the UCCP in the city. No traditional "Igorot" rituals were applied. Friends and relatives enjoyed each other's company. The carpenters and construction workers' spirits were lifted when visitors appreciated the beauty of the house they built. They also had their enjoyment through the spirit of alcoholic beverages.

"Who the hell is that moron doing stupid things?" A drunk old man said while pointing to Bart.

"Who the hell are you? Nobody knows you. And nobody gives a damn about you. The nerve of saying such things when you are merely a gate crusher," Mrs. Santos said to his face.

"Get the hell away from here," Mr. Santos said.

All of those present were pissed with the old man and drove him away for he was just a nuisance who disturbed everybody's enjoyment.

Bart went to the living room and stood while glaring at his grandmother Maria sipping coffee.

"Bart, why?" His grandmother said with a smile.

Bart was still in his position, glaring at his grandmother like he was pondering on something. Nobody knew what it was all about. Many tried to let him sit or offered him some food to eat in the kitchen but he was still with his grandmother. Bart got the mug and put it on the kitchen sink as soon as it was empty.

Wow, Bart is a good boy. Thank you. Grandma said.

Bart was giggling as if invisible fingers were tickling him all over.

Johnny was present during the house blessing. Nobody could detect anything peculiar about him. He and his family have been the occupants of the Santos residence ever since the Santoses left Kabayan for the city. He had three boys and the middle was his son with special needs. His behavior was similar to Bart's with the exception of speech. He could only comprehend simple reasoning. They wished to attend the house blessing but weren't able due to domestic problems. Johnny and Chaligto's relationship became hazy after years of marriage. Chaligto claimed that Johnny was a tub of lard and that didn't help with the home chores. She also accused Johnny of not caring enough for their needs, especially their middle child in spite of him working with the municipal government as a radio communicator operator. Johnny still had hopes of saving their marriage for the children's sake. Relatives and friends tried to intervene to fix the problem. He only quit when Chaligto got pregnant by another guy. The boys, with the exception of the middle child, were grown up enough to understand the situation and choose their father. Many in Kabayan were perplexed by what happened. They imagine the scenario of couples splitting. The mother was usually the one fighting till the end for the children to be in her custody. It was the opposite in the case of Chaligto. She was the one who cheated and left the boys with Johnny with any effort of getting them to her custody. Johnny left Kabayan with the three boys to start fresh. Mr. Santos helped him establish a life in the city by recommending him to his friend for a job. He even helped him get an apartment by paying his deposit and a couple of months' rent.

Many relatives were bugging the Santoses if they could stay in their house in Kabayan without paying any rent with their promise of maintenance. The Santoses turned them all down because if they allowed any of them to stay, the others would be envious. Kabayan was one of the beneficiaries of a Japanese based foundation project that helped special children in need. A vacant classroom was provided by the school for their class but the staffs were searching for a place to stay. It so happened that none of the "nipa" hats owned by the Kabayan local government and the storage facility were vacant and no other available spaces except for the Santos residence. Johnny knew the leader of the foundation in the Philippines and recommended to the Santos to let them rent their Kabayan house. It was better that somebody would be renting and maintaining the house than just leaving it empty.

The Santoses always went home for Christmas and New Year holidays. They were like celebrities every time the Kabayan people welcomed them back home. Many always gathered in the house to have conversations with them. They were eager to help them with Christmas preparations with the intention of pressuring them to host a party. Mr. Santos always bought his favorite animal, the goat to be slaughtered with alcoholic drinks for the party. They were always prepared with extra cash every time they went home. They always anticipated that similar situations would happen on their every homecoming.

"Dad, every time we go home, people are always expecting us to host parties and, and you always spoil them even when we only have enough money for us, for our expenses as a family. Mrs. Santos said.

"Let them be mama. You know they are less fortunate than us. Let them have their enjoyment. Maybe they only got to experience such food once in a blue moon," Mr. Santos said.

"Look, save some for an emergency. We are neither royalty nor billionaire to be throwing money around," Mrs. Santos said.

"Don't worry, I have savings. Don't worry we can manage," Mr. Santos replied.

Mrs. Santos did not respond but looked at her husband with a frown on her face.

Those people are enjoying our expenses while I am doing my best to save. I sew, I crochet, I knit and remedy everything I can for the household rather than buying those things again, Mrs. Santos told herself.

She also reminded her husband about the issue every chance she got.

The effect of what Mr. Santos' practices was feeding the unending notion of the people that they were "Bill Gates rich." It was Sunday, it was time for church. An aging man with his daughter was able to track the Santos residence. They arrived in an empty house with nowhere else to go. They appeared pitiful munching on cheap soda crackers without drinks. The neighbors saw what was happening and gave them more food. The Santoses arrived later that evening.

"You have visitors, and they have been waiting for you since this morning," a neighbor said.

They anticipated one thing; their visit was with the intention of money.

"Who are you? And what is the purpose of this visit?" Mr. Santos asked.

"We have been here for hours and we haven't eaten a proper meal since we arrived this morning. We even traveled far just to get here," the old man said.

They opened the locked door and let them in. They gave them leftover bread and coffee and let them rest in the living room for a few minutes before asking them more questions. Nobody was familiar with who they were, neither Mr. Santos nor Mrs. Santos. They were even debating on whose side of the family they were related to, acquaintance with or town mates. Nothing rang their memories.

"So, tell me who you are and what is your purpose for coming?" Mr. Santos asked.

"You have no idea who we are? You forgot about us? Your relatives," the old man said.

The old man's expressions and how he said his words irritated Mr. and Mrs. Santos' senses.

"No, remind me because none of us know who you really are," Mr. Santos said.

"Hey, it is me Albert and this is my daughter Eunice," the old man said.

"Dad, please talk to them nicely," Eunice told his dad.

"Listen to your daughter and tell us what you really want from us," Mr. Santos said.

"We need some capital for our farm. We don't have anything. We are poor," the old man said as he was sobbing.

"I am sorry. We don't have money lying around here. Do you know a capital for farming costs a fortune? We don't have such an amount and I don't even know where you are from," Mr. Santos said.

"We are from Nueva Vizcaya. We sacrificed our little money for the bus fare just to be mucked like this?" The Old man said.

"They don't care about us; we are just poor and uneducated," the old man told her daughter.

"Why did you come here without thinking first? I am sure there are many wealthy people near your place. Instead of coming here and causing some drama in my house," Mr. Santos said.

"Seventy thousand pesos only. Please help us. You are our only chance to save our farm. Nobody cared for us there and I thought you were the ones who gave a damn," the old man said.

"What? Seventy thousand pesos is only for you? Then why come to us if seventy thousand is really only with you. For us, that is a big amount. People like you don't seem to understand that we also have expenses to pay. Do you know Bart? He has special needs that are very expensive. You should have approached the wealthy instead of us who are also struggling," Mr. Santos said.

"But, it is all over, it is well known that you are the Chief of Police of the city and you can lend us any amount because you have it," The old man said.

The daughter just sat beside her father and Mrs. Santos didn't want to get involved and pretended to be busy in the kitchen.

"I told you we don't have that kind of money lying around! We have our own financial problems. Heck even the money used to build this house are loans." Mr. Santos said.

"No good relatives. You heartless relative. You don't want to help those in need." The old man blubbered as Mr. Santos' ears were ringing because of it.

The father and daughter did not have enough cash for their fare back and no place to stay that night. As much as Mr. Santos wanted to throw them away, he didn't and let them stay the night. The following day as everybody was preparing for the Monday rush, they let them have breakfast, and Mr. Santos gave

                                                    Lester Laoagan

them some fare money for their return home despite the old man's ranting.

Chapter XXX

Irene was a kind and friendly young girl. She never judged others by their mere appearances alone. She was not choosy about whom she interacted with. It was the reason why she had a flock of friends. She never failed to attend any of her friends' occasions. It may be a birthday celebration, baptism of her friend's relatives, the wedding of her friend's relatives, or just to hangout. Her circle of friends knew her birthday was near. They always wondered why Irene never invited them to their house. There were always excuses for ending up celebrating in restaurants, food courts and even in friend's boarding houses.

Irene was as wet as a fish with a dry spell throat. She knew her friends were aware of her birthday in two days' time. She kept on thinking of her next excuse for not celebrating her birthday in their house. At this point, she already used every excuse imaginable. She seemed rational on the outside but her heart was pounding every time she encountered her friends at school anticipating if her birthday would come-up in conversations. She became relaxed when none of her friends mentioned her birthday.

Irene's day finally came. Goat-based dishes were prepared together with other common Filipino dishes. Drinks were also available. Relatives, neighbors, and family friends were present without any of Irene's school friends. The celebration officially started when the birthday cake was delivered. Everybody kept silent for the prayer. Irene blew the candles off her cake and everybody sang the happy birthday song. A group arrived while everybody was enjoying the food.

"Surprise, we are here." Most of the gang was present. Bart was eating in the kitchen when Irene bolted and locked him on his second floor room with his food. She then directed her friends to the dining table.

"Grab your own plate and get whatever you want," she said.

Everybody had their eyes on Irene. A sudden banging was heard from the upstairs. A relative went to open Bart's room, and he went rushing to the CR. The smell of stink bombs was all over the house. Some visitors went outside for some fresh air while others opened every window and door.

"What is that smell?" A male friend asked.

"Yes, what happened?" The other female friend asked.

Suddenly, some loud heavy steps were ascending the stairs, and there was a large chubby guy naked from the waist down with a piece of tissue on his hand reaching out to Irene screaming.

"Go up Bart, go up," Irene said.

She followed him and wiped his bottom clean. Went back to her friends and apologized to them.

"I am very sorry for the disturbance," Irene said.

Some of her friends noticed her expression.

" Please don't apologize to us. It is okay," one of them said.

"He is your brother. Your relatives told us all about him. Don't be embarrassed by him," another one said.

"I am thinking that he must be the reason for not inviting us here. You shouldn't be ashamed. Stop doing that to your brother," one said.

"Sorry again, guys. It is just I am so embarrassed," Irene said.

"No, it's okay," another friend said.

Some friends and relatives helped with the cleaning after the party. Mr. and Mrs. Santos pulled her to the side to talk to her.

"What happened a while ago?" Mrs. Santos asked.

"What do you mean, mom?" Irene asked.

"You know what my father and I mean!" Mrs. Santos said.

"Oh, sorry, dad, I am just ashamed that my friends will find out about Bart," Irene said.

"There shouldn't be a next time. Because you should not do what you did with your brother anymore," Mrs. Santos said.

"It is late; we have to go to bed. Besides, we are all tired and please don't do it again," Mr. Santos said.

"I am very sorry," Irene said.

"Okay, let's go to bed then," Mr. Santos said.

The tutor was absent the next day. The Santoses assumed that the reason for her being absent was because it was a holiday. They expected her to come for the subsequent day but she was again absent. Her presence became inconsistent and schedule for Bart's tutoring was not followed. She would come for a week straight then never came for four days until one day she never came for almost a month. Mr. Santos tried to contact her but nobody answered her office number. He physically went to the office to check on what was happening with her. He asked the building guard if her office was open. It was revealed that she became late on her rent. She also took things from the office little by little every time she came. One day, she never came leaving your abandoned things that were generally trash, the unpaid rent and unpaid utility bills.

Bart discovered how to use a key to a padlock to open the door. Everybody guessed it was a knowledge he learned from his tutor. The Santoses kept the key out of Bart's sight to prevent him from escaping again. The problem was every time the keys were hidden, Bart would discover them and their hiding place. The key's hiding places were change every time it was discovered until he knew every possible hiding spot. Mrs Santos changed the key padlock into a number combination one in hopes of preventing Bart from escaping again.

The Santoses were confident that the new locking system will prevent Bart from escaping, that Bart will never find ways to break the lock. Their confidence was tested when one night Irene went to the kitchen to drink a glass of water and to the C.R. to do her business. She did not notice the busted pad lock and open door at first because she was rushing. The busted padlock and open door came to her consciousness when she was returning to her bedroom.

"Bart had escaped! Bart had escaped!" Irene shouted.

Jean, the new all-around help was in luck for she got to witness one of Bart's favorite activities. Everybody was restless and went out in the middle of the night to look for him. They could not ask for the police's help at the click of a button because Mr. Santos was at an out-of-town conference.

"Bart what again. Dad is not here," Mrs. Santos was thinking.

They went as far as they could, knocked on every household they found. Some expressed their worries and helped with the search while others were pissed-off because of the disturbances it caused. The search was on going when an owner of a karaoke bar suddenly called out for help.

"Sir, Please help. A large Korean guy just entered the bar drunk and is making a scene! He doesn't seem to comprehend English and he is insisting on speaking Korean!"

Two on duty cops were patrolling the area when they heard the cries. Their gut feelings were telling them that the individual asking for help was referring to the chief's special son. They went to check the situation, and they were right all along. One of the cops was Mr. Santos' relative, and Bart had seen before, not just in the city but also in Kabayan. He called Bart, to which he was responsive and they drove Bart home in the police mobile car.

"I'm glad I decided to return home to wait for anybody who will find him." Mrs. Santos said.

"Thank God you found him," Mrs. Santos added as the two cops were assisting Bart on getting off the vehicle.

"No problem, madam. It was good that we responded based on our gut feelings about a bar owner asking for help from a large Korean Guy drunk who was insisting on Korean when he was trying to communicate with him," one of the police officers said.

"Yeah, You Korean giant," Mrs. Santos said as she was smiling at Bart entering the house.

"Thank you very much. Come inside and have coffee or a snack or something," Mrs. Santos added.

"It's okay. It is part of our duty," the first officer said. "Thanks for the offer but we have to go. We are still on duty," the other officer said and they left.

Chapter XXXI

Martin arrived home from school on a Monday afternoon. He did not notice the door was unlocked, and started knocking on it. He saw the brightness of the light bulb in the living room. He again knocked on the door and it opened. Nobody was home; nobody was responding to his knock. He searched every room to see if anybody was present or maybe something bad had happened. He did not find a single soul, and then Bart came barging in with lots of chocolates, soft drinks and sweets.

"What the hell is going on?" Martin asked, expecting for Jean to follow but she never did.

Mrs. Santos came home later calling Jean to help her with what she bought.

"Jean, could you help me, please. I could hardly carry what I bought."

"Mom, she is gone," Martin said.

"You mean Jean?" Mrs. Santos said.

"Yes mom, I arrived at an empty house. Bart was not even here. He just arrived with a bunch of chocolates, soft drinks and sweets just seconds before I arrived," Martin said.

Martin explained to the rest happened. Mr. Santos was so concerned about Jean's welfare.

"I hope Jean is okay. I looked at her cabinet and all of her clothes were gone. My concern is what her loved ones will expect from us. What if they will come looking for her? There would be possibilities of blaming us if something bad were to happen to her."

The Santoses were thankful that they never received any devastating information about Jean. The only trouble was no one would take care of Bart while they were away. Mrs. Santos could only take care of him on certain days because she had her master's class. They pleaded with neighbors if they could just look after Bart on a temporary basis, before they could find a more permanent one.

A classmate of Mrs. Santos in master's class had disclosed about her cousin Soltana in one of their casual conversations. Soltana was a young adult in her early 20's who left their barrio to find opportunities in the city. It was also emphasized that she belonged to one of the major ethno linguistic groups of the region different from the Santoses. Mrs. Santos' classmate was having a problem with her because she was not able to find work and she was staying with Mrs. Santos' classmate. Mrs. Santos needed help for Bart so badly, she almost bargained and was willing to do any favor in exchange for her classmate to guarantee her cousin's approval to stay with them. Soltana turned up on a Saturday morning at the Santos' residence unannounced.

Who could be this lady moving towards the porch? Mr. Santos said.

"Anybody home? I am sorry for coming without informing you all first. I am Soltana and my cousin, Mrs. Santos' classmate, told me you need some help for your son Bart."

"So, that is Soltana. Let her in." Mrs. Santos said.

They interviewed her a little and Martin directed her to the room she will be staying in while carrying her baggage.

Mrs. Santos completed her master's degree. She applied for a vacant position in the City's accounting department. There were others who applied, but she was the one selected. Three of the applicants were bachelor's graduates. One was a fresh graduate without any working experience and the other applicant had the backing of a city-employed relative. Mrs. Santos knew a little about her fellow applicants and was sure that the one with the backing would be hired. Nonetheless, she tried her luck without Mr. Santos' knowledge. Much to her surprise, she was hired after they had gone through the proper selection process. The other applicants were so mad for not being selected. Again with the false accusations that Mrs. Santos being hired because of her husband's influence. The one applicant with the backing had the highest expectation of being selected. He accused his relative of not applying the "sip-sip" (get somebody's good side for a favor) enough to guarantee him a position. Just like the others, he also accused Mrs. Santos of using influence to win the position in spite of what he did. He also kept on accusing everybody of nonsense things just to justify the reason why he was not selected in the first place. Mr. Santos found out about Mrs. Santos' success. He wanted to show his appreciation by celebrating with the family at their favorite restaurant. Bart took off his pants and ran to the CR just as they were enjoying their meal in the restaurant. Soltana stopped eating and followed him.

Soltana came back running…

"Would you Martin come and help me? I already wiped Bart's bottom, but the loos are out of order so he took a dump on the….the….one…for peeing. Kindly flash the shit. I couldn't stay long because there were men entering. Thank you."

Martin went to the CR and flushed as many times as he could, and then returned to their table.

"Bart, what did you do? The restaurant smells. Hehehe!" Martin said.

"Oh, my son did not have a choice. It was an emergency hehehe," Mrs. Santos whispered.

They went home after enjoying the simple celebration. Irene and Martin prepared themselves for bed. Soltana assisted Bart with brushing his teeth and washing his face and feet. Mr. and Mrs. Santos stayed in the living room watching television while sipping their coffees. They heard a sudden knock at the door.

"Who is it?" Mr. Santos asked.

"Sir, sorry, to bother you but I need help," a voice said.

"Who is out there?" Mr. Santos asked again.

"Please, sir, this is Thomas from Kabayan, please, sir I need your help," the voice said.

　　　　　　　　　　　　　　　　　　　

Mr. Santos opened the door to a young man pleading for help. He was asking if Mr. Santos could order his men to release his brother, who was detained.

"Tell me what happened," Mr. Santos said.

"My brother is framed, sir. Just this afternoon, a group of drug dealers were in the same restaurant where my brother had his snack. The police included him in the arrest even though he didn't have any associations with the drug dealers," Thomas said.

"Sorry, I can't help you. It will jeopardize my position as the chief of police. Go to the address of this lawyer. He will help you." Mr. Santos said.

Thomas kept on pleading with Mr. Santos. He wanted Mr. Santos to take actions based on what he said. Besides, he reiterated that he could not afford the service of a lawyer and it would be faster if he would be the one to intervene. Mr. Santos explained his predicament again. Thomas left murmuring and began hating because of what Mr. Santos refused to do.

The next day was not any better. It was on a Saturday morning when two "jeepneys" full of men attacked the Santos residence. Mr. Santos was relaxed, sipping his cup of coffee, when an elder from the group confronted him. He demanded that a prisoner related to them must be released, or there would be bloodshed.

"Why would I release him? It does not work that way," Mr. Santos said.

"There is no use in coming here and threatening me. He must have violated the law for him to be behind bars. The police are not insane to arrest him if he had not done anything wrong." He added.

"We will avenge this! We will avenge this abomination!" The old man said.

"You do what you have to do, but there are laws of the land that every citizen must adhere to, and as a law enforcer, I must implement them. If you and your relatives, clan or gang or whatever you call your group violates any law then me and the police force must implement the proper punishment. Let this be a warning to you and your group," Mrs. Santos said.

Mr. Santos was ready for anything. The intruders weren't aware that the police were informed. They were hidden in strategic areas, ready to strike at any cost. Chaos was avoided for an unknown reason when the old man ordered his companions to go back to the "jeepneys" and leave. The entire neighborhood was prepared to help the Santoses in case all hell broke loose. They emerged from their houses as soon as the strangers left. The Santoses were surprised by the overwhelming sacrifice and help that their neighbors were willing to go through for their sake.

"Thank you guys, we were not expecting your willingness to help us. Again we really appreciate all your concerns." Mr. Santos said on behalf of the Santoses.

"Yes, we are willing to help everybody in our community if needed," A neighbor responded that it was seconded by everybody.

The Santoses also thanked the police officers who came to the rescue. Mrs. Santos was perplexed with what was happening in their life, with the problem due to her husband's position in society and the people constantly bothering for favors like they were machines that could solve everything. The stress was a bit much for her to take but she was a strong mother.

I must be strong for my son, for Bart. Also, for my family. Please Lord; give me the strength to move on with this life. Mrs. Santos told herself.

Chapter XXXII

Nothing was out of the ordinary when Bart stayed in his room alone. Irene was about to enter her room when she had a glimpse of Bart with the half-open door of his room. She saw his facial expression as he was enjoying himself. She wasn't sure what to do so she called Martin.

"Look at Bart. Look, what is he busy in the room?" Irene asked.

Martin opened the door without any warning. Bart pulled-up his pants and stared at Martin quietly for a few minutes. Martin was waiting for his next move but kept on staring at him. Martin discovered that the sheets and Bart's clothes were wet. He told Bart to take-off his clothes and requested for Soltana to remove the sheets and clothes for laundry. Martin assisted Bart with his bath while putting a smile on his face all throughout.

Mr. and Mrs. Santos were watching television when Irene told them what happened to Bart. They all burst out laughing.

"It is normal for a growing young man to do such an act. It is like menstruation to girls, the release of excessive manhood," they said later.

Soltana heard the conversation from the kitchen and remembered the time when he kissed a girl without the Santoses.

"Bart kissed her right on the lips as I was opening the door. She was shaken with her eyes widened. I thought she was frightened of Bart, but it turned out she knocked on the wrong door."

"Bart is becoming a man, Woooh! A man!" Mr. Santos said.

Mr. Santos revealed the exciting news that he was selected as one of the Philippine representatives at The International Law Enforcement Conference to be held in America. He was so lucky to be selected due to the program's strict selection process. There were only two of them selected from the Philippines. The other one was a "Fiscal" (The Philippine equivalent of a District Attorney in the US.) from the South. He was required to meet with the US Embassy before embarking on the wonderful journey. The Santoses were so thrilled for Mr. Santos because it was his first time to travel outside the country and the fact that his first time was in The United States of America. They weren't expecting how big a deal his trip to the US was that everybody would know about it.

Many relatives and friends were shamelessly requesting pasalubong (A Filipino gift giving culture from places one traveled to.) from American brand shoes to American brand shirts to NBA jerseys to chocolates to souvenirs and many more prior to his trip as if it was his main purpose for going to America.

What do these people think? I will travel to America for whatever they want? They didn't even give me cash for their demands? I will go to America for a conference. Mr. Santos was thinking.

He went on with the journey from Baguio City to Manila, where he met the lawyer/fiscal from the Southern part of the country for the first time. They had a connecting flight in the Middle East first before finally landing in America in the JFK airport in New York City, where they met other representatives from other Asian countries. The shuttle service brought them to the world-famous Waldorf Astoria Hotel, and they were in awe of how massive the building was and more with its majestic interior. Mr. Santos and the lawyer/fiscal were clustered with the other Southeast Asian country's representatives who stayed in one section of the hotel.

The highlight of Mr. Santos' trip was witnessing first-hand how the American government helped both children and adults with special needs. The American government had facilities that trained them with the skills such as carpentry, baking, cooking, dress-making and many other significant skills that they needed for employment and for being productive in life. There were also the existences of government-run schools for special children, complete with the necessary staff, highly specialized teachers and the necessary facilities for training. Grants or financial assistance were also given to families with special children from both the government and non-government institutions. He appeared to be his normal self when he witnessed everything that happened in front of him but in reality he had mixed emotions of joy for the Americans and envy for his home country of the Philippines.

People like my son Bart are taken good care of here. Wow, I wish the Philippine government will be able to provide such facilities and implement such programs also. Mr. Santos was thinking.

As expected, Mr. Santos' homecoming was met with the people's requests and wishes. A few had longingly awaited his stories about the trip.

"Dad, tell us about your trip, your adventures about America. Wow America, the best country," Martin said.

"My trip was great, I even witnessed those who are similar to Bart, and I am envious because they were taken good care of by the government. They work like normal people in factories, restaurants and retail businesses with the government's support. A family receives financial support from the government if they could not afford the finances for their loved ones with special needs. There are also existing facilities and institutions such as training and rehabilitation centers and schools that cater to people with special needs. I wish that programs like those will be implemented here in our country," Mr. Santos told his family as they were intently listening at the dining table

"Well, don't expect for that to happen if corruptions and dishonesty will persist here in our country," Mrs. Santos said.

The conversation continued until they were done with their dinner and went to bed. The Santoses have been disturbed almost every day since Mr. Santos arrived from America. Some visited with the excitement of hearing about his American adventures while others were asking for the "pasalubong" and even US dollars as souvenirs. Mr. Santos was irritated with the situation but over time it did fade away.

Mr. Santos received a letter from the US Embassy with the chance of a lifetime. He was offered a government-sponsored scholarship at Harvard Law School. He was so ecstatic to share the good news to his family however, he thought of them most notably his son Bart because he had to leave them for his study in the US for five years and if extended with the chance for a green card and later citizenship. He could petition his family as soon as he was awarded with the citizenship but, it will take so much time. He will miss taking care of Bart and his family. In addition, it would be very difficult for Bart to travel very long distances by air. He had to turn down the offer formally.

Irene was also busy with activities outside of school. She was open to every opportunity to "improve herself" or "to earn while studying". Cell phones with call and text features were still in their infancy stage in that era in the Philippines, the proliferation of "The Scatman" and "The Macarena dance craze." It became popular once the early models were released. Anybody with a cellphone in their possession made them look cool or appeared to be a member of the elite in the society. A female classmate of Irene was always displaying her cellphone on her waist or holding it in sight when she could be keeping it in her purse. The words ``open-minded" and "Do you have a dream that you want to achieve?" were always incorporated in conversations which she was involved with. Irene wanted also to be cool, to be the center of attraction, to be prosperous like her classmate. The classmate sensed Irene and had to communicate with her.

"I noticed that you have been eyeing me in class. Come to our office whenever you have time, and believe me, it will improve your life, big time," the classmate said.

"All you have to do is concentrate and just listen to the presentation they will give," she added.

I want her stuff. I want her demeanor. I am very interested in what they have to say in their office. Irene whispered to herself.

"It is better if we will go during our in-between class break," the classmate said.

"I have time to spare during lunch," Irene said with a smile of anticipation in her face.

"See you there and you can also invite some of your friends. They are also welcome to attend the presentation," The classmate said

Irene was looking forward for the office, her classmate had mentioned. She pictured the office to be a spacious room with a-state-of-the-art equipment and glamorous finishing. She wore a frown with a stony expression when she was in the actual office. It was an old abandoned hotel building converted into business renting spaces. Anyone can smell its ancient ambiance once inside. Old wood, rusting plumbing, old concrete, the whole nine yards. Her gut was telling her to leave but she didn't want to be rude to her classmate and stayed.

"Let me introduce myself. I am Robert, one of the wealth and life coaches here and your friend said that you are Irene, right?"

"Yes sir."

"Let's begin, so after I start with the presentation, I request you Irene to turn off your phone or put it in silent mode and focus, just focus on the presentation with an open mind."

Irene observed Robert's instructions and the business presentation began. From the explanation, Irene had to pay the required membership fee, in exchange for products that were primarily herbal food supplements and multivitamins. She can sell the product and gain profit or test the product by herself and testify its effectiveness to her potential future clients. It was told that she was only required to recruit two potential members to be positioned to her left and right side of the triangle-shaped diagram. Besides, wild promises of health benefits, wealth, travel, expensive belongings (cars, house and lot, cellphones, etc.), and remarkable rewards were promised in a short span of time.

Irene could not afford to pay the 9,500 Philippine pesos in full. The registration fee required to be a member. She only became a reserved member, meaning; one can reserve a position in the company according to the diagram for 500 pesos and be given a chance to complete the total fee in 1-2 months' time. She could ask her parents for the remaining balance but she knew they would have some protests of what she was associated with.

The Santoses were wondering why Irene was seldom home unlike before. She was too busy whenever she was home, and it did not take very long for her to be out again. Even during the night, she had a short amount of sleep. She was raising the amount of nine thousand six hundred pesos which was an expensive amount for a membership fee. She only bought the cheapest snacks whenever she felt hungry. She also brought food from home as her daily meal. She was trying to save up from her allowance. She also sold the leather shoes Mr. Santos brought from the U.S. and the blouse her aunt from Australia gave her.

"What is with you? You are never home. Even on weekends. You also miss church and if you are home, you are always busy with something. What are you busy about?" Mr. Santos asked.

"At school, dad," Irene said.

"No, I think you are busy for something else than school. Tell me be honest," Mr. Santos said.

"Dad, Actually I am sacrificing my time and effort to improve my finances. I am trying to have an extra income after school," Irene said.

"Extra income? You tell me what extra income is that and maybe I could also do that extra income you are saying, Mr. Santos said with an unusual overtone of his voice.

Irene got her "business book" provided used to introduce the company and the business structure, explaining how to become part of the business, how to earn and how to get bonuses and many more.   Irene tried to explain to her father with confidence. Mr. Santos immediately detected that the business structure was similar to a very popular scam called pyramiding scam.

"This is some scam you entered," Mr. Santos said.

"Dad, you are wrong. Many had become successful and let me show the testimonies. We are not on that part yet," Irene said.

"I know a scam when I see one. And where did you get the money to join?" Mr. Santos asked.

I sold some of the things you gave me from your U.S. trip and some of the ones Aunt Rhoda gave. The shoes, the dress, the blouse and I have saved some from my allowance, Irene said.

"What? Are you out of your mind? You just wasted your money and the clothes your Aunt and I gave you. Damn! Where is the office of this so-called business and I will confront them to pull you out! I don't want you ever to be active in such a thing. People may also think that you are a scammer." Mr. Santos said.

"No, dad, just as I told you there are proofs that the business is good and legit, please Dad, don't you want me to succeed?" Irene asked.

"Give me your business book. I am sure there is an address somewhere. Whether you like it or not, I will remove you from that scam!" Mr. Santos said.

Mrs. Santos was walking to the master's bedroom when she overheard the Father and daughter debate.

"What is going on here?" she asked.

"Look at your daughter. She joined some pyramiding scam and I am trying my hardest to make her realize that joining is a very terrible idea but she argues with me!" Mr. Santos said.

"Your father is right. You better get away from that scam. You even neglect some of your home chores here. I intended to tell you this but I kept forgetting. Don't you know I had to absent myself last Monday from work because nobody would take care of your brother? Because Soltana had to run for a family emergency. My boss assumed I was absent for no apparent reason at all and I am just making excuses. I knew you didn't have school that day because it was the school's foundation day. The school declared it as a holiday. You chose to waste your time with that scam you are involved with rather than staying home with your brother Bart," Mrs. Santos said.

"I am sorry mom, but what I do is not a scam. What I do is not a waste of time," Irene said.

"Look ma, I told you. She still doesn't get it despite what I said. And I am planning to visit the so called office of the company and remove her membership. I intend to refund the membership fee she paid," Mr. Santos said, grabbing the business book and handing it to Mr. Santos.

Mrs. Santos was scanning the business book saying. "I agree with you father. As I am looking at this book, I am seeing the ingredients of a scam.

Irene did not answer but she glared at them with protruding eyes and a frown on her face. She grabbed the book from her mother and retired in bed covered with her blanket.

"I will do what I said whether you approve of it or not," Mr. Santos said.

They left her room and closed the door with the hopes of her reflecting on what she got herself into.

Irene tried to stop her father from executing his plan. She wanted to reason out with him, but he refused to listen. He went to the location of the business the next day. He introduced himself, his position in the police force and confronted those who were present. He wanted a refund of what his daughter paid them and excluded her from the business. They tried to explain and convince him that his daughter was old enough to make her own decision and there was nothing wrong with her desire to succeed in life. He raised his voice a several octaves and reminded them who he was and his demands with the threat of using his power to shoot the business in all possible ways he could if his demand was not met. They again tried their hardest to reason-out, but eventually in the end, he got what he asked for.

Weeks had passed and Irene still had a little resentment toward her parents for thinking that they were an impediment for her financial success. The family with the absence of Mrs. Santos was watching the daily news in the evening when the regular programming was interrupted by "breaking news." It was revealed that the company Irene joined was on the brink of bankruptcy and the members were scrambling and threatening to sue if the company would not return their investments or rightful earnings. Mr. Santos stared at Irene without even blinking.

"You see what I was telling you. I was right, and I did the right thing because I didn't want your little head to be taken advantage of. Well, they already did. And still you showed disrespect and you are still angry at me at this point!" Mr. Santos said.

"I am very sorry, dad. Now I realize that you care for my welfare," Irene told his dad in tears.
"Forget about it, and let's move on. Let it be a lesson for all of us," Mr. Santos said.

Chapter XXXIII

The Santoses needed a more spacious car for the growing family. They had to get rid of the Volkswagen beetle first before acquiring a new one. A city employee was planning to purchase a motorcycle as his personal service. Mr. Santos spotted him and told him that the high percentages of road accidents were caused by motorcycles. It was to convince the individual to buy a car instead. He offered his Volkswagen beetle for sale. The guy was convinced because the vehicle was greatly maintained, which was obvious during the inspection.

Mrs. Santos was able to buy a second-hand Mitsubishi van. Everybody was couldn't wait to take the vehicle for a ride. Bart was laughing during the road test which indicated that he approved of the purchase. They decided to celebrate the new possession at their favorite restaurant. An old man from the other table near the door kept on looking at them. Mr. Santos was not positive if he knew the man. The man went to the CR and glanced at them on his way. He returned and talked with them

"My heart melted while looking at your son eating fried chicken," He said.

"Okay? I think I know you, but I am not sure?" Mr. Santos said.

"I owe my life to you. Remember? When I was being tortured in prison during the height of the dictatorship?" The old man asked.

"Yes, I was a young officer then and I remember! I didn't know why I particularly helped you. I just couldn't stand seeing someone being abused," Mr. Santos said.

He exited the restaurant before they could ask his name or converse with him more.

Mr. Santos asked for the bill when they were about to go home but the cashier said that the old man took care of it.

The excitement of the new car gave Irene the desire to learn how to drive. Martin, on the other hand, learned to drive in a driving school. Irene took it upon herself to borrow a car for the driving practice. Nobody knew how she was able to convince someone to lend their car to her, let alone a car for practice driving. She also convinced Martin to be her driving instructor.

Mr. and Mrs. Santos were out while the kids stayed home for the weekend. Irene convinced Martin for another session of driving practice. They decided to take Bart with them to let him experience the adventure leaving Soltana at home. They had their practice in a place called "atidug" (long). It was a winding road that was carved on the mountainside that was common in the highlands. The road was chosen for the reason of fewer vehicles and less traffic. It was also the alternate road going to Baguio from the neighboring municipalities. Martin allowed Irene to take the steering wheel. He was confident that no impending disaster would ever happen with his assistance.   The driving lesson ran smoothly when Irene kicked the accelerator by mistake on a sharp curve that plummeted the car into a five-foot ravine.

The car was upside down when they started screaming for help. There was no cellphone signal in the area and there were no government-assigned rescue personnel, as always the case. With the stroke of luck a delivery truck was passing and saw them in their situation. He immediately stopped and while he was attempting to rescue them, another man was running towards them to help. They rushed the siblings to the hospital just adjacent to the police station. It was miraculous that the siblings only had little scrapes and scratches. Mr. Santos came to the emergency room a few minutes later and saw Irene with a scratch on her forehead sitting in a wheelchair.

"What happened?" He asked.

Irene told her father everything and he checked on Bart lying on the emergency bed. Martin was also present lying on a hospital bed while the nurse was examining him. Mr. Santos' emotions wanted him to burst into anger, but he managed to stay as calm as he could. No life-threatening problem was discovered, and the doctor gave them the signal to go home with some prescription medications and home remedy advice.

The children went to the backseat never saying a word while Mr. Santos was driving. His anger grew, and he could not contain it.

"What the God Damn hell were you thinking?"

"You drag even your brother to danger! You are all lucky you didn't incur any serious injury or even die!"

"You even put me in a very difficult and shameful position! What will the car owner think now?"

Nobody answered and went straight home.

Some of the prescription drugs were bought by an on-duty police in a mobile car due to their unavailability in the hospital.

Mr. Santos ordered some of the police officers to inspect the accident site and the vehicle damage. Sadly, it could not be salvaged except for a few parts. He immediately set a meeting with the owner, explaining what happened and the situation of his vehicle. The car was a seventies box type, four doors model that the owner seldom used. Mr. Santos expected some animosity from the owner but he was calm and was willing to have a payment agreement with him. He went home without completing his working hours to have the rest and relaxation he needed but Mrs. Santos came rushing in.

"How are my children? Are they okay? Are they hurt?"

"Yes mama, they are okay. They only have few bruises and scratches on their bodies," Mr. Santos said.

"Thank God, they are all in good hands. I know the Lord saved them. God will never allow something worse to happen to Bart, I am sure of it," Mrs. Santos said.

"Don't go to their rooms, let them rest," Mr. Santos said.

The Santos residence was flooded with nosy people once the news of the accident went out. The odes of it was those genuinely concerned were not badgering the Santoses with stories of the accident. The church service and prayers intended for the Santoses nearly did not happen. It was because of many people that the house could hardly accommodate. Mr. Santos kept his cool but it was the last straw as he witnessed what was happening. He held nothing and blurted all out not caring even with the presence of the pastors and church-members.

"Hey, let the church visitors sit! Let them conduct the service! Yes you! You know whom I am referring to! Those who have nothing to contribute, and are just here for their curiosity! Just get out! Let those who really care to stay!" Mr. Santos said.

Many realized what Mr. Santos was saying and left. Others left because of fear. But others still stayed. The Santoses could only count, close friends and immediate family members who were really concerned for Irene, Martin and Bart.

The pastors and church-members did nothing but conduct the church service. When the service was over, the Santos served snacks and had conversations.

It was divulged that during infancy, Bart behaved the best compared to his brother and sister. Irene and Martin cried a lot. They cried when their diapers needed to be changed. They cried when they needed to be fed or when their lampins needed changing. They cried all the time. On the other hand, Bart was a gentle, quiet baby. He only sobbed whenever his lampin needed changing or when hungry or when he felt uncomfortable. A simple sway or rocking on a hammock or simple lullaby always did the trick for him to go to sleep. His sibling were the opposite. The problem was noticed when he did not talk even when he was six or seven or the stage he was expected to say his first word. He could not say papa or mama until the present days, only those unintelligible words.

A visitor was the daughter of Mrs. Santos' very good friend. She was a sight of wonder with fair skin, soft cottony lips tinged with strawberry delight, and shiny ebony hair. Bart went to the living room and surprised her with a kiss. Everybody giggled at what had just transpired. The young lady never uttered a word, smiled, and her cheek went from fair to rosy. He then cleared the sofa by pulling those seated up and laid on it like he meant business.

Everything was back to the way it used to be after the accident issue had faded as they thought so. Bart welcomed the morning with an awkward walk and a mad dog grimace on his face. Each step was partnered with high-pitched screams. The later movement was in slow motion.

"Oh, Bart! My goodness! My son! His foot is swollen!" Mrs. Santos said.

"We should give him an anti-inflammatory and pain killer medication," Mr. Santos said.

Bart went to the dining room by himself despite his physical condition. They let him have his breakfast first before giving him his hot Milo mixed with medication. Mr. Santos speculated what was causing Bart's suffering upon further inspection. A regular sufferer himself, the first thing on his mind was gouty arthritis. He also gave Bart an anti-gout medication tablet, and he chewed it followed by a glass of water. Bart became active again after a few minutes which validated Mr. Santos' suspicion. He got out when Soltana was entering with the dried laundry and got a bottle of 1.5 Coca-Cola and a bar of chocolate.

Chapter XXXIV

Signs of the next millennium were apparent. Things that could only be felt in dreams and seen in Sci-fi movies were taking shape. The first cyborg, TV phones, computers, electric pets, and no stick shift cars were on the run. The Santoses purchased a personal computer set, complete with an internet modem and universal printer and scanner that helped a lot with Irene and Martin's studies. Research became easier; errors were avoided compared to typewriters, and computer skills incorporated to the modernization of the school curriculum. Mrs. Santos took advantage of internet access to research Bart's condition. She asked for help from Irene and Martin for the operation of the internet system. She found many articles, cures, and remedies online. She didn't care much about the authenticity of the information. The sad part of her research was most of the studies and treatments she found were only available in the first world countries or the western part of the world, such as Sweden, The US, Australia, Germany, and many other advanced countries. No studies were found readily available in the Philippines, and many "experts'' were not knowledgeable enough about the condition.

Social media platforms were still unavailable in the early stages of the internet. Communications through chat rooms were the available means of internet communications. The older generation was not-up-to-date with the flourishing digital age. Traditional mail or the term "snail mail" that was coined in the era was still the primary method for a long distance communication seconded by landline or "long distance call" that cost extra than the normal rate for a regular phone use. As it was the case for Mrs. Santos. She was informed about her cousin Leah in New Zealand about her trip to the Philippines through a long distance call. She was not very particular about "pasalubong" even after her cousin asked what she wanted to receive from her. What was important for her was her cousin's safe travel and seeing her again for the first time after many years of being apart. Mrs. Santos and Leah were not only cousins but also best friends. They practically grew together, and souls connected. Leah's family was less fortunate compared to Mrs. Santos. Mrs. Santos' family often helped Leah's family with their finances, food, and she often gave her cousin the hand-me -downs of clothes she outgrew, for she was a bit larger than her cousin.

Ms. Leah stayed with a friend for two days when she arrived at the capital city of Manila first before heading to Baguio City. The Santoses were responsible for her stay in the city for her immediate family were in her and Mrs. Santos' hometown of "Bokod" where there were no means of communication but only through letters. Leah stayed with the Santoses bearing "pasalubongs". Perfume for Mrs. Santos, a cowboy hat for Mr. Santos, t-shirts for the kids, and New Zealand chocolate brands for everybody to enjoy. Mrs. Santos took a leave of absence for a week to be with her cousin's company. They went their favorite spot during college and enjoyed the night. They also tried to visit one of the students' hang-outs during their college days in the late 70's-early 80's, but unfortunately it was out of business that Mrs. Santos wasn't even aware of. They relieved their younger years together. Mr. Santos with the family wanted Leah to taste the "Igorot '' dishes with new twists that she was missing in the Santoses' favorite restaurant before leaving for her hometown. Leah promised to see the Santoses again before going back to New Zealand. Weeks had passed, but she never visited the Santoses, which they suspected that she had already returned to New Zealand. The Santoses received a package from her containing chocolates, used clothes and kitchen gadgets but mostly herbal medicines for Bart.

As Bart was maturing, he became aware of the usage of money for the transaction. One time, he went to a store with a change that he put on the counter and grabbed some chocolates.

The store owner smiled as he was leaving. The amount was not enough to pay for the chocolates he got. Bart met Mrs. Santos as he was returning home. She accompanied Bart home and asked for Soltana to pay the rest of what Bart owed.

"Oh, My boy. He already knows the use of money but he is not knowledgeable enough to know how much chocolates cost," Mrs. Santos said.

"But Ha! Ha! Ha! He thinks one peso can afford a bar of chocolate that costs twelve pesos!" She added.

It was part of his enjoyment of being driven around the city. Police officers took turns driving Bart on the same route every day. Mr. Santos would give the assigned police officer for driving Bart some cash for Bart's goodies or whatever he got from the store.

Mr. Santos received a text message for a clan reunion. The reunion Mrs. Maxim was trying to initiate. It was always held once a year with mostly the same faces and only few new attendees present. Host families became difficult due to locations and financial constraints. The majority agreed to the suggestion that the clan reunion would be held every other year. In the latest clan reunion, a niece of Mr. Santos approached him during meal time.

"Uncle, can I ask a favor?" She asked.

"What is it?" Mr. Santos asked.

"Well, I have a cousin in prison because he was accused of theft. Can you please help him in any which way possible?" She asked.

"Okay, let me see what I can do. I hope it will not interfere with my position as Baguio City's Chief of Police," Mr. Santos said.

"Uncle, he is imprisoned in La Trinidad Provincial Jail if I am not mistaken, and I believe it is a different jurisdiction from Baguio," she said.

"You are right. Let me do what I can. Anyway, we need somebody to babysit Bart," Mr. Santos said.

"Thank you very much, uncle," she said.

Robinson was a cousin that Mr. Santo's niece mentioned. It was again a great timing for Soltana to be requested by her family to return home to their province because her ailing mother needed someone to help her around. Robinson stayed with them as soon as he was bailed while waiting for his scheduled trials. He was excellent at cooking. He drove Bart around, cleaned the house, and did other chores without expecting a salary. In short, he was an all-around good guy. The problem arose when he befriended the neighborhood guys. He was influenced to drink, gamble and go to clubs. He was willing to be told what to do as long as he was provided free drinks, "pulutan" and fun. His acquired habit interrupted his obligations with the Santoses. He became lazy, oftentimes hung over, and seldom drove Bart. Recently, he preferred to sleep in the Santoses' vehicle at night. The main reason was to sneak out to neighbors or to the drinking establishments without the Santoses' knowledge.

A noise in the darkness of the night was heard throughout the neighborhood. Mr. Santos went to check it out from a safe distance before calling for the police. It was Robinson being pummeled by two men. One was hitting him with a piece of wood while the other was kicking him while he was down on the street. The perpetrators ran when they heard the police sirens. Robinson was rushed to the hospital with swellings and bruises primarily on his head and a few minor injuries on the rest of his body. His wallet and the wristwatch given by Mr. Santos were missing. He was lucky that the beating was interrupted. It could have caused worse injuries or even fatal if the beating lasted longer.

The doctor asked Mr. Santos if he would stay in the hospital for a day or two for further observations or recover at home. Mr. Santos chose the latter.

"I am tempted to slap him while scolding him at the same time, but he is not my son," Mr. Santos was thinking.

"Please don't be so careless not only for your sake but also for mine! Do you know that by bailing you out, I risked my career big time? Please cooperate! Look, instead of you taking care of Bart, it is us who are taking care of you!" Mr. Santos said the minute they arrived home.

"I am very sorry, uncle. Please forgive me. I will be good next time. Please give me another chance," Robinson said.

"I will give you another chance then, but please don't ever do it again! Martin is even far humbler than you, the fact that he is my own son! My own flesh and blood, but you are only living with us through the plea of my niece, your cousin!" Mr. Santos said.

Robinson bowed his head and listened to Mr. Santos, for he was so ashamed to look Mr. Santos eye to eye. Robinson was still persistent in his ways of drinking at night with the neighbors. It was after his full recovery and after what Mr. Santos had reminded him. The difference was this time, he was very careful about being caught. He also made certain his duties during the day were accomplished; those were the important things that the Santoses saw and cared about.

Chapter XXXV

The Santoses were in their routine days of bonding together in their favorite restaurant with Bart. It was unanimous for them to try something new. Bart was never part of the Santoses' grocery team. They decided it was time for him to be part of a new activity. The supermarket had two sections of selection, the locally made goods and the imported goods. Bart had his eyes wide open, staring at the displays while pushing the cart slowly. He touched every item they passed. He wasn't getting anything, and the rest of the Santoses were just waiting for his next move with smiles on their faces. He then stopped to look in the direction of the imported goods section and ran towards it. Mr. Santos told Robinson and Martin to go after him. They tried to stop him, but they couldn't. He grabbed as many chocolates as his massive hands could carry.

"Those imported chocolates are very expensive. Return the ones Bart did not taste and exchange them with a cheaper local variety. Anyway, Bart wouldn't know the difference," Mr. Martin said.

"Robinson, go and return those chocolates he placed on the cart while his focus is on something else." Mr. Santos said.

Bart never complained. He just enjoyed his day. He fell asleep in the family van as they were on their way home.

Men clearing the vacant lot just before the Santoses greeted them with smiles and hellos. As they were unloading the groceries from the van, the guy who seemed to be the eldest approached them.

"Sir, can we ask for a favor?" He asked.

"What is it?" Mr. Santos asked.

"Can we leave the equipment in your house for safekeeping?" He asked.

"It's okay with us; just list all the equipment so that we will be aware. We will take care of it and hide for safekeeping," Mr. Santos said.

"One more thing, sir. Can we temporarily share electricity for our equipment and water for the concreting later on? Don't worry, we will split the bill with you," the man said.

"No problem, everything is set," Mr. Santos said

The men gave thanks and left for another working day. They were expecting the construction workers the following day, but nobody came. They were so anxious about the equipment they were holding for the construction workers. They were worried that it might get lost or in a more terrible condition as compared to when they received them. The equipment was abandoned longer than expected. The property owner came about a month later with a different set of men except for one whom Mrs. Santos interacted about the equipment with.

The construction created some problems for the Santoses, especially with Bart. Screeching sounds, nail pounding, and the noise of a construction site were overheard throughout the neighborhood. Martin and Irene had to stay in the school library or internet cafés to study and do their assignments. Bart screamed and behaved badly like a frustrated drunk person each time the noise was unbearable to everybody's ears and consciousness. Sunday was the standard day-off for any construction in the Philippines, but not for the neighbors. Most often, the construction work would last from very early in the morning to very late at night. The Santoses could hardly rest and concentrate on their daily activities. Mr. Santos requested the foreman to let his crew have their day-offs on Sundays or stop the work at five pm in the evening or six tops. The foreman obliged Mr. Santos' request because he wanted to be neighborly, or maybe he knew about Mr. Santos' position in the police force that he didn't want to upset him in any form of the matter.

The newly constructed house was supposed to be the retirement castle for an old Filipino man who was a US navy veteran from Hawaii. Sadly, his children were feuding on the property while he was still alive. The completed house was unoccupied for more than a year before it was sold to Mrs. Fecora and her family. They could not immediately move in for there were many repairs needed. The Santoses and Fecora families were like one household. They shared whatever they had. They also helped each other in their time of need. Mrs. Fecora often gave Bart some "pasalubong" whenever she came home from work. She also became the "chismosa" (refer to a woman who engages in gossip) of the neighborhood they settled in. It was not uncommon in the Philippines to have "chismosa" in every unit of society.

Bart was screaming so loud it could be heard from miles away. Mrs. Fecora was inspecting their newly built house next door. She side tracked to the Santoses a bit to inspect what was going on. She saw Martin and Bart who were alone in the house.

"How is Bart?" Mrs. Fecora asked.

She saw Martin was holding a bottle of soy sauce in his right hand and a pair of scissors on his left while moving them closer to Bart's face.

"Why? What are you doing?" Mrs. Fecora asked.

She ordered Martin to quit what he was doing to Bart.

"Aunt, it is illogical. Soy sauce and scissors? What's wrong with those? Why is he screaming every time those items are close to him?" Martin asked.

"Just stop it, Martin. Maybe he just doesn't like those. But stop it," Mrs. Fecora said.

Mrs. Fecora and her family were planning for the house blessing. The pastors and church workers of UCCP were invited to conduct the blessing ceremony. Invitations were relayed through social media. Everybody, even the neighbors whom Mrs. Fecora and her family had never met before, were welcomed on the occasion. The house was jam-packed, and people overflowed that the Santoses had to open their house for the guests that could not be accommodated in Mrs. Fecora and Family's residence. Many were elated with congratulatory greetings for Mrs. Feroca and her family for finally possessing their own residence after years of renting. In a stroke of coincidence, Johnny and his three boys visited the Santoses for a separate reason. Mrs. Fecora knew who they were and invited them to have some food before proceeding to the Santoses.

James checked every room upstairs. He saw Bart in one of the rooms and didn't move when their eyes clashed for a few seconds. When Bart started screaming, James shut the door and took a couple of breaths with the expression on his face that could not be explained in words.

"What was that?" Johnny asked.

"It's Uncle Bart! Shouting! Angry!" James said.

"Come here and let him be!" Johnny said.

"Leave your uncle alone!" Johnny added.

"It's okay. It's not his fault," Mrs. Santos said.

Johnny and his boys were already a part of the Santos family. Mrs. Fecora and her family too considered them as blood relatives. Johnny could not express his appreciation enough for the two family's gestures.

Several of Mr. Fancesco's relatives and friends stayed for some karaoke and drinking sessions. Mrs. Fecora invited the Santoses and whoever was present to join in. Besides, she gave some leftover food to them. James saw the food on the kitchen table and took a bite of each. Bart also went to the same table when he saw plenty of food. He was like a giant devouring the flesh of his prey. James stopped chewing and stared at him. Bart almost screamed, but James continued his meal in the living room. They could never be left alone together. There were always palpable tensions between the two. James ended up looking around as if he was searching for something the minute he was done with his meal.

"Lola! (Filipino term for grandma) Where are my dad and brothers?" He asked Mrs. Santos.

"They are at your "Lola" Fecora. Our neighbor," Mrs. Santos said.

"Lola Fecora?   What....uhhhmm...Who is she?" James asked.

"You have another "lola" next door. You're Lola Fecora. The one who gave you the food," Mrs. Santos said.

James paused and took a deep breath, then said. "Okay! So, can I go there?"

"Yes, you can! I am sure you are welcome," Mrs. Santos said.

As James was entering Mrs. Fecora's house, he went straight to the living room and started introducing himself to everybody.

"So, this is James, one of our grandsons. Go to the kitchen and get whatever is available," Mrs. Fecora said.
She knew what had happened to them. She knew the separation of Johnny and Chaligto but she did not bring it up despite being a "chismosa" to avoid upsetting the boys, especially James. The boys slept at the Santoses while their father enjoyed the drinking and the overnight karaoke marathon the whole night.

Chapter XXXVI

A family went to the Santoses to seek financial help, which was sadly the norm. The Santoses were not always at home, even on weekends, for their restaurant routine on Saturdays and Church attendance on Sundays. The visitors arrived in an empty house on a Saturday morning. Mrs. Feroca welcomed them and let them wait in their household. When the Santoses finally arrived, the visitors offered to carry the groceries with smiles on their faces. Mr. Santos already got a hint on what the purpose of their presence was the minute he saw their gesture.

"Okay, thank you very much for helping us with the groceries and your visit. You can now go back to my sister's place and I will have a chat with all of you a bit later," Mr. Santos said.

"Sir, actually, it is you we came here for," a middle-aged man said.

"Me? Let's go inside at my place then," Mr. Santos said.

The middle-aged man entered the Santos residence with a woman and a young boy. They introduced themselves and they turned out to be a family. The middle-aged man did most of the talking while his wife and son were on the side listening. The Santoses were not familiar with them except for their family name. Mr. Santos prepared himself for it was again one of the moments they can't shake from their family reputation.

"The only thing that is familiar with you is your family name. I believe I never met all of you, and if we did meet, I am sorry, I don't remember. If what you are saying that we are related is true, then why do I only know about you just now? And why the sudden visit when you only need help?" Mr. Santos said.

The visitor never had a response and just listened to what Mr. Santos had to say.

"Now I remember, one of the wealthiest men in the city has the same family name as yours. You must be related to them," Mr. Santos added.

"Why won't you go to them and ask for the money? It's what you are here for right?" Mr. Santos asked.

The family never answered with the look in their eyes acknowledging Mr. Santos' suspicions.

"Sir, we are ashamed to ask them because we are not that close to them. Besides, they don't give a damn about us, the less fortunate ones."

"But we were never close! I don't even know you at all! But you are not ashamed to approach us! Give me a break! My family is not even that rich! We only live from paycheck by paycheck!" Mr. Santos said.

Mr. Santos convinced the visitor to go with him and Martin for a ride. He explained that the money was sitting in the bank and withdrawal was needed. He engaged them in conversations to avoid any suspicions from them. They finally stopped on the side of the road at the frontage of a towering building. He left the vehicle to inform the guard that a relative of his boss needed some assistance. The visitors were reluctant to exit the vehicle, but they did it anyway. Mr. Santos drove immediately as soon as the guard approached them and never looked back.

"We must not let people abuse us like this. We must not spoil them. They need to know and learn the reality," Mr. Santos told his son.

What transpired did not sit well with Mr. Santos. He entered Mrs. Fecoras' residence, and confronted her.

"I left the visitors to their relative's building! What the hell were you thinking welcoming them?" Mr. Santos asked.

"Sorry, my brother, I don't know. They told me who they were, and I was familiar with the man's dad. They were our neighbors a few blocks from our house way back when. But I have no idea what their purpose was. They just told me they needed to see you. I am very sorry," Mrs. Fecora said.

"Next time, call me whenever I have visitors when I am not around!" Mr. Santos said

He went home for his much-needed rest.

People don't just get it. We don't have the fortune to give around. Was tingling his mind before taking his nap.

The early morning was not different. A family member of their back neighbor was peeping on their living room window.

"Hey, What the? What are you doing there spying on us? You don't even have the decency to hide," Mrs. Santos said as she was startled by the little boy's large round eyes and unwashed face.

"Auntie, can we borrow fifty pesos? My mom said," The little boy asked.

"Fifty pesos? Why?" Mrs. Santos asked.

"I don't know. My mom told me to ask any of you fifty peso," the little boy said.

"You wash first before coming here. Your breath even stinks. But okay, wait there, and I will still get the fifty pesos you are asking for," Mrs. Santos said as she went to their bedroom.

What a shame. The little boy's parents kept on producing children when they couldn't afford to feed their children even for only fifty pesos. Mrs. Santos thought.

She got a hundred pesos, for she didn't have the exact amount the little boy was asking. Martin was staring at the little boy and handed him some chips stored for Bart.

"Fifty pesos, please," The little boy said.

Martin and the little boy kept staring at each other. Mrs. Santos was going downstairs.

"Mom, what is he talking about? He kept on saying fifty pesos," Martin said.

"Here, give it to your mother," Mrs. Santos said as she was handing the money to the little boy.

"Go and clean yourself. You are very dirty," She added.

"What was that all about mom?" Martin asked.

"He was just borrowing fifty pesos, but I gave him a hundred and I am not expecting any return from them," Mrs. Santos said.

"Weird, they should pay because they borrowed. They will be spoiled if we continue to do such a thing," Martin said.

"Martin, just let it go. They are the ones who deserve help and besides it is only a hundred pesos not like others who are expecting for us to dole out hundreds of thousands of pesos or something," Mrs. Santos said.

"And, ugh…most of them belong to well-off families or have close relatives that are way richer than us," she added.

"I almost forgot. Go and wake Robinson, for it is already getting dark. Tell him to cook soup with meat and cabbage for our dinner."

Chapter XXXVII

Robinson went outdoors to buy something personal well, according to him. Not long after, an old lady in the neighborhood was looking for something or somebody. Mrs. Santos entertained her, and she broke the news. She wanted to let Robinson know about her granddaughter's pregnancy.

"You are back. An old lady was looking for you. According to what she told me, you are the father of her granddaughter's unborn child," Mrs. Santos said.

"Old lady who?" Robinson asked.

"She said that her granddaughter Darla is pregnant, and you are the father," Mr. Santos said.

"What? I mean, I don't know any Darla. Honestly, I don't," Robinson said.

"Don't be like that! Don't Goddamn play with me!" Mrs. Santos said.

"Hum….maybe?...Don't know…maybe…it's Darla…the girl I met in a bar," Robinson said.

"Okay, what I appreciate is some honesty," Mrs. Santos said.

The discussion never went further. Robinson went on with his ways, never expecting anything. In the next days, Robinson drove Mr. Santos on a trip by themselves. The trip was a mystery to Robinson, but he was so shy to ask for details. He just abided with Mr. Santos' directions. They arrived in a small community atop of a hill. Robinson never saw Darla's grandmother in his entire existence. So, it was reasonable that he didn't have any reaction at all when she was surprised by their arrival. The old lady let them enter a modest "nipa" house and dashed to the neighbor for sweet potatoes and native black coffee. A moment later, two old men arrived asking who among them was Robinson.

At that moment, Robinson knew what the trip was all about. Not too long later, Darla arrived and surprised by Robinson's presence. Her small stature of about less than five feet could hardly accommodate her baby bump. Robinson was sweating and trembling on his knees when the old men begun doing rituals. He thought that they were applying the "gamod" (curse) upon him, but it was actually the ritual of blessing. They allowed the old men to finish their ritual before explaining their purpose of being present, which the old men already knew prior. Mr. Santos let Darla sign the marriage papers, and Robinson was a bit reluctant to sign at first but was forced to do so later. He was mostly fearful not at Mr. Santos but of the old men and the possible "gamod" they would inflict on him. A simple wedding ceremony was held at the city hall with the judge as the officiating official later. The event was mostly attended by Darla's relatives with the Santoses and three pairs of principal sponsors on Robinson's side. Robinson and Darla later stayed in Robinson's province and the Santoses never heard from them again.

Rose was hired in place of Robinson who used to work for a grocery store. Bart was well taken care of, but she must be instructed all the time for the rest of the household chores. Every day was the same story. Bart was good but the house was untidy. They tried to give her a chance but the longer she was with them the worst it became. She became neglectful not only with the chores but also with Bart. She always watched television or was busy with social media all day long. Mr. Santos even had to yell at her in order for her to do her job.

The blasting ringing of the phone disturbed the sweet rest of Mrs. Santos in the middle of the night. The person on the opposite line was her cousin just a few miles away from the Santoses. It was in the lower area of the uneven terrain of the housing community. Mrs. Santos and Martin went to sway Bart to come home. They saw him lying on his uncle's living room couch.

The uncle and the female cousin who called lived in a duplex apartment where Bart ran into.

"Bart knew where to go. He missed his uncle," the female cousin said.

"Yes. I believed so aunty," Martin said.

Bart was laughing and looked like he was enjoying just lying down. Martin tried to persuade him to go home, but he refused. Mrs. Santos tried it too but without any success also. Martin called for back-up, but when he tried again, Bart just stood and walked home.

"Sorry for the disturbance, uncle, auntie," Martin said.

"Yes, sorry for the disturbance," Mrs. Santos added.

"It's okay, no problem. The important thing is Bart's safety," they said.

Rose was sitting on the sofa playing with her phone when Mrs. Santos and Martin arrived. They contacted Mr. Santos to inform him that Bart was found and he didn't have to request the police force service.

"Look what happened with your negligence. Bart had escaped. It was good he went to a relative's house," Mrs. Santos said.

"I would have blamed you if something bad happened to Bart. You were the last one to go to bed, and all you should have done was simply check if the door was locked and the keys were hidden," she added.

Rose just kept quiet and did not say a thing while her head was in a bowing position.

"You wait for your "manong." And while waiting, make sure you lock the door and do it right this time." Mrs. Santos said.

Everybody went to their bedrooms but Mr. Sandman did not visit for the remainder of the night. They had their breakfast and relaxed for the rest of weekend. Mrs. Santos hand-washed the underwear in the upstairs CR and hung it to dry on the balcony at Bart's room while he was lying on his bed. Bart became uneasy, rolling on his bed and screaming at the top of his lungs.

"Hey, Bart! Why do you keep on screaming? You sensitive fool! Mommy is just hanging underwear and most of them are yours! Hey! Stop it!" Mrs. Santos said.

"What a sensitive being you are? I am just drying these underwears!" Mrs. Santos said.

A cat must have entered through the opened balcony door, making some purr sounds. Bart grabbed it like a lifeless object and flung it through the window. It turned a complete 360 degree with its limbs stretched out like a propeller before it landed on the concrete pavement outside.

Mr. Santos was in the living room surfing the television. A typhoon warning was in both local weather reports and international stations. The Philippines was one of the major areas to be affected and within the country affected was the Cordillera Region. Mr. Santos had to report to the station. The Santoses were prepared enough for anything the typhoon would throw at them. The very afternoon of the announcement, strong winds without any rain started coming in swaying, the trees and blowing the unsecured things across the community. The strong cloud that wet the land came the night of the very same day. Electricity was shut down as the Santoses stayed at home anticipating if the weather would get better or worse through the battery-operated radio. They were startled by a loud sound from the outside. Martin peeked through the window and saw a couple of galvanized iron swiped by the strong winds on the parked family car in front of the house. Martin went outside, to remove those things from the car thinking all along that he locked the door but Bart escaped without any regard for his safety in the bad weather they were experiencing.

"Bart! Bart!" Martin screamed.

Mrs. Santos and Irene went after him. Bart was in the rain without any protection running and paused for a moment when a tree fell just a few inches in front of him. It did not dissuade him from moving forward and trying to force himself on the closed stores. Mrs. Santos tried to pull him home, but he was so stubborn with his hands anchored on the handle of the closed gate at one of the stores. Mrs. Santos was so pissed and got a piece of a long branch, and whooped his ass. Martin, Irene and Mrs. Fecora went to help get him, and through the unity of their power, they managed to force him back home.

"Shit! Damn shit! You were willing to risk everything just to go to the store! Why did you do that! Bart! It was so stupid of you! You could have died!" Mrs. Santos said.

"All of you take a shower and include Bart!" Mrs. Santos added.

At the police station, everybody was required to report to assist with city rescue groups and the city chapter of the Philippine Red Cross with the rescue and retrieval missions. They received a message through the radio communicators from the Red Cross that they needed some assistance in a landslide-prone area of the neighboring municipality. Mr. Santos was supposed to stay at the station as it was always the protocol for the department heads to function as the head commander but for some reason, he opted to go to the site with some of his men, leaving his second in command in charge of the police department.

There were already rescue groups helping an old lady survivor when they arrived at the scene. It was the muddy side of the mountain slope on the brink of collapsing into the ravine. They helped the rescuers with the retrieval of her husband, whose hand was sticking out from the rubble of rocks, piles of house materials and mud. Mr. Santos noticed that there were several men with civilian clothes who were neither members of the rescue groups nor the paramedic and definitely not one of their own who were seemingly helping with the rescue. He thought at first that they were men from the nearby village who came to help. He was dead wrong; he got a glimpse of one of them putting some things washed with the mud hidden from sight. Another was seen by a member of the Red Cross rescue team running away from the site holding an object that must belong to the elderly couple. He became suspicious because of what he saw and what the rescuer had told him. He immediately called his men's attention and successfully arrested some of the civilian men. Wet and muddy, they all entered the police mobile while the other arrested men rode with the Red Cross' rescue vehicle. Mr. Santos ordered some of his men to let the arrested men stand in line inside the police station. He beat each of the men who were in line with a nightstick on their midsections that forced them to kneel in pain which was a good example of police brutality.

"What were you thinking about stealing from the victims! You!....hmmm!...devils!....no souls....! They were victims of the typhoon and all of you were thinking of taking advantage of them! You excuses for human beings!" Mr. Santos said.

He attempted to hit them again with the nightstick on the back of their heads kneeled down bowing with their hands tied on their backs. As he was about to execute the first strike, everybody stopped him from ever doing so. They advised him to dry and go to his office to calm down and they detained the arrested men.

The typhoon brought so much damage to the affected areas of the country. The Santoses thanked God for the least damage caused by the disaster and watched over the family with the special mention of Bart. Whatever happened he still had the sense to avoid dangers. Prayers were also offered for the victims, survivors and the entire country.

The typhoon was finally over. Everybody was supposed to enjoy the great outdoors after experiencing the hell of the weather. Martin's room was loud with high screams, belting, deafening riffs, and hard-core rock and roll. In the other room, Bart was screaming, biting his hand and could not keep still.

"Martin! Martin! Stop that noise! You are disturbing everybody, especially Bart!" Mr. Santos said.

Martin could not hear his father knocking and shouting. The door was unlocked and Mr. Santos killed the loud tune.

"Hey! What was that all about?" Martin said.

"It's me! Martin! Never play that kind of music when everybody is present or at least lower the volume," Mr. Santos said.

"Why won't you come out from your room and enjoy the sunshine or help us fix whatever damage incurred from the typhoon like anybody else," he added.

"Sorry dad. I thought it was Irene." Martin said.

"It doesn't matter. Just remember what I told you." Martin said.

"Yes dad," Martin said with a frown on his face.
He went and joined the rest of the Santoses with only Bart locked inside the house.

Chapter XXXVIII

"May I enter? I just want to have a chat." Were the words heard from the outside.

Leonor was the newly employed all-around help of the Santoses. She saw a lady holding a mug with visible steams coming from it. She was unfamiliar with the lady, and she was unsure of what to do on whether she would let her in, or ignore her.

"Is anybody home? Let me in please. I just want to chat with anyone in there," the lady said.

"Oh, that must be their Aunt Fecora. They are our next-door neighbors. Let her in," Mrs. Santos said.

Leonor opened the door, but she was surprised by Bart escaping outside.

"I am sorry. Bart has escaped. I didn't know," Mrs. Fecora said.

"It's okay. Martin went and followed him," Mrs. Santos said.

The only open store was the one near the computer shop that was further than the two closed ones. The store owners were a couple with four children. They were kind to Bart and let him take his time to select what he wanted. Martin had a bit of a chat with them and they seemed to be kind and well-mannered people. Martin and Bart were able to go home without any incident.

It was a different mood the second time around. The store had a different atmosphere. The head of the family was boiling and looking at Bart as if looks could kill.

"Bullshit! That abomination of a being is a jinx to my business! Remove him! Get him out of the store!" The head of the family screamed as he punched the door injuring his fist.

Martin stood at the entrance and witnessed all that happened. Irene and Leonor were on their way to help. Martin kept quiet and tried to pull Bart out, but his power could not do it. Irene and Leonor also saw what was going on and the three of them managed to extricate Bart from the hell hole that was the Double Dose store as it was the owners' family name.

"I heard what the Double Dose did to Bart! The ungrateful bastards! You see, the mother was pregnant with their first child when she was about to be detained. I have read from the complaint that she was charged with fraud and estafa. I talked to the complainant, who happened to be my second cousin's daughter. I pleaded with her to drop her complaint and just have an agreement with her for the payment of what she owed her. The complainant informed me that she was really a scam queen. She wanted to give her a lesson and prevent her from ever doing it to others. I pleaded to the complainant more for humanitarian reasons because the culprit could give birth anytime in prison without health facilities, which could be detrimental to the infant. The complainant was forced to denounce her complaints, and I let the station secretary construct an agreement between the two and let it be validated by a notary public lawyer and be formally presented to the court," Mr. Santos said.

"Let them be. It will blow into a bigger problem if we confront them because of what happened. They will have their time with God. God knows what he will do with them," Mrs. Santos said.

The habit of Bart escaping could never be stopped. It can be avoided by locking any exits but sometimes the Santoses as human beings made mistakes of forgetting to lock the doors. Bart again went to the Double Dose store regardless of the presence of other stores. Nobody understood why he liked going to the Double Dose store in spite of their terrible treatment of him. Mrs. Santos was alone when she followed Bart. It was only the mother who was present in the store when Mrs. Santos entered to retrieve her son.

"Why, my son? Why do you like coming here! They will kill you if they want to!" Mrs. Santos said."

"Sorry, madam. I am very sorry," The mother said.

"Bart, come! Why do you insist on coming here? People are evil! They will kill you!" Mrs. Santos continuously said disregarding the mother.

 "I am very sorry, madam, let him be," the mother said.

But Mrs. Santos insisted that Bart must get out of the damn place.   With her high degree of anger and maybe adrenaline, she was successful in physically wrestling Bart out of the store, even with his towering girth and size.

"I am really sorry," The mother said.

Mrs. Santos went on with her son like nobody was trying to communicate with her.

"Why, Bart? You always like going to that hell hole! Please! Quit doing that! Please don't go there anymore. They will kill you! You stubborn boy!" Mrs. Santos kept on repeating, hoping that Bart would understand even a little through the practice of repetition even when they were at home.

Is it God's will? Is it bad karma? Or are they reaping what they sow? The Double Dose family's economic condition was going downhill. Their business was not doing well. Their bakery became the community's joke on low-quality baked goods. The mother passed away due to an undisclosed reason. The attitude of the father blew like the wind in everybody's consciousness in the community. Only a few remained as his friends. He tried to run for a barangay position, but he got the second-lowest votes ever in the history of the Barangay election in the City of Baguio. The family became the joke of the community.

Unhealthy habits and lack of physical activities purged Martin's body to gain weight and fats all over. He could not move due to his ballooned foot. A material as light as a feather could trigger the throbbing pains that shoot, all over the body. A slight movement was not possible. Even a simple activity like drinking water or going to the CR was so difficult. Martin was alone in his room, and Bart was in his room also. Leonor was so busy with the laundry on the ground floor that any sound was masked by the loud noise generated by the washing machine. Martin needed to drink water from the bottle near his bed, but he could not reach for it. He tried his hardest, but he could not endure the pain.

"Bart, good boy. Come," Martin said.

"Good boy! Get the water! Give! Good boy! Give!" Martin pointed at the bottle of water.

"Bart! There, get and give! It is very much obvious where I am pointing at! The water! Get and give!" Martin said.

Martin's pointer finger was inches away from the bottle and the foot felt like it was going to explode anytime when Bart finally got the bottle and handed it to Martin.

"It is very simple and obvious! I was almost touching it, you useless boy! I called you to get the damn bottled water so that I could drink it! So that I don't have to move with the pain in my foot! Very simple instruction! You can't even follow!" Martin said.

After a few days of medications and rest, Martin's swollen foot had subsided. He could already walk in a normal manner. The first thing he did was to hug his brother Bart and apologize for the insults he told him due to the pain he was suffering from.

Martin could now join the educational trip that was required in his school curriculum. He can't wait for the scheduled trip to Metro Manila; the capital city, for it will be his first time to experience the place. In an untoward circumstance, the help left without any permission from the Santoses. Nobody available could temporarily take the role of a babysitter while they seek another. Martin was so down with emotions, but he had to stay for his brother.

In the outskirts of the city, a taxi driver was preparing for work when he noticed through his apartment window that the pile of leaves on the adjacent vacant lot was moving. He did not pay much attention to it with the thought that it might be an animal, or the wind was causing the movement. He was about to leave and go to his taxi when he had a second look at the pile of leaves and saw a barely moving exposed human arm. He rushed to his landlady's living space and informed her of what he saw. They went to inspect the area and found a young teenage girl with obvious scratches, bruises, and hematomas present all over her body. They helped her inside the land lady's space, and the landlady gave her a sponge bath because she was too weak to stand or sit for a regular bath. She was given some tea, and mentholated ointment was gently rubbed on her body. The landlady didn't have clothes that fit her so she just let her rest on the sofa covered with a blanket. The taxi driver drove to the police station to report what they had witnessed. He led the responding police officers to the apartment. The police officers reported to Mr. Santos about the young girl that was found. He requested a city hospital ambulance to go and pick her up for her much-needed medical attention.

The young lady was questioned by the police when she gained her strength back. She was asked first about her name and background. She revealed that her name was Juliet, and she was from "Pangasinan" (one of the provinces near the Cordillera Region). Her family lived in a moderate sized "nipa" house on a rice field owned by her parents. A high-ranking retired military official was claiming their property and the neighboring farms. He managed to bribe some Municipal officials, employees from the land title office, properties division and some cops to help with his dirty deeds. Some of their neighbors were convinced to sell their land at a low price, while those who resisted, including Juliet's family, were met with violence. Many were tortured and massacred, including her parents and a younger brother. She was raped repeatedly by the dirty cops and some men of the retired military officer. They left her in a forest area to die, but she survived and forced herself to walk with the fear of them going back and finally finishing her off the moment they learned that she was still alive. The next thing she remembered was lying on a pile of dried leaves while a man was carrying her inside a concrete house.

"I got a proposal for you. You have seen my special son and we need someone to take care of him while we are at work and school. You will also be the all-around help in our household while your case is ongoing. If, it okay with you?" Mr. Santos asked.

"The previous companion appeared to be driven away by Bart's escape which she could not handle," he added.

"That's fine with me, sir, I can do that besides I have no place to stay within the city....and I am also afraid to go back to our place at this moment because I am afraid that those who did all of these to me and my family might return and finish me off," Juliet said.

"You can call me uncle or "manong" instead, and don't worry you are safe with us. I assure you," Mr. Santos said.
"Thank you very much, uncle. You are very kind," Juliet said.

Chapter XXXIX

Mrs. Fecora was so excited about her son Grim's birthday. She could not contain her mouth that the news was disseminated all over. At school with Grim's teachers, with Grim's very good friends in the neighborhood even those who were not close to her son were invited. Martin and some of Mr. Francesco's relatives were requested to wake early on the day of the celebration for the food preparation. Many guests were too early while preparation was still going on. Some guests opted to help while others enjoyed the preliminary drinks and "pulutans." The main dishes were served one at a time in accordance with what was prepared first. Mrs. Fecora and her family's house were jam-packed that the Santoses opened their doors for other guests who came later. The main celebration started with a prayer. The candle blowing and happy birthday singing were almost neglected because many were already filled with alcohol while others were already full. Mrs. Fecora called for Bart, accompanied by Juliet from next door to join in with the celebration. They were enjoying their meal at the dining table when Bart saw the 1.5 liters of coke, grabbed it and went back home. Juliet followed him just a moment after. Mr. and Mrs. Santos had conversations with relatives, friends and Mr. Francesco's relatives before heading back home. Martin stayed and had drinking sessions and karaoke with those who stayed. As a dentist, Mrs. Fecora noticed the poor condition of Bart's teeth. She went next door to again inspect his teeth.

"Brother, I want to check the extent of the damage to Bart's teeth and if I could do something about it, but for now, he is asleep." Mrs. Fecora said.

"Yes, I will wait until he wakes up and besides go back to your guests and enjoy," Mr. Santos said.

Mrs. Santos was sleeping on the living room sofa waiting for Martin. He was so hammered he could hardly carry himself as he was entering the house.

"Martin, you are drunk. Go to your room first before getting naked," Mrs. Santos said.

She gave Martin a boost, and he entered his room without any clothes on.

Martin woke early the next day with a throbbing headache. He went to the second floor CR for his business and emerged to see Bart's room wide open with Bart looking at him screaming.

"What's with the anger my brother?" Martin asked.

He noticed that the floor was carpeted with his clothes and vomits that stench the entire room. He cleaned the vomit with the clothes on the floor first before cleaning it again with a mop and a bucket of bubbling detergent. Bart stopped screaming but still stared at him with the unexplainable sense of weirdness emitting from Bart. It was the moment when he was bare skinned. He finished the cleaning and went back to the CR to take a bath.

Martin went downstairs feeling refreshed.

"You were very drunk last night," Mrs. Santos said.

"Yes. I didn't even remember most of what I did," Martin said.

"It's good you were drunk next door at your Aunt's place. Be cautious next time, especially when you have drinking sessions outside," Mrs. Santos said.

"Yes mom. I am sorry," Martin said while having his breakfast in front of the television set.

"I remembered that a "perya" (carnival show) is coming to the city for the first time," he added.

"Of course the carnival. I saw the set-up within the park. I planned for all of us to go visit one of these weekends when everything is ready," Mr. Santos said.

Everybody he knew was planning to go to the opening program of the carnival show. On the other hand, he planned to take his family on any other day than the opening. He didn't want the hustle of keeping up with lots of people with Bart's presence. It was a great strategy, for they went the weekend before the carnival left the city.

Irene and Martin were amazed at the carnival rides, and the amusement park setting for it was their first time experiencing it. Martin went ahead to the entrance but a carnival crew guarding the entrance stopped him.

"Where is your ticket?" The carnival crew said.

"Ticket?" Martin said.

"Yes, ticket. You should buy your ticket first before you are allowed to enter the premises," the carnival crew said.

"Martin, what are you doing? Come here first and let's buy our tickets," Mr. Santos said.

The ticketing booth was on the right side of the entrance and on the window. A piece of white bond paper with the words "50% off, Ride all you can" written was posted on the glass above the open space on the cashier's window.

I was right all along. I knew the price would be slashed, and people would be few. Mr. Santos told himself as he was paying for the tickets.

The first ride they saw was the train. Mrs. Santos asked the operator if Bart could ride the train or any other rides. The operator saw Bart.

"I don't know. Your son is a large dude. He may be too heavy for all the rides," The train operator said.

"Please be considerate and let him ride. He is a special child with a condition. Please," Mrs. Santos said.

The train operator took a look again at Bart. He was skeptical at first but he allowed him to ride the train alone due to his weight and size. Bart resisted initially but the Santoses forced him because they wanted him to experience the ride even once in his lifetime. Bart sat on the train when Martin accommodated him. Bart was screaming with laughter as the train moved round and round and in and out of the tunnel.

"My boy Bart, did you enjoy the ride?" Mrs. Santos asked.

"Mom, he seemed to enjoy it. He laughed and laughed during the ride," Martin said.

"Good Boy Bart," Mr. Santos said.

The Santoses noticed the presence of tourists of different races. There were caucasians, there black people and Asians. Martin noticed that the Asians were staring at Bart and some of them were bowing in his presence.

"Look at the "intsik" (Filipino term used to call people of Mongolian race primarily referring the Chinese.) tourists. Notice their reactions whenever they cross paths with Bart," Martin said.

"Oh yeah, I see what you mean. They thought Bart was one of their own for appearing like a fat Buddha or even sumo wrestler," Irene said.

They went on laughing as they were looking for other rides

They both caught the attention of the rest of the family and joined in with the laughter noticing what Martin had initially noticed.

"Oh, Bart. You must have been born in the wrong country. Your kind knows about it. You must be originally Chinese or Korean or Japanese," Mr. Santos said, holding his hand while walking.

The Santoses enjoyed most of the rides. They ended their enjoyment when Bart's large body showed signs of fatigue. Mr. Santos parked in a restaurant near the carnival for their dinner. Bart screamed and refused to get out when he was forced to do so. Martin tried to pull him out of his seat which was the right side of the back seat but he wouldn't budge.

"Let him be. Order some take-out food instead and we will be heading home," Mr. Santos said.

Juliet stayed at home and slept. The house was completely dark, the inside and the porch. Mr. Santos was banging on the door while the rest were shouting "open the door, please," but there was no answer. Mrs. Fecora and her kids noticed what was happening next door and went to inspect it. Bart took off his shorts and attempted to take a dump in the dark. Mrs. Santos took him next door to do his business and clean his bottom.

"What is happening with Juliet? Why doesn't she open the door?" Mrs. Fecora said.

"I am sure she is inside, and I never saw he left," she added.

"I don't even have the spare key with me." Mr. Santos said.

"Stay here for a moment while waiting for her to open. Call for the others also. Maybe she is fast asleep," Mrs. Fecora said.

They were about to go next door when the living room light was switched on, followed by the porch light.

"There you are. I almost invited them next door. Hehehe," Mrs. Fecora said.

Mr. Santos, Martin, and Irene entered, followed by Mrs. Santos and Bart from next door.

"I am sorry I overslept and did not hear your knocks," Juliet said.

"It's okay, but what is going on with you? You didn't want to join us at the carnival show then?" Mr. Santos said.

"Before answering that we bought take out and prepare it for our dinner," Mrs. Santos said.

They were having their dinner when Juliet revealed that the final verdict of her case was scheduled on Monday next week.

"Yes, I forgot about it. I hope those who did you and your family wrong will get what they deserve," Mr. Santos said.

"I am sure God will not allow for them to get away from what they did," Mrs. Santos said.

"Sorry for not coming with you to the carnival show and for not opening the door immediately. I am so nervous about it," Juliet said.

"It is okay. I am sure justice will prevail just like what I said," Mrs. Santos said.

"I am sure about it," Mr. Santos said in agreement.

Irene and Martin did not join with the conversation but listened instead while having their dinner.

"Guilty!" with the pounding sound of the gavel was music to Juliet's ears. It was a bit sad that not all the perpetrators were convicted. The good news was the involved police officers were stripped of their positions and convicted without the luxury of bail and without any possibilities of parole. The other convicted suspects had the same fate. The success of more than two years' trial was not possible without the efforts of Mr. Santos and the City Prosecutor Office for their role in insisting the trial be held in Baguio City to avoid any whitewash and for the speedy serving of justice.

"You finally won the case. It is up to you to decide if you will go back to your hometown or to stay with us," Mrs. Santos said'

"Uncle, you and your family have been good to me and treated me like part of the family. I decided to stay and enroll to the newly implemented program of the state university, the Open University System where classes are held every Saturdays and Sundays and some evening classes on the weekdays. I am asking your permission if you would allow me," Juliet said.

"Yes, of course. Why not. Just give us a copy of your class schedule after your enrollment and we will work something out," Mr. Santos said

"You and your family are very kind uncle and auntie. No amount of thanks can equal what you did and still willing to do for me. Thank you very much," Juliet said.

"No problem. Just always remember that you always have a place in our family," Mr. Santos said.

"Anyway, how is your family back in your hometown? And your properties?" Mr. Santos asked.

"Uncle, I asked my relatives to sell the rice fields that the land grabbers were not able to acquire. I also encouraged them to migrate to another municipality or province if possible. It is difficult to ask but it is for their safety. They can also track other relatives from other places to stay with if possible. Many relatives and associates of those evil people who did the evil acts to us are still in power." Juliet said.

"My murdered parents are buried in the public cemetery of the neighboring municipality at my request.I sent some cash for the expenses.My uncle; the younger brother of my late dad, is also in the city working as a baggage boy in one of the large grocery stores," She added.

"It will take time but I am glad everything is going back to normal." Mr. Santos said.

Chapter XL

Loud music stretched throughout the neighborhood. It was a non-stop music, primarily love songs, ballads, operas and other genres with melodic sounds.

When the music on the radio became heavy rock, Bart got agitated, jumped around the house and screamed so loud neighbors peeked through their windows to check what was going on. The Santoses would turn off in complete silence, and he would revert back to silence.

Mrs. Santos with Juliet was cleaning the house. They were checking on the things lying around to see if they could be used again or go to the trash. Mrs. Santos saw old newspapers and magazines with Bart's scribbles.

"He used to draw when he was young but he became lazy now that he became older," Mrs. Santos said.

"It is better for him to be busy with something than lying and making loud noises just like when he screamed and jumped around to the tone of that rock and roll," She added.

"Yes, I surely remember when he used to draw figures like trees with trunks and triangular leaves, the logo of "ABS-CBN" (one major TV stations in the Philippines) TV network but without the letters, one that looks like a lolly pop and there were even images that look like heads and legs. Maybe that's how he sees the world? But, yes I totally agree with you. What a waste that he does not draw anymore." Martin said as he heard what the two were talking about.

"So sad we never saved some clearer work of his. All we have are these old newspapers and magazines. Let's try to save these as remembrances and evidences of his work. We never even maintained his interest because we became so busy and lazy. We should have given more time. What a waste," Mrs. Santos said.

Juliet was still busy with the sorting of things but she managed to listen to what Mrs. Santos and Martin were talking about.

Mrs. Santos planned to ignite Bart's passion for writing again. They had lessons every time she had time to spare. Mrs. Santos would write words such as Bart's and the Santoses' complete names to immitate. Bart became agitated and burst into screams every time he had difficulty copying the words. The neighbors could hear what was going on, but they understood enough that they tolerated such noise, with the exception of one. The neighbor with an infant appealed to the Santoses to minimize Bart's screaming because it always startled the baby into persistent cries. The Santoses tried to conduct the lesson without agitating Bart into screams but it was not possible. His lessons were sadly halted to prevent any creation of noise.

The Santoses were frustrated because they could not find any experts or institutions that aim to help people with developmental disorders. Members of a non-profit organization were required to acquire police clearance or NBI (The Philippine equivalent of FBI) or court clearance as one of the prerequisites for their application for a permit to operate. It caught Mr. Santos' eye while reviewing each member's application. He tried to approach the said organization, but they stated that Bart was not qualified for being 19 years old. They only cater to children 18 years and below. His high hopes were shattered. He had no choice but to adhere to the organization's policy.

The Department of Social Welfare and Development established schools for children with special needs such as Autism, Down Syndrome, low IQ and similar clients with mental and developmental disorders. They also catered with gifted children or children with special abilities. Mr. Santos enrolled Bart in the program. He had the highest expectation for Bart's improvement because the program was well funded by the government. He requested Juliet, if it does not interfere with her schedule to stay and observe Bart's class and document what she observed for the first few days.

"Uncle, I observed that the lessons given to Bart and the other students are not sufficient. Bart was only allowed to play with the toys while lying around at the same time. He writes a little and has snacks during breaks. Plus, the students are not separated according to their conditions and needs with appropriate teachers," Juliet said.

"I almost forgot, parents or guardians or any representative are required to participate in the "Work for a cause" for the construction of the school's new building," she added.

"What a ridiculous policy. It is a government program and they should provide workers for that. There are many unemployed who need work. I am sure the funds allotted are again going to the pockets of the officials. This is totally nonsense," Mr. Santos said.

Mr. and Mrs. Santos decided to keep Bart away from the government school program. For they concluded that taking him there was useless with the school routines they discovered. Besides, his classes could not match their busy schedules.

A group of nursing students were visiting every household with permissions from the barangay officials. They arrived at the Santoses' household with Mrs. Santos present to entertain them.

"Good morning, madam. We are nursing students from the University City System. We have our community-based practicum and we are required to have our initial visits and surveys of every household in your barangay," one of the students said.

"Come in, and we will do the interview inside," Mrs. Santos said.

"Can I give you all some snacks or something to drink?" She added.

"No, thank you, madam. We are all okay," one of the students said.

Another student was taking the interview when Bart went down stairs naked from the waist down, holding a tissue.

"Excuse me. That is my son. He needs help doing some of his personal hygiene, for he has autism," Mrs. Santos said.

"Madam, go on and do what you must," the student who was doing the interview said.

Mrs. Santos wrote all the required information for the form and answered all the questions of the students. The students asked permission if they could return the next day to focus on Bart and Mrs. Santos agreed.

The nursing students came the following day to interview Mrs. Santos regarding Bart. Other medical-related students came pouring in the following days and weeks for the same reason. The Santoses became tired of the disturbances brought by their visits. It was about the ninth or tenth visit when Bart began to scream with jumps that shook the entire house. Mrs. Santos was accommodating when she was present for the first couple of visits. Other visits were accommodated by either Juliet or the Santos children. Mrs. Santos became available again for the Medical-related students to interview.

"I don't want any more home visits! Don't disturb us! After you students get what you need to pass your subject or course, you leave us hanging without any follow-up on my son's progress! He even gets overwhelmed with the large number of people that often disturb him!" Mrs. Santos asserted without giving the group of students a chance to introduce themselves and ask permission.

The students expressed their apologies and exited the premises. Other attempts were made for the same visitations but the Santoses were not welcoming anymore.

Two individuals were knocking at the Santos residence when Mrs. Santos peeked at the window.

"What? Nursing students again? Or Psychology students? What do you need from us?" She asked.

"No madam. We are from the barangay to conduct the annual census," one of them said.

Mrs. Santos opened the door and welcomed the two.

"I am sorry for my rude attitude. I thought the two of you were nursing students for psychology students or any of those medical-related students who were always disturbing us. They always came to interview us about Bart just to fulfill their requirements at school. They never had follow-ups on what Bart was doing or offer some help for him," Mrs. Santos said.

"He he he! I know how you feel. They even disturbed us when we were busy. I have a nephew with down syndrome at home and have the same experience with those students," one of them replied.

"Anyway, can I offer you some coffee or something to drink or snack?" Mrs. Santos asked as she was filling up the form.

"No, we are okay. Thank you," The other one said.

The two left as soon as Mrs. Santos completed filling the census form.

Mr. and Mrs. Santos were contemplating and searching for a specialist from time to time. The only available they found on the internet was located in the capital city of Manila. They were discussing it often before going to bed. They concluded that the risk was not worth it. They could not afford the expenses for the check-up and lease for the place they will be staying. The worst risk they will be facing was the travel condition and safety of Bart from Baguio to Manila. Sadly, they had to throw out the idea.

Chapter XLI

A glimmer of hope came for Bart when Mr. Santos heard about a female Physician specializing in "Childhood Disorders" that included Bart's condition with its scope. Mr. Santos set an appointment with her to check on Bart. The Santoses were in full force in accompanying Bart to the specialist's clinic. He entered the hospital without any resistance. He even waited with the Santoses in queue. He shakes and throws a tantrum when the specialist's assistant attempts to take his blood pressure and temperature. He was holding on to the sides of the door when Martin and Mr. Santos tried to give him a little push to enter the specialist's main office. His screams and cries caught the people's attention except for a few foreign nationals who were waiting for their turns.

"Let him be. Don't force him. Sorry but you have to bring him back home and do this some other time," the specialist said.

"People should not look at him like that, never," the specialist added.

The specialist advised the Santoses to introduce Bart to the clinic room in a slow and steady manner. They should not force him in a crude manner all at one setting. They should give him time to familiarize himself with the place and to establish that the clinic was a safe zone. The Santos adhered to the advice, and Bart had his physical check-up and developmental evaluation on a twice-a-week basis. He was also taking medications that kept him calm and relaxed most of the time. The Santoses were positive about Bart's development, but it was cut short. The specialist migrated with her family to Canada without any warning at all. She was the only known available specialist in the entire region. Bart's progress was discontinued, and reverted to his old ways of staying at home doing nothing. The Santoses never stopped with the specialist prescriptions. The Santoses wanted to implement the diet recommendations without the specialist's help, but they were not successful.

On the other side, Juliet completed her studies with the course of Bachelor of Science of Education Majoring in Elementary Education. She was struggling with whether to accept the job offer she received in the lowlands or to remain with the Santoses. She let the initial offer pass her without the Santoses' knowledge. She was still struggling with the major decision of her life. Her desire was to really help her people to fight poverty through the power of education and to give them the push they needed to strive more in life. She had many chances to ask permission to leave but again she did not. She was assisting Bart with his bath and stared at his face more than usual. The conflict within was really bothering her, for she fell in love with him as a brother and with the Santoses like her own biological family .One day, the Santos noticed that something was bothering her through her actions.

"What's the matter with you?" Mrs. Santos asked.

"Auntie, I want to tell you something and I hope you will understand," Juliet said.

"It seems that something is bothering you? What do you want to tell me?" Mrs. Santos asked.

"I....I am....uhhh!...planning to go home with hopes that everything is settled. I want to visit my parents' grave and teach some poor children, those who can't afford to go to school," Juliet said.

"How noble of you. Of course, it's okay with us. The important thing is that you know someone who will take care of Bart,"Mrs. Santos said.

"Don't worry, auntie, I will look for my replacement." Juliet said.

Bart stood in between Juliet and Mrs. Santos, seated in the living room, having a conversation. He was facing Juliet, which made her notice something peculiar on his lips. He scratched the surface of his lower lip in a violent manner until blood spurted from the exact spot. Irene also noticed the blood all over the sheets thinking that the injury was so deep and wide.

"Bart, What did you do with your lip? Come here. Come here. I said! Let me clean your wound and put some Band-Aid on it. Please don't remove it," Irene said.

"What happened?" Martin asked.

"His usual self, he scratched his lip. Hope he won't remove the band aid that I applied." Irene said.

Not a minute long, the Band-Aid was removed and blood was all over Bart's shirt. Mrs. Santos noticed his bloody shirt, let him change, then applied an anti-bacterial ointment before putting gauze secured by micro pore plaster.

"What happened to Bart?" Mrs. Santos asked.

"Mom, I cleaned and put a Band-Aid on his lip, and again, he removed it! It won't heal if it continues," Irene said.

"Bart, no Bart, never remove that on your lip please," Irene told Bart and pointed at the affected area.

The Santoses got weary, and sure enough the gauze was removed, then some sort of flesh replaced the blood from the cut. The wounded area grew like a tumor as time went by. The Santoses was right all along to have an appointment for its removal. The first private hospital they went to had to cancel due to the specialist's unavailability on the set operation date.The second government hospital did admit him the evening of his check-up, with the operation set for the next day.

Bart had no idea about the operation. He just screamed every time they extracted blood for testing. The hospital decided to incorporate the oral operation that his parents agreed upon with his Aunt Fecora. The operation went great without any complications. Mr. Santos took a picture of Bart and Irene posted it on social media. It blew up. Many expressed their love and concerns through their comments. It could be categorized as a viral event. Some of those who could spare their free time went to visit him the moment they learned about his hospitalization.

There was much love and care for Bart, including the hospital staff that came to know him.

The love and concerns still overflowed days after Bart's discharge from the hospital. It was expressed on social media and whenever a member of the Santos came across with someone they knew, concerns about Bart were the initial words that came from their mouths. *What is it? Is it a genuine concern, is it out of curiosity on how a person with his condition handles such a situation? Or Just human nature, we tend to give our hearts to the underdogs?* Whatever it might be, the Santoses could not shake it off for a long time.The phenomenon slightly faded away as time passed.

Juliet was finally out of the Santoses' lives. The supply of help continued from the Cagayan source of manpower. Elizabeth was hired with Juliet's recommendation. She did the typical house chores with the excellent job of taking care of Bart. Nothing irregular was observed in her working attitude. What's important was her good treatment of Bart.

Bart developed a habit of taking photographs from the photo albums and keeping them in the drawer. Everybody was clueless about why he did such action.

Maybe there was a connection to the presence of Elizabeth?Maybe it was his way to combat boredom? It became somewhat of an annoyance to the family because well-kept photos full of memories throughout the years were disarranged or misplaced.

"Bart, what are you doing with the photos? Look some are forcibly removed from the photo albums. Some are even torn,"Mrs. Santos told Bart as he was staring at her with a blank expression. There was nothing to be done, and Bart continued with his photo habit.

Mr. Santos saw their picture at the beach with his sister Fecora's family on the floor. It triggered his craving for swimming and relaxation. He wanted to try the newly opened mountain resort located in the Municipality of La Trinidad, the neighboring town often mistaken as part of Baguio City. He invited his sister Fecora and her family. Johnny and the boys were also welcomed to join. Nothing can hide the excitement written in the boys' expressions. It was a wide and long swimming pool with a depth of five feet to five feet nine inches with a separate kiddy pool and shaded booths for hire around it. The pool had no hotel or restaurant available, only a sari-sari store. Bart was expected to love dipping in the pool, but it was the opposite. He only sat at the booth eating or just walked around the sides of the pool. Even the shallow kiddie pool was not spared from his refusal to get in the cool waters. Everybody who accompanied Bart only drenched him from time to time to prevent sunburn from irritating his skin.

"What's wrong with you, Bart? I decided to have a family vacation because you were caged in the house for quite some time and for you to enjoy a different environment but it seems you never enjoy anything. You used to love the waters,"Mr. Santos said.

"Yes Bart. You used to love swimming but now why? What happened to you?"Mrs. Santos said.

The whole gang tried to force him into the water one last time but he screamed. The people around were focused on him. He persisted in his screams even biting his hand. Elizabeth and Bart were driven back home to avoid ruining the rest of the family's enjoyment.

Chapter XLII

Mr. Santos found the land titles, plans and other pertinent documents of lot ownership mistakenly placed unconcealed in their room. It has Mrs. Santos' name on several of the documents. Others had evidence of the transfer process. Mrs. Santos entered and caught Mr. Santos reading the documents.

"You found a lot of documents. Those are cheap enough for me to afford on an installment basis. My coworkers and friend were rushing to sell," Mrs. Santos said.

"Wow, now you are wealthy with many properties. Hehehe," Mr. Santos said.

"You are laughing like a joke. I bought these properties as investments. We don't have savings to be used in cases of emergency. What if something happens to us? We can sell and the good thing is properties appreciate. We can demand higher prices," Mrs. Santos said.

Mr. Santos did not utter another word, and they both went to sleep.

Mr. Santos was surprised when the police station received a "balik-bayan" box (Which literally means return country; A package that is usually sent by Filipinos abroad for their loved ones and friends to the Philippines which contains everything one can think of from chocolates, clothes, grocery items and items that could be legally sent.) addressed to him from Cora his half-sister from Germany. Mr. Santos requested some of his men to bring the package to their place. He texted the rest of the family not to open the package until everybody was present.

"Good, we are all home. Open the package and take all that you want from it," Mr. Santos said.

"Okay, you are so excited as if you had never received a package before. Your sister Fecora did not even arrive yet," Mrs. Santos said.

"Just as I said, make sure to take whatever you want available in the package, and if there are chocolates and groceries items, take it all but share some next door enough for them to taste," Mr. Santos said.

"Why can't you wait to open the package? As if we can't afford all of these things," Mrs. Santos said.

"You know Fecora. You know how she is if we don't get what we want ahead of time. She will not divide the package fairly and she will get the good ones and only give us the leftovers," Mr. Santos said.

Mrs. Santos burst out laughing while the kids were rummaging through the pile of items from the package. Irene got a shirt and a pair of leather boots that fits her perfectly and Martin got a pair of jeans and shirts that were a bit large for him but he loved baggy clothes anyway and as for Bart, he did not care for anything the important thing was he got his sweets and chocolates.

Irene opened her social media account and searched for her Aunt's account to thank her. She encouraged her parents and brother to do the same.

The Santoses went next door to give their share of the package.

"Wow, imported stuff from my sister Cora. Wow. I love it," Mrs. Fecora said when she received her share.

One of Mrs. Fecora's joys in life was rummaging at "balik-bayan" boxes. Her senses glow every time she receives a box or two. There weren't any moments that she held herself from inspecting the contents of a box, even if it was intended for her family and the Santoses.

Mr. Santos was reminded about the latest incident they were handling. He warned everybody, especially the children to be careful when walking alone in the streets, for they had received information about a white van driving around kidnapping children. It was also alleged that the kidnappers were also harvesting the organs of the kidnaped children and selling them in the black market.

The police force and other law enforcers were well aware about the potential danger brought by the fear of kidnappings. Check-points were set all over major roads. Police and "tanod" (Barangay police) are patrolling their jurisdictions, especially at night. Other than those safety measures, life was normal.Leonor was cleaning the frontage of the house when a little boy of about six or seven years old scratched-up and dirty all over, went straight inside. Elizabeth did not notice him at first, but she saw him trying to take a piece of bread from the kitchen. She then stopped the boy and bathed him. She clothed the boy with one of Martin's shirts and gave him a Milo drink and a piece of bread. She texted Mr. and Mrs. Santos informing them of what was happening.

"He is a cute little boy. Where did he come from?" Mr. Santos asked.

"I don't know, uncle. I just saw him roaming around as I told you in my text message," Elizabeth said.

"I am very suspicious. Maybe the kidnapping thing but we are not certain," Mr. Santos said.

Mr. Santos asked some questions when the little boy was awake. He asked his name and where he originated from, but because of his very young age, he did not remember that much. He only knew that he was called Richard by his family and his mother's name was Diane, and his father's name was Bob. Mr. Santos also asked what the little boy could remember about what happened to him. He only answered with uncle and white broom-broom as it was how he described the vehicles.

Mrs. Maria made a surprise arrival at the Santos residence without any companions. She went to the city to claim her husband's death benefits. She asked for any of the Santoses who could help her fast-track her claim. Mrs. Santos accompanied her mother to the appropriate office during her long break from work. Mrs. Maria did not go back home after her mission to the city was successful. She stayed for a couple more days for the weekend. Mrs. Santos accompanied her again to visit some relatives her mother missed. Richard's presence made Mrs. Maria's heart miss her grandchildren's company. The Santoses allowed her to bring Richard to the province. They thought that he would be better off in a clean and peaceful environment and it was difficult for the Santoses to have a child around with Bart's presence.

Mrs. Santos had to purchase a newer cell phone models because she needed an update to fit the more modern times. The new model had a camera and video recording features that were absent from the old one. Mrs. Maria was a devoted active member of the Catholic faith but still believed in the traditional "Igorot" ways of living which were very far from the spectrum. Mrs. Santos sent her old cellphone to her mother who wasn't well versed in technology. The one who was practically using was a relative. She would call or text Mrs. Santos with Mrs. Maria's instructions. The majority of time was for personal use because the load bought would be wasted if not used to its maximum limit. Mrs. Santos received a call from her mother inviting them to attend a "canao"(Igorot celebrations for weddings, thanksgivings and healing rituals) because according to her, Richard was restless and could not sleep at night due to the presence of his father's spirit. He was always dreaming of him requesting for his presence in the afterlife, and contradicting such occurrence is to adhere to whatever the "mambunong" required, which were the "canao" and the immediate family's presence or, in this case the guardians. The Santoses acknowledged and were proud of their "Igorot" heritage, but they were not 100% firm believers in the rituals and traditions due to practical reasons.They did not agree with the idea, but they didn't want to be disrespectful to Mrs. Maria.

Mrs. Santos' ancestral house was full of people, animals being slaughtered, and smoke from the burning firewood.

Everybody was so busy except for the elders inside who were settled in. The Santoses were just fresh from their trip when the "mambunong" required the immediate family of the hostess to dance the "tayaw" (A traditional "Igorot" dance performed during "canaos.").They all complied with the requirement to the extent of Bart throwing a tantrum because he was forced to participate. He did not complete the dance and ran to the store. It was not long after the Santoses' surprise when he was walking towards them with a 1.5 liter Coke. He went inside to drink the entire thing. Richard tends to follow him around except when he needs to go to the CR or eat his meal. Richard always got excited when Bart was around. Nobody could explain why the case is not even the elder or the "mambunong." A drunken male relative suddenly fell in front of the house. Everybody suspected that what happened was only due to too much alcohol consumption. Two men were trying to fix him into a more comfortable position and location when he suddenly stood like nothing had happened. His actions and demeanor were like someone who was not drunk at all.Many who knew Benjie noticed that he started acting like the deceased. He started confessing and being apologetic for what he did with Benjie's voice. He even pleaded with relatives to take care of his children.

"Please take care of them! Please take care of them! He was repeating.

He then followed with "It's cold out here!" which was interpreted by the "mambunong" as his spirit is cold on his way to the afterlife that traditional woven "Igorot" long enough to drape Benjei's thumb is required.

The immediate family members were required to bring the blanket, a portion of the slaughtered animal specifically for him, and some "tapuy" offerings the night when Benjie's spirit manifested in one of the relatives.

The drinking and celebration continued throughout the night. Bart was not able to have a good night's sleep due to the noise. He laid on a bed for a few moments, then went down and up the stairs like he didn't know what to do. He ate a little, then went back to bed and went downstairs again to pee and back to bed and went down again, drank a glass of water, and went on through the night.

Practically, everybody had little to no sleep except for those who had too much to drink.

Chapter XLIII

Mrs. Santos' younger sister Lady and her family moved to the Municipality of La Trinidad one of the major neighbors of Baguio, City. They were to live in her husband's province in the lowlands but she could not stand them being discriminated against for being "Igorots". They occupied a parcel of land on the hillside of the farthest Barangay as squatters. The house they were living in was made from leftover timbers, and temporary galvanized irons as roofing and walls. The Santoses helped them however they could. They were even the first in mind every time they had extra clothes, extra food and people to invite on occasions.

We are helping strangers and other distant relatives. Then why wouldn't we help my sister. She has a close family. was on the mind and heart of Mrs. Santos.

There were rumors of Mr. Patrick having a land located near where Mrs. Lady and her family were staying. Mrs. Santos went to check if the rumors were legally binding. It was discovered that the lot just a few meters north of Mrs. Lady's residence was actually purchased by Mr. Patrick years ago. There were a few temporary occupants who were staying on the property for significant amounts of time and were resistant to leaving the area. Mrs. Santos had to acquire court orders with police power for them to vacate or she, her sister, and their mother threatened them to file suit. Mrs. Santos was ready for anything possible to happen. She got a copy of the land title, she had the court order. She had the backing of the police with her husband's support, and she was willing to be violent with the occupants if needed. Mr. Santos was not present during the actual issuance of the court order to the occupants, but he ordered some of his men to accompany the court officer and his wife. Mrs. Santos was very thankful that the occupant understood what was going on and asked for time for them to leave. A one-story house was built on the property, which gave Mrs. Lady and her family a decent place to live in.

Mrs. Lady was a kind-hearted woman. They did not have much but she was helpful to others. A cousin with the name of Alvin, had a motorcycle business in the city. He repaired motorcycles, sold motorcycles, and motorcycle parts. He was doing okay and could afford to rent an apartment space. The problem arose when the building across from his building opened a similar business. His business was involved with original Japanese motorcycles while his competitor was selling cheaper "made in China" replicas that customers preferred. He was forced to close his business and could not pay his rent. The landlord gave him an ultimatum that he must leave his unit on a given date. He was sitting on the bench within the La Trinidad "jeepney" terminal when he saw his cousin lady waiting for a ride.

"Hey, "manang" Lady," Alvin said.

"Oh, it's you Alvin. How are you?" Mrs. Lady asked.

"I'm glad we crossed paths," Alvin said.

"You did not answer my question," Mrs. Lady said.

"I am fine. Thanks," Alvin said.

"Are you sure? You don't look fine. I can see how you look at me. C'mon tell me what is going on with you?" Mrs. Santos said.

"It's just, my business is bankrupt, and I don't have any other source of income, and my landlord is asking me to leave. I have nowhere to live," Alvin said.

"Is that it? No problem. You can live with us," Mrs. Lady said.

"Are you sure?" Alvin asked.

"Yes, we have extra room, and you can stay until you can stand on your own two feet," Mrs. Lady said.

Alvin stayed with Mrs. Lady and her family helping with the chores and maintenance of the house. He tried to apply for work, but sadly, he was unsuccessful. When Mr. Santos knew about Alvin, he asked him to be his driver. He would drive Bart around when Mr. Santos needed his driving services with allowances given by Mr. Santos. It was better than receiving nothing at all.

The kidnapping issue was still hot when bodies were discovered in the outskirts of Baguio, City. Another was discovered on the same trail within the territory of the neighboring municipality of La Trinidad. Hours later, another body was found in the municipality of "Bokod."The discovered bodies must have been connected because the heads and hands were decapitated and were missing .A joint task force was organized with the National Bureau of Investigation and The Philippines National Police. Upon the investigations, some of the bodies were identified through their tattoos, identifying marks on the bodies, and the clothes they were wearing. Those identified had criminal records of rapes, sex molestations, sexual assault, and other offenses pertaining to sex. Further investigations revealed about a female college student who was a rape victim who belonged to the "Kalinga" tribe."Kalinga" tribe is known as the most violent sub tribe of the "Igorot."All the "Igorot" sub tribes practiced head hunting, but "Kalinga" were the fiercest. They would seek revenge to somebody who did wrong to their kind through beheading and bring the head to their respective community as a trophy and a sign of their victory.

The investigators knew about the reason for the beheadings but they were puzzled on why the hands were also removed. An Uncle and a cousin of the rape victim were traced and invited to the police station for their statements.

They confessed and were so proud of what they did because, in accordance with them, the massacred victims deserved their fate due to what they did to the members of their clan. They revealed that the reason for removing the victim's hands was to make their bodies unidentifiable. They also made the mistake of mentioning their accomplices with the confidence that they would be released because they adhered to tradition.

They were outraged when they were detained, and the accomplices they mentioned joined them later. They were given a fair trial as the law dictated. The trial proceedings were similar to the American style but with the absence of a jury. The presiding judge rules the court and makes all the case decisions. Trials were full of tension, especially from the suspects' supporters. The situation became worse when the suspects were convicted.

"These are all non-sense! The ones killed deserved what they got! Those who made the killing must not be convicted, mad they did what is right according to the tradition of revenge!" One of the elders of the convicted felons' clan said. The incident became a circus controversy nationwide.

With all of what's happening at work Mr. Santos still managed to drive his children to the premier restaurant within La Trinidad. It was nostalgic for him because it was the restaurant that started many things in the food industry in the Cordillera region in the late 50's.The restaurant invented many standard dishes in restaurant menus which were imitated by other restaurants. The primary showcase menu was the "Rice Toppings." These are dishes that are partnered with steamed rice.For example, the (name of the restaurant or eatery) rice; the basic components are "chopsuey" (stir fried vegetables), lechon kawali (deep fried pork belly), a piece of fried chicken and steamed rice topped with a sunny-side-up on the side. Another on the menu is the "chopsuey" rice, "lechon" rice, and others. There were also different soups and side menus that the restaurant invented or made from traditional Filipino food with twists. Mr. Santos called for his wife, who was attending her master's class at a university within La Trinidad. Mrs. lady and her family were also invited to enjoy the moment with them .Bart went to the display stand of cakes and pastries and grabbed a choco mousse cake. The rest ordered the rice toppings with an order of "pancit" and a half order of fried chicken for Bart. Mrs. Lady and family met them first before Mrs. Santos came for her lunch break. Mrs. Lady's kids ate some "pancit" and fried chicken while she and her husband had the same order as Mr. Santos'. Mrs. Santos went back to her master class when she was done with her beef and broccoli meal. The rest parted ways when it was time to leave the restaurant. Mr. Santos had to stop in a meat shop located at the side of the road on their way home to buy some wild boar meat. It was a special establishment because they were one of the few meat shops that sold wild boar meat by schedule due to its rarity .A guy who was a little bit tipsy in civilian clothes approached Mr. Santos on the driver's side while Martin was in the shop doing the actual buying.

"Hey! Don't you know that it is prohibited to park here?" The guy said.

Bart went out to pee, and it aggravated the guy.

"Hey!I am the boss here! I am the police! I am the law! Peeing is prohibited in this spot!" The guy said.

"Sorry for parking here sir. I am just waiting for my son who is buying meat. It won't take long and my son who just peed is a special one so please be considerate enough to let it be,"Mr. Santos said.

"Ah! No one is above the law! Give me your license or let me have five hundred pesos and all of these will go away! "The guy said.

"Hey! What is your name? Where are you assigned? I am Baguio, City's police chief and what you are doing is illegal! I will track you and report you to your superior!" Mr. Santos said.

"Sir, I didn't know! I am very sorry! Please forgive me!" The guy said.

"No! I won't let this pass!I promise you! Police like you are the reason why the organization has a bad reputation! I will see to it that you will be removed from the service! Get out of my way or I will do something you might regret!" Mr. Santos said.

Martin entered the vehicle, and the drunken guy was still pleading for Mr. Santos not to pursue what he was planning, but he pretended like nobody was talking to him. He started the vehicle and went on, almost side-swiping the drunken guy. When they were settling from their day at home, four visitors came knocking at their door.

"Who the hell are these again?" Mr. Santos said.

As the door was opened a middle-aged man entered and immediately stepped into the living room. He felt like he was oozing with confidence and acted like he was very close with the Santoses. His companion followed in the living room as well.

"Hello! Insan we are here to invite your family to my sister's wedding! She will marry a man from the United Kingdom!" The middle-aged man said.

It became obvious that he was the spokesperson, and he looked at Mr. Santos with a smile like he was not serious about anything.

"What wedding? Who's wedding? And who are you?' 'Mr. Santos asked.

"What? You forgot who we are! You lived in Kabayan for many years! And you have no idea who we are! You must have a poor memory! He! He! He!" The middle-aged man said.

He started introducing himself and explained who they were.

"Okay I am familiar with your family name and some of your relatives but I also don't remember you and your companions."Mr. Santos said.

"Well, it must have slipped your mind, but we brought you something anyway. It is a bit worn-out, and some paints have stains on it but it can still be worn," the middle-aged man said.

They saw Bart coming out of his room and the middle-aged man said, "Good timing. Those clothes I gave will surely fit him."

The Santos were so pissed that they never offered them some snacks, and they went on their way until they left.

"He is so full of himself! Who did he think he is! These clothes he gave are just trash!" Mr. Santos said and threw the clothes in the trash bin.

Chapter XLIV

Mr. Santos was at the university faculty room where he was teaching as a part-time college of criminology professor. He stood from his sitting position but sat again. He tried a second time but shoot chunks of vomits. They painted the entire room and laid on the floor with his face down. Some of his colleagues carried him outside to the parking area for air, while others went to the clinic and sought some help. Mrs. Santos was also contacted while giving medical attention to Mr. Santos.

Oh, my God! Please Lord! Keep my husband out of danger! Hope this is a minor thing! Mrs. Santos' prayer.

Mrs. Santos left work without any signs of trouble. Mrs. Fecora was already at the hospital when she arrived. Mr. Santos was in the Intensive Care Unit. There was the presence of a large glass in front of the room that made everybody visible. A few hours later, Mrs. Alexia Mr. Santos' sister, arrived from "Potia, Ifugao." (One of the municipalities and provinces within the Cordillera Region)The last time they have saw each other was about seven to eight years ago during their brother Jewel's death. They seldom see each other because of the distances between them. It was about an eleven to twelve hours trip from "Potia" to Baguio, City.

Oh! God! Oh! God! Thank you! My brother is not dead! The words played in Mrs. Alexia's mind while waving at her brother.

One visitor at a time was allowed to enter the ICU with proper protective equipment such as a face mask, head-gear, gown and footwear provided by the hospital must be worn at all times while inside. Mrs. Alexia opted to enter after her short chat with Mrs. Santos and Mrs. Fecora.

"My neighbor back home died of a similar case. Her sibling from abroad didn't come to visit her initially. The sibling opted to send her money for the hospital expenses and decided to come home later, but it was too late. My neighbor died a day before her sibling arrived. I thought of the same scenario with us. So, I abandoned my class and immediately came before it's too late,"Mrs. Alexia said.

"Sis, you are exaggerating, for my diagnosis is only a mild stroke, nothing major .Thanks for coming anyway anyway,"Mr. Santos said with a soft voice.

"I am very relieved that nothing major bad happened to you, brother," Mrs. Alexia said.

A representative from the mayor's office handed Mrs. Santos some cash for his hospital bills. Mrs. Santos was touched by the gesture and thanked the representative, hoping it would reach the Mayor. The following day, two off-duty cops came to visit and handed some amount that was collected from the Baguio City Law enforcer's Cooperative that Mr. Santos pioneered. Again, Mrs. Santos was overwhelmed by their kindness and expressed her appreciation. The University where Mr. Santos teaches awarded him with the employee's sick benefits. Other financial contributions poured in from private individuals. Mr. Santos was discharged after four days of hospital confinement. The police department approved a six-month-sick leave from work for his much-needed rest.

The police station was so surprised when Mr. Santos went to work a few weeks after he was discharged. Everybody was concerned about his health.

"Sir, you shouldn't have come for work. Your sick leave for six months is approved anyway," a police officer said.

Similar concerns were expressed by coworkers, several city officials, city employees, friends, and relatives. He insisted on working because there were cases in which he had to supervise himself. The police force only allowed him to stay in his office and never gave him any case or situations that could trigger so much stress.

The organization formed from the clan reunions did not achieve its aim, which was to raise funds to help the less fortunate relatives. Meetings were only held every after annual family reunions. Implementing programs was difficult due to the busy schedules and distant locations of each relative. As such, family reunions became redundant parties with the same faces. For these reasons, the organization's intention to donate cash contributions for Mr. Santos during his hospitalization did not materialize. There were only a few relatives and friends who contributed little monetary help.

The Santoses had the tradition of going home to Kabayan every Christmas, but after what the Santoses experienced that year, they didn't have the enthusiasm to go home for a holiday. They understood that they might have saved more if they celebrated within the city. Everybody was preparing for the "Noche Buena" (Christmas Eve) relatives, friends, neighbors, and communities were greeting each other a Merry Christmas. Unfortunately, the unrest notion of the Santoses being too wealthy set in. The house was filled with people who were mostly for free stuff and a few who were sincerely present to celebrate with them.

"Uncle, Merry Christmas. You see I only have enough money for a one-way fare here. So, can I have some cash money for the fare? It will be sort of my Christmas gift from you. Thank you," a relative who traveled from a faraway place said.

"Cousin, me too. I don't have a place to stay and I don't have fare to go back to my place," another one said.

Few other relatives had told the Santoses about their situations with the mission for asking money.

"What the hell are you all doing wasting your lives and dragging me with your nonsense!" Mrs. Santos said.

"Christmas is a time of relaxation and good times, and there, you all ruin it!" He added.

Mr. Santos had no option but to give them some cash. He didn't give a damn if it was enough for their needs. It would be a bigger problem if he refused to give. Mrs. Santos on the other hand claimed that she had no cash to spare and did a great job of portraying it.

"They came here with nothing at all! The food and the party were free. They did not have to contribute, and yet they wanted more! What kind of attitudes!" Mrs. Santos said.

"We need to be assertive sometimes because they are not our obligations," She added.

The children were listening from the other room. Bart was also present but the Santoses never knew if he had a concept of what was happening around him at all. He was again craving food and went to the dining room to put an Everest on his plate. With his usual eating habit, He stuffed everything in his mouth. A few minutes later, it backfired; he spewed chunks on the floor, on the sink and painted the CR.

"Bart! We kept on telling you to eat properly! Eat slowly! Bite what you can chew and swallow small pieces at a time! Look what happened! You vomited!" Mrs. Santos said.

Elizabeth cleaned the vomit, and Bart went puking again. She gave him a bath the second time around to clean him completely. He insisted on eating again after a few moments but Mrs. Santos prevented him from doing so. He kept on insisting but Mrs. Santos managed to force him to go to bed with Martin's help.

Bart's birthday was on the 2nd of January , the day after the New Year. The Santoses always sees to it that they never missed celebrating his birthday. They wanted their special boy to feel his special day the best they could. In spite of being the year where many asked for cash, draining the Santoses pockets, canceling Bart's birthday was never an option. The meager amount left was budgeted wisely to purchase the essentials. A birthday cake was purchased, and there were many leftover ingredients from the holidays that were created into several dishes. The unforeseen number of guests kept coming but their love for Bart was overflowing because there were only very few who came empty handed.

"Thank you everybody! We can feel you really do care for Bart!" The Santos' simultaneously said

"We really do have a place for him in our hearts," one of the guests said.

"Of course, I wouldn't miss it for the world," another one said.

"For Bart, we do anything," those were the responses of the guests present during the party, while others nodded their heads in agreement.

Chapter XLV

I rene could not wait to live college life. No more with the fixed eight to five schedule. No more with the school uniforms. It's the stage of her life when she was transitioning from a girl to a woman. She could almost do whatever she wanted. The enrollment could take forever to be completed. The weather was humid, and the lines were long. She felt every discomfort it brought but was relieved but a "hottie" passed her way. It seemed that every movement, every walk, and every aura of the "hottie" were in slow motion, filled with a glistening atmosphere around him.

"Oh! Holy! Papa!" Irene's best friend said.

She stared at the tall guy with a charming face and a presence that could make the atmosphere pleasant in any situation.

"He is looking in our direction!" She added.

She started shaking and appeared like somebody was tickling her all over.

Irene was at her back, not saying a word, and wanted her best friend to stop what she was doing. She wanted to go as far as possible from her best friend, but she didn't want to leave the line. The "hottie" passed them without glancing their way. Her best friend could not keep still and continued with what she was doing, which annoyed the others who were inline. She kept quiet when the others in line threatened her with violence. Irene and her best friend parted ways when they completed their enrollments. Irene went to the "jeepney station" and saw the guy as they were both entering the same jeepney. They sat opposite each other, and the guy smiled at her. She responded by raising both of her eyebrows (a common gesture in the Philippines when somebody recognizes another, just like what a wave means.)

Irene never thought that she would encounter the guy again.She found-out later that they had the same course in Psychology and he was in her every class. The guy's name was Melvin; his father was Austrian, and his mother was Filipina as he revealed in some of the classes, which required introducing themselves. They started talking every time they were in the hall, waiting for their next class that ignited their friendship. Irene often made Melvin repeat his words because she could not fully understand him due to his heavy accent. She and her best friend didn't see much of each other because they had different courses located in different buildings on the campus.

Her best friend suspected that something was more going on between her and Melvin other than friendship. She became so envious of her and accused her of taking advantage of the situation.

"Hey! Irene! What were you doing? You know that I am the one who is attracted to him. Trying to get the man of my dreams for yourself! You selfish bitch!" The friend said.

Irene was so surprised by the attitude by her best friend towards her. She never expected this kind of unacceptable demeanor from her best friend. She thought nobody could be trusted at that point in her life. Besides, she wasn't interested in Melvin as a lover. She was okay with her and Melvin being good friends. Her best friend also warned Melvin not to associate himself with Irene because they were a family of deranged creatures. Bart was her reference, but Melvin resented what the friend said.

Irene never talked to her best friend after the incident and for the rest of their lives. The so-called best friend crossed the line. Their friendship was never repaired, and they never reconnected with her again. She learned in the succeeding years that her best friend and her family migrated to Canada without completing college in the Philippines.

Irene knew how attractive Melvin was and that any woman would die to be in his arms. Their relationship was based on the "more than a friend but less on a lover" premise. They valued each other, they were intimate with each other, and they were brothers and sisters. This was a unique concept. The Santos even became Melvin's family in the Philippines, for he didn't have any relatives in the city. He had his own place, but he was always welcomed in the Santos residence. He also became close to Bart that chocolates were often given every time he was in the Santos' residence. Irene and Alvin were always mistaken as lovers everywhere they went, which they only shrugged off. Their kind of relationship went through their college years.

They were finally going to graduate and make their journey in real life. Martin could not be seen during their graduation rite. Irene went looking for him in the crowd, but he couldn't be found. She was expecting his name to be announced with his presence on stage, but it did not happen. After the graduation ceremony, she went to his apartment but it was empty. The landlord had informed her that he packed his things and left without ever giving him any advance notice. What the landlord cared about was his completion of his rental and utility payment. Santos was saddened about it, for they never had the chance to say their goodbyes. It was assumed that he went back to Austria but it was never proven.

Martin knew Melvin as a member of the Santoses and he was grateful for being extremely good with Bart. However, he was not too attached to him. He had his own life to enjoy, and one was having with friends having drinks at a karaoke bar. They were celebrating a friend's birthday. They enjoyed it so much that most of them were as drunk as a wheelbarrow except for Martin and a friend from the group. Martin pretended to be drinking at the same pace as the others, but he was controlling his alcohol intake. Maybe the other friend who was not also wasted also did the same thing. They didn't have any idea what was going to happen. The group seated at the opposite table was staring in Martin and his friend's direction.

"Hey! The family of crazies! The family of dumb stupid people!"Were the words heard from the opposite table?

"Shit! Your dad was the reason why my grandfather died!" One of them said.

"Who does he think he is? Shouting and making noise!" One of Martin's friends said.

"Yeah! Hell yeah! Should we give them a piece of our fist? He wants to challenge you in a fight Martin!" The other friend said.

"No, let him be. For as long as he doesn't physically attack us. We don't retaliate," Martin said.

"But we must be careful at all times. Maybe he and his buddies will be physical with us when we turn our backs on them," Martin added.

Martin entered the CR, and after doing his business, fists were swinging and bottles were thrown all over while everybody was kicking each other's asses. Martin grabbed some of his friends and dragged them out of the bar. The other friend, who was also in control, did the same. They ran as far as they could from the violence. Some of them insisted on continuing with the night out but could barely stand it. Martin and the other sober friend hailed a taxi, stuffed their wasted friends and paid some amount to the driver. They didn't give a damn if the driver drove them in the right direction or the cash they paid was enough to cover the fare.

"Let's go for the last bottles of beer. Let us catch up, for we haven't seen each other for a long time and we never know when we will see each other again," the friend said.

Martin agreed, and they went to a cleaner and more decent bar in the city.

"What's been going on with you, my friend?" Martin asked.

"Well, after high school, I went back to my hometown and worked on our vegetable farm," the friend said.

"That's good for you and I am not against education, but I think nowadays, it is not necessary to have a degree to survive. I think being wise and resourceful in life is important," Martin said.

"I believe so! But if given a chance, it would be nice to have a college degree," the friend said.

"Anyway, what was that all about? The bar brawl a while ago?" He asked.

"Honestly, I have no idea, but I suspected that it had to do with my dad's job of being a cop," Martin said.

"My friend, please don't be offended but the guy was shouting about your family being a family of crazy. Do you have family members with mental disorders?" The friend asked.

"Nope, but we have a special child, my younger brother," Martin said.

Their conversation went with the friend revealing that he also had an older brother who had seizures. His brother's logical thinking declined every time he was attacked by seizures. Martin also described his brother's condition. They felt each other's sympathy and love for their brothers. Each one had one more beer before they left the bar.

Martin was surprised to wake up early in the morning. He was expecting to have a hangover and tired body. He took a warm shower to get rid of any unwanted effects of alcohol and the dirty body discomfort. He didn't think of anything at first but the warm relaxing effect of the water cleared his mind. He was reminded of the night before. His father was going to the kitchen to have his breakfast Bart followed and was joined by the rest of the family.

"Dad, may I ask you something?" Martin asked.

"Sure, what is it my boy?" Mr. Santos responded.

"Do you remember the recent arrest of an old man, who eventually died?" Martin asked.

"Let me think, Yah, a seventy-seven years old man had a heart attack while in detention. I can't remember his exact name but let me see the records. Why do you ask?" Mr. Santos said.

"Dad, actually, the birthday I attended last night was drinking with my bodies in a bar. I thought it was at my friend's house at first but anyway somebody recognized me and shouted at my family for being crazy and…and he blamed you for the death of his grandfather. I don't know?" Martin said.

"If I am correct, his grandfather was a rapist! He sexually assaulted his nine-year-old grandniece! The sad part was their relatives didn't want to press charges against him because they said that it would bring shame to their clan if it was brought up! The judge convicted him anyway for the child's sake," Mr. Santos said.

"The judge even told the relatives present in the courtroom that they were worthless and pretentious creatures, for they prioritized their reputation in the society rather than the safety and welfare of the child. The judge also added that there's no way that the child consented and enjoyed being sexually assaulted. It was sad for the child to be taken by the City Social Welfare and live like an orphan but the judge wanted her to get away from her heartless family. I also expressed my sentiment for the victim and supported her. I was one of the instrumental components for the old man's conviction," Mr. Santos added.

"Really. How sad, and maybe his death was God's punishment but I would like for him to suffer in prison," Martin said.

"If it was up to me, the old man should have suffered in prison, including the relatives who were on his side!" Mr. Santos said.

The rest of the family did not say a word and just listened to the father-son conversation. They finished their breakfast and prepared for their normal day.

Chapter XLVI

Martin had nothing to do for the day. He had neither class nor anywhere to go. He bathed Martin while Elizabeth did the laundry and cooked for lunch. He also cleaned both the ground floor and the second floor CR. He was still surprised at why he had so much energy and did not suffer from a hangover. He also conducted writing and puzzle arrangements with Bart like a proper lesson.

"What's with me? I am not usually like this. All of a sudden, I have the urge to do some activities with Bart?" Martin was thinking.

Bart took a nap late that afternoon as it was his routine. Martin almost forgot the speech assignment they had to deliver in English class. The topic of the speech must be based on the question of "What is/are your aspiration/s in life?" He was thinking hard as he was trying to construct his speech. The paper was blank as he did his best to think. It went on for almost an hour and still nothing.

This sucks! I must complete my speech to be delivered tomorrow! He kept telling himself.

The heavy-footed Bart was coming downstairs with a tissue in his hand signifying that he needed his bottom wiping. Martin did the cleaning of his brother's bottom, and washed his hands and face then it was there that his mind formed ideas for the speech. It was because of Bart and the smell of the CR for some odd reason. The speech was made around the idea of Bart.

It was Martin's turn to deliver his speech in class. He was in front of the class without any external signs of nervousness, but his heart was pounding like a drum. His mind was confused. He was unaware of his environment. With his amazement, the first word of the speech went well, which gave him confidence to continue. His world with his Brother Bart was opened. His speech revealed about his brother's condition and his perspective on it as the brother. He stated that his desires in life were more focused on his brother. He hoped that he would be strong enough emotionally and physically to step-up when their parents became old or leave this physical world for his brother. He also included in the speech how the profound the "Hope that your future wife will understand your brother's situation" that his parents kept on telling him. He never thought much about those words when he was younger, but he knew better as he got older. Many of Martin's classmates were shocked. Some tears were dripping especially with the ladies. Most of them were emotional hearing Martin. They said some comforting and encouraging words as Martin was going to his place. The teacher appeared unaffected by the speech but during Martin's in-between breaks, she revealed that she was touched by the message of the speech. She also revealed about her cousin with down syndrome. She was sympathetic with him even though she could not fully understand how it felt to be in his shoes.

"Come to the canteen. Tell me what you want and I'll take care of it. "The teacher said.

"Lechon mami (lechon noodle soup) please, "Martin ordered.

"Thank you, madam," he added.

"You are very welcome," the teacher said.

He was not joined by the teacher of the worries of others misinterpreting the scene they would witness. He became shy of that moment that prompted him to excel in her class.

The medicine and Psychology department hosted a free lecture on childhood disorders, genetic abnormalities, and mental health, anything that involved the human brain, and the factors that altered its normal functions. It was posted for several months on campus. Martin was thinking back and forth about attending the lecture or not. He wanted to know more about Autism, but he thought he could research more about it on the internet. He attended anyway besides, it was a coincidence that he had some time to spare. He was only interested in the Autism topic of the entire lecture. The lecturer sounded like talking in an alien language at the beginning of the lecture. Martin's attention span drifted away. He felt like he was in some science fiction movies that were not necessarily his favorite because of the medical terms used. He only came back to the realm of reality when Autism became the subject. He was so attentive that he had written some terms he did not understand to search for their meaning later. After the autism part, he made an excuse to do his business to the C.R. but it was actually his way to escape.

He went home to find his cousin Kate. She is Mrs. Lady's first child from her first boyfriend. He talked to her and did not think much about her presence. He only assumed that it was just a casual visit. She was fresh from the province and will be staying with the Santos family. She was a shy, cute girl at the beginning of her stay. She was obedient and very studious. She never had a problem taking care of Bart if needed. The problem arose when she learned about city life. She began hanging with the wrong crowd and became a bit of a teenage rebel. She would cut classes and go drinking. She had a relationship with an out-of-school guy who smoked and drank a lot. Mr. and Mrs. Santos learned that she was not attending school and not qualified for the next school year. She had to repeat the same year level.

"We don't need another problem. We already have Bart. If only she did well at school," Mr. Santos said.

Mrs. Santos agreed and sent her back to the province.

Eddie was employed in the police department as an all-around civilian employee. He got employed because of Mr. Santos' recommendation. He was a relative of Mr. Santos from Kabayan. He was responsible for the cleanliness of the police station and functioned as a typist if needed. Mr. Santos would also ask him to drive Bart around sometimes. Just like the habit of most of the guys in Mr. Santos' hometown, alcoholism set in. He reports mostly with hangovers. The office would smell like it was disinfected with alcohol. His alcoholism almost put Bart in danger every time he drove him around. Mr. Santos had to recommend his termination of employment because of those reasons.

I am done. I will never recommend anybody for employment anymore. My good name will suffer. Mr. Santos told himself.

There was a moment in Bart's life when he often cried the night away, disturbing everybody around him. It went on for several nights already. Everybody became sleepy whenever they were at work or at school. They wondered what could be the reason for his behavior.

They wanted to keep Bart quiet for their much needed, but they were forced to put up with his noise.

Elizabeth prepared boiled black beans with "kinuday" dish for lunch. The Santoses enjoyed their meal and even claimed to be "the best black beans and kinuday dish" they ever had. The following day, Mr. Martin and Bart could not leave their respective beds due to their swollen feet. Gout had again attacked the joints of their feet. Mr. Santos called the police station, informing them that he would not be able to go to work due to his swollen foot. He requested one of the police officers to purchase medications and he will reimburse him or her once it was delivered.

"Hey look, Bart is behaving. He! He! He!" Irene said.

"Yeah, I thought he would cry more because of the pain," Martin said.

"Leave your brother alone! Let him rest!" Mrs. Santos said.

Elizabeth became busier with Mr. Santos and Bart's conditions. She gave Bart a sponge bath, and she had to deliver their meals in their rooms on the second floor. She was always alert incase Mr. Santos called for her or if Bart needed something.

Everybody was home from their day. It was bed-time already, and Bart was quiet unlike the previous nights. Mrs. Santos had to say something to her husband just before bed time.

"Dad! Please! Be disciplined with food the next time! Look, instead of giving attention to Bart, then you are added to be taken care of!" Mrs. Santos said.

"You are right, mama, but I find it difficult to make myself as disciplined as possible in terms of food. The food served before me is tempting," Mr. Santos said.

"Dad! This is no more a joke please! Do your best to avoid food that is bad for you!" Mrs. Santos said.

"We already have Bart to think about! Please don't wait for your health to worsen! Please don't wait for the day that you will need some assistance or caregiver for the rest of your life before living a healthy lifestyle!" Mrs. Santos added.

Mr. Santos just stared at Mrs. Santos and they both went to bed.

Chapter XLVII

he Santoses considered Bart as considered as the Angel that bonded the family. They were very positive that he was with God all the time. They only wanted to make it official through baptism. Most of the relatives and friends were present. Mrs. Lady and her family were present, Johnny and the boys were present, and many others were in attendance.

Mrs. Lady's children were well behaved and sat throughout the baptism rites, but James could not conduct himself well and kept asking questions.

"What are they doing, dad?" James asked.

"They are baptizing your uncle, Bart," Johnny said.

"What is baptizing? And why are they getting his head wet?" James asked.

"Just because, you are asking so many questions. Here are some candies, and you can go outside to play!" Johnny said.

James went outside and played in the parking lot while sucking on the candy.

Bart was cooperative during the baptism. The water poured in his head did not bother him a bit. In fact, he smiled and clapped his hands and the attendees smiled in awe. Elizabeth and Johnny went to the reception ahead to check if the hall was ready. There were 50 seats with 20 on standby. Guests who did not attend the baptism were pilling. Elizabeth and Johnny became so worried that the seats and food would be enough. The guests from the church came not long after. All the guests present were accommodated. The food was more than enough extra that everybody was welcomed to go for a second round. The usage of the hall was only limited to four hours. Others who tried to attend the reception in later hours went home after realizing that they were late.

There were still some extra foods left. The Santoses gave a few to the staff and brought some home. Johnny was about to hail a taxi and go home with the kids when Mrs. Santos invited them to their residence for more desserts and snacks. Both the Santoses and Mrs. Lady wanted to take the opportunity to bond with Johnny more. They imagined when would be the next chance for them to bond given their busy schedules. James sat at the front with Johnny while the rest were at the back of the van with Mr. Santos driving. James smiled and kept on staring at the Jollibee mascot dancing in front of the fast-food station while moving forward. Bart sat at the back most part of the van, which became his permanent sit. Many were anticipating his negative reaction to the jam-packed van, but they were surprised that he behaved all throughout the trip. Everybody went straight to the Santos residence once they arrived. James entered the Santoses' with the rest but immediately went to Mrs. Fecora and her family's residence. He discovered that the Santoses' house was full of people and he had to be in close proximity to Bart. He played and enjoyed his time next door at Fecoras for a few minutes.

"James! James! Where are you?" Johnny said.

"James is here playing!'' Mrs. Fecora said.

"Let him be! It's okay! He is enjoying himself!" She added.

"Tell him to come here! His grandpa will give him something!" Johnny said.

"Okay, then!" Mrs. Fecora said.

Mr. Santos gave the brothers five hundred pesos each which excites the brothers except James who was staring blankly at the paper money. Mrs. Lady's children were not the exception and also given five hundred pesos each.

"So, this is what? What will I do with this?" James asked.

"That is money. 500 pesos. You can buy anything you want," Johnny said.

"I can buy paint and cartons?" James asked.

"Yes, not only cartons. Even proper painting materials for what you love to do," Johnny said.

"Keep it, so that it won't be lost," Johnny added.

"Hey boys, what will you say to your grandpa?" Johnny asked.

"Thank you, Lolo," (grandpa, granduncle in Filipino) the boys said in chorus.

They all said their goodbyes to the Santoses and waved goodbye at Mr. Fecora as they were passing by.

"Hey, come here for a while and wait for Knoll! He will be going in the same direction as you are all heading. He will use the car and he's just by himself. All of you can ride with him," Mrs. Fecora said.

Knoll glanced at them every now and then but his main concentration was on the road while driving.

"Can I ask something?" Knoll asked.

"No problem, shoot. Give me your question," Johnny said.

"Can you tell me something about yourselves? It is because I don't know you that well and yet we see each other sometimes," Knoll said.

"Ah! Is that it? My mother and Auntie Trisha are first cousins," Johnny said.

"What are the names of your boys?" Knoll asked.

"I am Sam, this is Steve, and this is James."

"Oh, I see! And James?" Knoll asked.

"He is like your cousin, Bart. The only difference is he can communicate," Johnny said.

"This is your uncle Knoll, and if you see him, say hi to him or you can even ask for jeepney fare if you have no money. Hehehe!" Johnny jokingly said.

"Hahaha!" Knoll burst out laughing.

Johnny and his sons got off the car at the city mall area. Knoll went on to where he was supposed to be.

The Banged family lived just a few blocks from the Santos. They were good to Bart. The brothers Russell and Bryan were High school and elementary classmates of Irene and Martin. They were not so close, but when it came to whoever needed help, they were willing to render some.

Russell was still a friendly lad that tended to have conversations with any of the Santos about anything under the weather. He would go to the Santos on numerous occasions, unlike his younger brother Bryan whose routine was home and work most of his time. Family tragedy of losing their father coupled with him being victimized by illegal recruiters for his application to work abroad triggered his mind to lose its sanity. He began speaking in nonsense manners by himself or when talking to others.

He went to stores grabbing anything he wanted without any payment. Some neighbors saw him in surprising places and often wondered how on earth he entered establishments and offices such as the mall, the police station where Mr. Santos worked, the hospital, some restaurants and others. The police knew him and gave him some food to eat every time he visited and so with the other places he went to.

"I wish we could do more to help Russell but he has his family to help and love him. Maybe they accuse us of meddling with their business when we attempt to help," Mrs. Santos said.

"He must have missed his father because he lost his sanity the moment they buried him," she added.

"He goes to the station sometimes just to sit, and we let him be! We also give him food whenever we can," Mr. Santos said.

"I hope nobody in the outside world will harm him. Besides we never saw him being violent," Mrs. Santos said.

"I totally agree. Hope his family and the government will help them," Martin said.

They gave Russell some food or change every time they encountered him. The important thing for them was his safety. They also had the hopes of abled people understanding and caring more for the less fortunate and disabled ones.

Chapter XLVIII

Irene was job hunting. She had her resume and requirements ready at all times. Every job opening she tried was filled, or she was "overqualified" in accordance with the recruiter or employer. The major reason being was her lack of experience in the workforce.

Oh, My God! If all categories and disqualifications can be implemented, then what will happen to fresh graduates like us? Damn! Irene told herself with anger in her heart.

After being unemployed for a significant amount of time, she planned to apply in the capital city of Manila. She gave it another go for the last time. It was statistically difficult for her being a Psychology major in college, for there were few non-existing industries involving her field of education. Even when she was willing to take any job she could, that too was not easy to accomplish. A newly established German company that dealt with forensics considered hiring her since there were few applicants whose backgrounds fitted the field of industry. The company sponsored trainings for her and other qualified applicants to enhance their skills in the budding field. The company relied on the contract with the Philippine National Police crime lab division for the business to keep running. The industry was sadly short-lived due to the high expenses that the Philippines government could not afford. Irene was forced to return to Baguio City and stay unemployed with her parents.

"Got some bad news everybody," Irene said.

"What bad news?" Mrs. Santos asked.

"Let me tell you," Irene said.

"The company that I have been working for almost three years closed. The industry was very expensive, and their services were seldom needed. A single chemical reagent for single usage only costs for about one thousand five hundred pesos, even up to ten thousand pesos. The government contract can't keep up with the payments, so they had to cut ties and cancel the existing agreement," Irene added

"That is very sad! I am even very excited about the usage of new technology for crime investigation but it is what it is,"Mr. Santos said.

"It's okay, don't give-up you will eventually find another job that suits you," Mrs. Santos added

It was like everything happened with a purpose. Elizabeth went about her normal day-off on Sundays but never returned. Irene took over the responsibility until they found a new all-around help.

Foreigners in the Philippines from both English and non-English speaking countries were at their height. Baguio, City is considered the "Summer Capital of the Philippines" and "The Educational Center of the North." It became one of the main choices for tourists, both local and foreign, to have their holidays, at or for the non-English speaking foreigners to study at. Schools offering English as a second language course, became wide-spread. The Santos needed a new all-around help the moment Irene expressed her attempt to apply for an English teacher job.

Carla, the relative of Mrs. Santos and the Santoses' neighbor, was always a reliable help .She took care of Bart whenever a babysitter was not available on a temporary basis. It took two weeks before hiring a more permanent help. Rachael was from the wonderful place of "Bagao, Cagayan Valley. Many workers such as maids, babysitters, helpers, plumbers and others seem to come from the same place.

Being an English teacher to foreigners was not a high-paying job. Irene went on being one because she had no other choice of employment. Her students were mostly Koreans, Japanese, Chinese, Thai, and a few Vietnamese and Taiwanese. The only positive she got from teaching foreigners was she was able to learn more about their cultures and had friendships with them. It was okay for her to be so friendly with her students, but she maintained their teacher-student gap when they were at school. A Korean student was eyeing her. Irene noticed that there was something about the guy every time they interacted. She believed the Korean guy was attracted to her, and she was right all along. The Korean guy even attempted to invite Irene for a date, but just like the other students, she maintained the teacher-student and friendship relationship only.

Rachael was so kind to Bart. She loved the coke brand soft drink. There were no chocolates in the Santos household during her time. The only sweet substance in abundance was the 1.5 coke variety. Bart did not hate coke. He only preferred chocolate. With only coke available to satisfy his sweet tooth, he came to love the drink.

"Coke? Why?" Mrs. Santos asked.

"Auntie, it might be me because he drinks my coke little by little until he likes it so much. Sorry," Rachael said.

"No problem, I am just curious," Mrs. Santos said.

Bart escaped when coke was absent. It was great timing when he entered the store whose owner understood his condition. Again with the timing, the store owner just purchased the items for sale and did not arrange them yet for display. Bart stayed for a while and arranged the items for sale. The store owner was just watching him with a smile on her face.

"Bart just get what you want, and let's go!" Rachael said.

Rachael tried to convince Bart, by giving him the chocolates and coke available at the store.

"Let him be. He is a good helper of the store, he he he!" The store owner said.

Mrs. Santos was worried about why Elizabeth took so long to get Bart. She followed them to wherever they were.

"Where is Bart?" She asked.

"Auntie, he is inside arranging some items for sale," Rachael said.

"Did he take anything?" Mrs. Santos asked.

"Surprisingly, nothing at all. He is just busy with arranging," Rachael said.

They just let Bart continue what he was doing when the store owner was okay with it. He got a bottle of 1.5 coke when he was done with the arranging and went with Mrs. Santos and Elizabeth home.

Mr. Santos went to the National Police Headquarters in the capital city of Manila. Mrs. Santos was alone in the master bedroom that night. The locked windows just above the headboard were slowly opened. Some guy applied ninja-like movements to avoid any detection. Mrs. Santos smelled something funky that woke her up, and she was about to sneeze when she was face to face with a guy trying to grab her purse beside her.

"Who the hell are you?" Mrs. Santos said.

The guy was not intimidated by Mrs. Santos' shouting, but he immediately jumped out the window when he heard heavy steps and giggles coming towards them. Martin and Irene went into the room without any movements from Elizabeth's room.

"Thank God nothing happened! I was so worried that the thief might have a weapon of some sort and hurt Bart!" Mrs. Santos said.

"What happened?" Irene asked.

"He was attempting to grab my purse, but he failed. I am wondering how he was able to open the locked windows. Maybe he is a professional thief. He must have done this before," Mrs. Santos said.

"I am glad that nothing bad happened to all of you and especially Bart who entered the room first," Martin said.

The Santoses were too anxious to sleep through the night. They went into conversations and had some snacks till dawn instead. After a day, Mrs. Santos recognized the thief among the guys playing billiards. It was near the "jeepney" station just meters above the Santos residence. Another resident from the same barangay was certain that some other guy from the same billiards hall was a thief also. One of the guys playing overheard what Mrs. Santos and the lady said.

"Are the two of you positive that the guys you are referring to are really the thieves that have been stealing from our community? Some of my personal possessions were stolen too and they might have been responsible for it," the guy said.

"Yes, I can't forget a face," the other lady said.

"Me too!" Mrs. Santos added.

The guy Mrs. Santos and a lady talked to approach the other guys at the billiards hall in secret. The next thing that Mrs. Santos and the lady saw was the suspected thieves were on the floor while the rest of the guys were stepping on them.

"God damn! You almost fooled us ! You are the ones who have been stealing from us!" One guy said.

"Be honest! Admit it! Both of you are thieves!" The other guy said.

"Get away from our sight! Don't ever show yourselves here or worse will happen to you!" Another one said.

The two fled and were never seen again within the "barangay". Subsequently, the incidence of stealing was also reduced.

A commotion was present in a "jeepney" on the busy street of the National Highway. A guy snatched a lady passenger's purse and tried to run away. The driver kept on driving until they reached a nearby police station. The victim was a fast derby runner that caught up with the snatcher. The other passengers called the attention of law enforcers on the side-walk. The snatcher was successfully apprehended. He was processed to be found out later that he was one of the burglars lurking in Mr. Santos' barangay community.

Chapter XLIX

A noise resonated from upstairs. I sound like Bart with high pitched scream that could shatter glass.

"What the hell is happening? What's wrong with your pee?" Martin asked.

"Why is Bart screaming? What is wrong with him?" Elizabeth asked.

"Bart had difficulty peeing, and his pee is dark and smelly," Martin said.

Mrs. Santos went to check what was going on. They were all worried about Bart's condition. They reduced his sweet intake, especially soft drinks, Milo, and chocolates, and increased his water intake. The problem was Mr. Santos. Every time Bart got his way with his father, whatever he desired was always granted.

"What the hell is this coke again?" Mrs. Santos asked.

"Uncle let Bart out and get some from the store when he had his tantrum," Elizabeth said.

"Dad! Why? Can't you see he has difficulty peeing and we are reducing his sweets intake and here you are ruining our efforts!" Mrs. Santos said.

"Mommy, for this once only," Mr. Santos said.

"Once only? Once only! It is not once! He always manipulates you. He always throws a tantrum every time you are home. We are reducing his sweets intake not just because we just thought about it but for his own good! Look! He has difficulty peeing! Please, help us also! Please, dad! Don't wait for the worst thing to happen to him! Please!" Mrs. Santos Said.

"No, this once only. I am not always providing him with sweets always," Mr. Santos Said.

"Oh my God! If that is the case! Then kill your son! To get over it!" Mrs. Santos said.

The argument went on with Mrs. Santos exaggerating things with the intention of making a point. Mr. Santos lost the discussion, with him, keeping quiet at the end. Everybody was aware of what Bart was doing whenever his father was present. They argued with Mr. Santos and continued to reduce Bart's sugar intake.

It was not the first time they had argued. Mr. Santos tended to have the attitude of "bahala na" (come what may). He always argued that he only got to taste a better lifestyle as opposed to his childhood. He claimed that he and his family could hardly afford food. Just like Bart, he stuffed himself with the delicious food he could afford.

Mrs. Santos, on the other hand, came from a higher middle-class family. Her father had a high position in an American-owned construction company in Baguio City and her mother was a school teacher, which was rare during the 50's - 70's. Most "Igorot" during those times were uneducated and mostly involved in agriculture. But it was not her intention to control food. It was for health reasons. She would always utter these words to Mr. Santos, "Please look out for your health. We don't want any of us to go first before Bart, don't we?" That Mr. Santos always agreed with, but his lifestyle said otherwise.

Mrs. Santos was alarmed because Bart's condition had been persistent for more than a week. She consulted a doctor and explained Bart's circumstance and his underlying condition. The doctor requested a urine test and instructed Mrs. Santos on what to do at home and must bring the specimen herself to the hospital. He also loaned a glucometer to measure blood sugar that can be used at home and explained the proper procedure on how to use it. His suspicion was right; Bart had high blood sugar content.

Mr. Santos' phone rang in the middle of Mrs. Santos' speech about an arrest order brought to his jurisdiction about an alleged rape of a psychologically disturbed young lady. It was revealed that the suspect was his second cousin from Kabayan.

The suspect's father and uncle wanted to talk to him to ask a favor for his cousin. Mr. Santos ordered the police to offer not to give the suspect and his loved ones any favoritism and to apply the process that must be done to the suspect, and his loved ones must adhere to it.

"Who was calling you late at night?" Mrs. Santos asked.

"Nobody, just my police officers asking for some advice about the station. Let's just go to sleep," Mr. Santos said.

The suspect's father and uncle were very persistent in asking a favor from Mr. Santos. They wanted him to mediate for the victim's family and not to continue their charges. They even wanted him to talk to the judge when they learned that the two of them were good friends.

"What the God damn do you think I am? A fool that you can just boss around!" Mr. Santos said.

"Why aren't you willing to help a relative? We are practically family," the father said.

"The nerve! The nerve! Family? Family? Really? You want me to risk my job! To risk my position! To destroy my good reputation to just bend the law for your rapist son and nephew!" Mr. Santos said.

"Get the hell out of my office and let the law take its course!" He added.

The father, and uncle stayed without any plans of going out. Mrs. Santos had to order his men to escort the two in order for them to leave.

Mr. Santos was invited for a relative's house blessing the week after. He was welcomed by the home owners and many other relatives. An old man with signs of intoxication stood in front of him.

"Hey, Santos! What did you do with my grandson! You stole his freedom! He had a lot ahead of him! His future!" The grandfather said.

"Shut up! Please! Shut up!We are here to celebrate with our relatives! Don't you dare ruin the moment!" A relative said.

"So, cousin! We are not particularly fans of those two but since they are relatives, we let them, since they are already here. In fact, nobody invited them," the relative told Mr. Santos.

The grandfather was at it again. The other relatives were holding him back, restraining him from the possibility of hurting Mr. Santos or being hurt himself. Mr. Santos was quiet and waited for the old man to calm down. When the old man could not be contained and was about to shout at him again, then he broke his silence.

"Who do you think you are telling me those things! Your grandson is a rapist! It was proven with strong evidence at the court of law! I just did my job! How about the young girl he raped!

"Instead of being sympathetic towards her! You strongly defend your horny grandson with your life! Did you ever think of that! Or you are so dumb that you don't distinguish between what is real and what is fantasy! I will never compromise my job for anybody! The law must be implemented! Do you even have a conscience! Are you that evil? "Mr. Santos said.

The entire crowd was stunned and listened to every world Mr. Santos said. The father was so drunk he didn't know what was going on. The grandfather didn't say another word, pulled his son into their vehicle, and drove-off. Maybe he realized that he was wrong? It was the hope of everybody who listened to what was going on. Mr. Santos apologized to the hosts and many other relatives who were present. The majority hated the father and son and their family, for they were full of controversy that caused troubles within the clan. The celebration continued without any major troubles except for a few drunken men.

Mr. Santos was on his way home from the family occasion when he received a text message from Ms. Dulnuan Bart's godmother requesting him to pick some goodies for Bart from her place of business at the La Trinidad, Strawberry fields area.

She had a grandson who lived with her who had down syndrome. She handed snacks of treats such as toasted "mamon" (Filipino cupcake-like pastry) "pilipit" (Crunchy Filipino churroslike fried treats), local chocolate treats, and Ube candy (purple yam) and many others. It was not her first time to adorn Bart with gifts and not just some simple gifts but large numbers of goodies, fruits, and vegetables.

The Santos had constant communication with her over the years. With everybody being busy, the communication shriveled until there was none. They tried to reconnect with her, but in a sad event she died for more than a year without the Santoses ever knowing it.

"It is sad that Ms. Dulaman passed away without informing us. I am sure she is in a good place with God. She was such a sweet lady," Mr. Santos said.

The family visited her grave and offered a prayer.

Mrs. Santos was reminded of how short life was. She did her best to let her husband eat healthy at home or whenever she was present, but doubtful if it was being implemented whenever they were apart.

"I kept telling you! Please be mindful of your health!" Mrs. Santos said.

"It seems that if I follow the diet, I don't have enough energy for the day!" Mr. Santos said.

"You again with your reasoning! Do you want to go ahead of Bart! Please, for Bart's sake!'' Mrs. Santos said.

Mr. Santos never responded and went to sleep.

"You should listen to me because it is not only you that suffers! The whole family suffers! Instead of focusing on Bart, you do this!"

Chapter L

Mr. Santos bought a new lamp for their room. The very important factor to consider is the term the Santoses coined "Bart Proof" meaning items in the house must be durable enough to withstand Bart. To withstand Bart's destructive behaviors such as jumping, running, and moving around. One day, they all noticed that the glass lampshade was broken.

"What the hell did you do with the lamp? You broke it! Nothing is ever safe in the house! Even when we did our best to things from you!" Mrs. Santos said.

Irene and Martin were listening intently trying to find out why their mom was so angry at Bart. They saw pieces of glass on the floor and a broken lamp shade. Mrs. Santos was about to sweep the pieces of glass when Irene got the broom and dustpan and went on with the sweeping.

"This is the third time your brother broke the glass lamp shade. Remember?" Mrs. Santos said.

"Yes, those two, and it is exactly the same," Irene said.

That's the reason why I am so mad," Mrs. Santos said.

Bart snuck in that very same night without the knowledge of the Santoses. The next morning, Elizabeth went out to throw the trash. She noticed shredded pieces of tissue papers scattered all over the front yard. She wondered about how the tissue paper got there. She checked the back door, and it was locked. She even checked for Bart if he was in his room, and there he was. She just shrugged and cleaned the mess.

She heard a knock just after she was done with her cleaning and entering the house. She peeked at the window to see who it was or what was going on. The timing couldn't be right for the Santoses were descending the stairs. Elizabeth asked the Santoses if they knew the couple but nobody recognized them.

The couple asked to talk to them and was given the assurance that they had no bad intentions.

"What can we do for you?" Mr. Santos asked.

"Do you have a large son? I assume you are the father. Who has a condition or is mentally retarded?" The lady asked.

"Yes, maybe its Bart you are referring to," Mr. Santos said.

"There he is in the kitchen. That's him, right?" Mr. Santos added.

"Yes, let me tell you. We are in one of the residences a few meters down there. Last night we saw a large man mumbling and stomping his feet in front of our house. Our daughter was so afraid that bad things might happen. We turned on the light because there was an unexplainable feeling that he, your son might have mental retardation because I also have a brother with such condition. My husband accompanied him somewhere here. He is not sure because your son just ran towards here in this direction then my husband returned home after. My daughter is traumatized. She won't leave her room in the dark. She became afraid of the dark in general. We just want to see your son and assure our daughter that it is okay. That's it, nothing else," the lady said.

"I am very sorry for what happened .It is very shameful that none of us knew about this. How can we help?" Mr. Santos asked.

"Don't worry; we just want to see your son. We understand and we just want to let all of you know all of these things," the guy said.

"We are deeply sorry .If you need anything at all, here is my contact number," Mr. Santos said.

"By the way, can we offer you coffee or bread?" Mr. Santos asked.

"No thanks. We will go now," the lady said.

Bart looked at everybody and they smiled at him.

"Hey! What did you do last night? You scared a little girl. Don't ever do that again. Be a good boy please," Mrs. Santos said.

"Yeeeh! Bad! Bad!" Martin said.

Bart glared at them without any expression. He went on to eat alone and didn't mind his surroundings. He was assisted by Rachael in taking a bath then nothing extraordinary and went back to bed. He did not fall asleep nor took a nap again; he was just conscious blubbering in his own words that nobody understood.

The door was forgotten to be locked again when someone went out for just a few seconds. Bart was storming from the second floor towards the store with a freshly delivered coke which he detected from a few blocks away. He was like a hound sniffing his target. Elizabeth went after him and met him on his return with two bottles of 1.5 liters of coke. He became more accustomed to coke as his primary love over chocolates.

Mr. Santos learned about the internet and social media. In fact, he bought his own personal laptop with the recommendation of some of the police officers. Elizabeth and Bart arrive at Mr. Santos seated on the sofa browsing his social media account and watching some videos on his laptop in the living room. He came across the post of the clan reunion. It was indicated to be located at the Santos resort in "Kalinga" province, which was a twelve-hour trip from Baguio City. It was the resort owned by Mr. Santos' first cousin, who got married in the area. The Santoses and Mrs. Fecora's family decided on a joint rental of the largest van they could find with a driver included for the trip. The Santoses left Elizabeth and allowed her to have her vacation for as long as she made certain the house was secured, and she was present the moment they arrived back.

The van had enough space for all who would attend. Bart owned the entire last row of the back, complete with blanket and pillow. Mrs. Santos led a prayer for their safe trip before starting their journey, and yes, it was a journey indeed. They never expected what they encountered along the way. Most of the route they went through hard road repairs and constructions that delayed their movement. Lighting struck a tree that almost fell on the van but they were able to avoid it thanks to the diver's vigilance. It was almost dark, and they thought nothing could go wrong for they were almost at their destination when they heard a burst. The driver went to check it out, and it turned out to be a flat tire on the left rear of the van. They were in the middle of the highway without any houses, and very few vehicles passing. The skies turned into darkness and made their situation even more difficult. The driver changed the tire with Martin holding a small flashlight that barely lighted what the driver was doing. They continued with their trip only to find out that there were no streetlights present and if there were it was not functioning.

There should be a sign "Kalinga Province this way" with an arrow pointing in the right direction when they reach a fork. The darkness of the night and the small writings on the sign made it difficult to follow the correct direction. They went straight to "Cagayan Valley," the neighboring region, instead. It was a long trip that added an hour more than the anticipated twelve-hour trip. Constant texting and calls were received by Mr. Santos and Mrs. Fecora asking how they were and why they didn't arrive yet. The relative's worries, especially the host, can be noticed with their constant communication through calls and texts on the situation that they were in. They finally arrived in everybody's relief, asking them what had taken them so long. They told the entire story, which they laughed over dinner.

There were relatives who attended the reunion for the first time or relatives that knew the Santoses but were not aware of Bart. He became the main topic of discussion. Everybody had theories on how he acquired the condition. There were theories that were out of this world, like evil spirits caused him to be who he was, or someone put a curse on Mrs. Santos during pregnancy, and others the possible theories like Mrs. Santos was sick during her pregnancy, or she might have taken some drug during her pregnancy and others. The reunion was a success with everybody's delight.

They all arrived home late in the evening. The Santoses were met with an empty, locked house that had no indication of human presence for a few days. Elizabeth had not returned from wherever she was. Mr. Santos called her and learned that she was on her way back from her hometown. After a few hours, she arrived with two men.

"Who are they?" Mrs. Santos asked.

"Auntie, these are my brother and my nephew. They will sleep here first before going to their jobs here in the city. I hope it is okay with you," Elizabeth said.

"Do we have a choice? Since they are already here, please show them the room where they can stay," Mr. Santos said.

"What's with the idea of Elizabeth bringing her brother and nephew without our permission first? Who does she think she is?" Mrs. Santos asked her husband when they were left in the living room.

"Let them be. We have no choice. They are our responsibility now. It will be if we kick them out at this late hour. They might be put in harm's way. They may get sick or injured. It will be our problem if that is the case," Mr. Santos said.

"Yeah, you have a point there, but still." Mrs. Santos said.

Chapter LI

The extra help in the Santos household was not necessary. Elizabeth's brother and nephew's stay was longer than expected. The Santoses assumed that they already had a place of employment according to Elizabeth's explanation. The neighbors were concerned about strangers going in and out of the Santos residence.

"You know, your house is full of strangers every time you leave them. My concerns are that strangers with unknown backgrounds could just enter your house. You never know what they will do," a neighbor told Mr. Santos

"The two guys in your house left Bart on the terrace of his room and locked the door. He tried to escape by climbing towards the next room's window which is very dangerous. I was so mad about it and screamed at them while watching their precious movie in the living room," another one said.

"Talk to them, or better yet, send them home," another said.

Many other observations were brought to the Santoses. Martin took the initiative to talk to the guys, which they did not take lightly. They packed their belongings and presented the Santoses as being heartless for forcing them out the neighborhood. Many of the neighbors did not believe their drama and just let them be. Mr. Santos expressed his anger towards Elizabeth and made her choose between leaving like his brother and nephew or remaining with them. She chose the latter. She was given another chance with the warning of termination once she made the same mistake.

Elizabeth only did her duties whenever the Santoses were around. The house was so dirty and the chores were not completed. Bart was also not taken care of. Bart did not take a bath and did not eat proper meals. She spent many of her hours at Mrs. Fecora's residence when they were away just to pass the time. She only completed her obligations whenever she realized that it was almost time for any of the Santoses to arrive home.

"I want Elizabeth to leave, but I don't want to offend her because she might spread negative rumors against us." Mrs. Santos told herself.

Bart managed to escape again when the opportunity presented itself. He ran so fast that too many street dogs were chasing him. He did not care about dog bites because he was running away from the person who was chasing him.

"Bart, don't ever run! The dogs are chasing you, and they might bite you! Walk!" Martin said.

Bart seemed worried by his facial expression about Martin preventing him from reaching the store than the dogs around them. Martin swung a twig around to scare away the dogs. The store owner helped him repel the dogs by shouting.

"Be very careful. Next time don't let your brother just run away like that. There were several times that your brother was almost bitten. As we all know, there are many dogs scattered everywhere in our neighborhood," the store owner told Bart.

Martin noticed Bart's natural body odor that indicated he did not take his bath yet. Elizabeth rushed to give Bart a bath as soon as they returned.

"Hey, I came home earlier than I was supposed to, and I observed twice that Bart did not take his bath. What's with that?" Martin asked.

Elizabeth did not answer and went on to cook dinner.

Martin was so pissed off, but he did not push the issue.

Mr. Santos was having his lunch at home with Martin and a police officer with Elizabeth giving Bart a bath when he received a call on his cellphone.

"Sir, there are two representatives from the national office and a representative from the justice department for a surprise inspection," the caller said.

"There is even a representative from an animal rights organization or something?" The caller added.

"What the hell are they doing in our station?" Mrs. Santos asked.

"Sir, they demand reports of the crimes and cases that our station has resolved," the caller said.

"Why? You know our performance! We are one of the best law enforcers in the country, and no doubt about it!" Mr. Santos said.

"Entertain them and give them what they are looking for to get over with. We will be over there," he added.

The second-ranking official gave the visitors what they were demanding, but the visitors insisted on talking to Mr. Santos. Other police officers offered them some coffee and lunch at the nearest restaurant, but they declined and waited for Mr. Santos in the station.

The investigative group threw the issue at the Baguio City Police regarding their refusal to raid businesses involved in the trading of dog meat. There was a law passed by the lawmakers against trading and eating dog meat. The Cordillera, the highest dog meat consumers in the Philippines, refused to implement such a law. Politicians, Judges, Government lawyers, and the local police did not participate in the raid and filing of charges against the restaurants serving dog dishes and dog meat market except for the minority who were allies of the seated administration. The national government investigative group made their intentions clear to Mr. Santos. They were not alone for they brought with them police officers from the national headquarters to raid several restaurants and meat shops that Mr. Santos had no intention to divulge their locations. Still they had their ways of finding the establishments.

"That anti-dog meat trade law is ridiculous to implement here in the Cordilleras! If the national government gives us an order, then we have to do what we should do! That is not to implement the order because if we did the scenario, the dog meat traders will be arrested by dog-eating policemen then will be investigated by dog-eating public investigators, and then persecuted by dog- eating judges," Mr. Santos said.

The government group despised him because he was a strong opponent to the law and its implementation compared to others that were subtler. They proceeded with the raids and successfully closed many restaurants specializing in dog meat dishes. Meat shops all over the city and its neighboring municipalities within the region were inspected, and dog meats were confiscated. The dog trade and consumption stopped for several months when the issue was still hot. The industry resurfaced within the Cordillera and Ilocandia region when the matter spiraled from being the flavor of the month issue. The difference from before was the method of ordering a dog meat dish. A dog-meat specialty restaurant served other dishes as a cover. Customers must ask the food server for the specific dog dish to be included in the order. Slaughtering the dog was also done in secrecy.

On the other hand, Mr. Santos was not afraid to be public for his love of dog meat. He ate at dog meat specialty restaurants and purchased take-outs for his family whenever he had the craving. All members of the Santoses also consumed dog meat. Mrs. Santos ate dog meat, Irene ate dog meat, Martin ate dog meat and also with Bart, no exception. It was ingrained in their culture and their way of life.

Irene's search for employment brought her to the province of "Pangasinan." She first informed Mr. Santos, who gave his seal of approval in spite of the controversy his police department was facing. The rest of her family was also fine with her decision provided she was safe in her new place. Her recent employment was near a beach, a different environment from the mountainous area of Cordillera. Her employment schedule and location gave her the opportunity to enroll in a master's class. She took the opportunity not only for employment but to experience a different environment from what she used to. She was residing in an apartment unit all by herself for more than a year but accepted a roommate later. Sally, as it was her name, was from "Pangasinan" in a more secluded area of the barrio. She opted to have her own place in the city center because of her work schedule and the expensive ride going to and from her hometown.

"Hey, we have been roommates for several months now, I still don't know a lot about you. And I believe you don't know a lot about me either," Irene said.

"Yes, we never talk that much. We are both busy. Okay, since we are here and we still have time, we can ask what we want to know from each other," Sally said.

Their conversation turned into question and answer dialog with the common topic of family background. Where they are from, how many siblings are in the family, parents' occupation and much more personal informations. They discovered commonalities between them. They both have sibling with special needs in their families. Irene has her brother Bart, and Sally has her brother Sam. The common denominator made their bond tighter like sisters. Sally was more adjusted to the area they were living in that moment because she grew in a similar setting of tropical hot weather, beach, seafood-based diet, and cheaper lifestyle versus the mountains and more expensive cost of living in the highlands.

Sally had to take part-time work aside from her main one just to make ends meet. Unlike Irene, her family sends her money whenever she made requests due to lack of finances. She also took care of Sally's part of the bill to be repaid later. A break from work and school was their opportunity to go home to their respective families. Irene's arrival was met with her dad in the hospital caused of his undisciplined eating habits. A heart problem was detected, coupled with gout and borderline high blood sugar. Her vacation was extended for a week due to her father's condition.

"Dad, you must watch your diet. Realize what is happening to you. You want to die or compete with Bart that our family needs to care for the rest of our lives because you are disabled," Irene said.

Mr. Santos was silent while looking at her face and hearing those words coming from her mouth on his hospital bed. His face said it all that he was the concern, and agreed with all Irene was telling him.

Chapter LII

Irene returned to "Pangasinan" to resume her job and life. She was late the next semester for her master's class. She had to wait for the semester to end before she was allowed to enroll in the next one. She had more time to spare which prompted her to find a part time-job. She observed that her roommate was not in the apartment.

What is happening to Sally? she asked herself.

She tried to look for Sally at the park, her workplace, and in the public areas around town but she was nowhere to be found. She asked for their neighbors within their apartment, but nobody had seen her lately. She remembered that Sally's room was locked all the time. It should have been the first place she searched. She knocked at the door, but nobody answered. She knocked the second time around but still nobody answered. She heard somebody moving from the room. She stood there for a few minutes calling for her name before she finally opened the door.

"What's happening to you? What's the problem?" Irene asked.

"Well.....Uhmmm....My brother died. The special in our family. I am so guilty for not doing more for him. I can't even imagine," Sally said.

"You have nothing to be guilty of. I am sure you did love him. All you should do now is to be strong for your family and for yourself," Irene said.

"Let me see if I can squeeze some free-time. Let's go to your place together. You are not alone with this," she added.

Irene understood their pain of Sally. She imagined her brother Bart with every drop of tears they shared. Both went to Sally's hometown. The only public transports available were buses going to the main town. There were no available rides going directly to Sally's community. The methods of travel were only either by foot, hitch hike if lucky, and hired public transport such as tricycle, "jeepney" or taxi. Irene tried to find a tricycle that was willing to escort them to Sally's with the regular fare rate, but nobody was accommodating. They must negotiate a price agreement with a driver in order to take a ride. They found a tricycle with the lowest price possible. A separate passageway from the main highway leading to Sally's was a long rocky dirt road which made Irene understands the tricycle drivers' sentiments. They arrived in the middle of a field just about a kilometer or so from the ocean with a small "nipa" hut made from bamboo walls and a hay roof with temporary shades around it. She tried to check her cell phone to see if she had received important messages or missed calls, but there was no signal. Irene stayed through the night and felt a weird feeling that words could not explain. The wake was nothing like what she used to experience in the highlands. It was a bit like the generic one. The casket was in front of the living room with the mourners or guests facing it, and that was about it. The Catholic Church led the holy prayers and singing while snacks of cheap cookies with diluted coffee were served. The meal was simple with only rice and viand of mostly fish or vegetables. She saw the simplicity of what was going on and the low economic status of the family. There was one major surprise that she never could imagine in someone's wake was the presence of a karaoke machine. Everybody was welcomed to sing anytime they wanted except during Christian services.

How weird it is that they have to hire a Karaoke machine that was out of place, but they could hardly afford the expenses and provide snacks or food for the people attending the wake. Irene told herself.

Irene's heart wanted to help Sally's family by giving a more significant amount of "abuloy" (cash donations that were dropped in a box), but she only had enough money for the ride back to the apartment. She could only stay for an extra few hours because she had to go back to work the next day. Her boss in the department store where she was working as an accounting clerk was kind enough to give her some leeway, but she didn't want to abuse the kindness shown to her. She was very thankful for the good treatment her boss was giving her without any expectations on her part. He was a faithful family man who understood her situation for he too had a member of the family with special needs. It was his niece with Down syndrome. What a crazy alignment of their universe that made the connection stronger through common situations in life.

Irene was able to enroll in the next master's class while working. Sally returned after a week of absence from her work as a food server in one of the eateries commonly seen on the side of the main highway. Unlike Irene's boss, hers was not a considerate one. Every absence she incurred was deducted from her salary. Every damage or lost utensils were also deducted from the employee's salary. Her performance at work showed that she was still in mourning for the loss of her brother. It did not sit well with her boss, and as impatient as he was, she was fired. Irene learned about it and was willing to take responsibility for the apartment while Sally was searching for another job.

"I can't anymore. I hardly have part-times. I am ashamed of you for taking care of the bills. I am ashamed of you for taking care of me. I must go home now," Sally said.

"I don't know what to say. That's your decision, but you must think about it a lot before doing anything," Irene said.

"Yes, I will go home. There is no use staying here. I got fired, and my brother is already buried. I have no one to support. I will take time to think about things," Sally said.

"Okay, good luck and may God bless you," Irene said.

Sally went back home while Irene completed her master's degree and then stayed in "Pangasinan" without a roommate for more than a year before going back home. Their only communication was through social media, but it seldom happened because of the lack of signal and the absence of internet connection in Sally's hometown. Irene stayed in their house unemployed and went out with friends sometimes or just hung out with several applications whenever the job openings were interested on her. One application was approved, but she had to refuse it due to the absence of Elizabeth, who went home without the Santos' consent. It was agreed initially that Elizabeth would only be out for a week before returning, but she did not fulfill her end of the bargain.

"Sorry, kindly take care of your brother for a few days more. Let's give Elizabeth an opportunity, a few days to return. Don't ever text her or let her know that we need her. I don't want her to have the impression that we are desperate. She might use it against us and demand many things she wants. We better search for another," Mrs. Santos said.

"It's okay mom. I am not busy anyway. Besides, he is my brother," Irene said.

No news was heard from Elizabeth for another five days, which prompted the Santoses to look for another all-around help. Elizabeth went back to the city, but it was too late for her to return to the Santoses. She was replaced by a relative of the Santoses who was willing to work with the regular schedule of Monday to Saturday and was also willing to include Sundays when needed to.

Constancia was an excellent help. She always completed her chores and barely sat throughout the day. She also relaxes sometimes but is also busy with something else. For instance, she watched her favorite telenovela recycle old newspapers into pots or she just sat and relaxed while converting plastic bottles into something useful and the like. The downside was Bart became so spoiled and lazy. Constancia did it all for Bart. She would bathe him, which was not unusual. She would cook for him, wash his clothes, and even literally feed him. She would scoop a spoonful of food and put it in his mouth. The Santoses noticed what was happening to Bart.

"My heart melts whenever I see Bart. It is not his fault why he had the condition," Constacia said.

She asked permission to attend a family funeral but never returned.Some of her personal belongings were never recovered from the Santoses.

Irene had to halt any plans she had before finding another help. It was a sad situation for her because it offered both long-term and temporary employment. She was hoping that the next help would be willing to stay with the Santos for a longer period and never have tricks on her sleeves.

Irene somehow discovered a property in the Longway Barangay area. It was one of the properties she never mentioned the transaction to her family until 50% of the payment was completed. It was sold by a coworker at a rock-bottom price because her family needed the fund for her father in the hospital. The coworker also offered the neighboring property that was excluded from the initial purchase, but Mrs. Santos declined. She could not afford to spend another peso even when the offer was also at the lowest price possible. She offered to help her coworker to sell the property, and it was bought by her cousin and some relatives of her husband. They would visit the area as a family during their free time, usually on weekends and on holidays. Bart was allowed to run around the area for there were no sari-sari stores present and immediate neighbors that he would disturb.

"Look at that large building. Who in their right mind would erect a building like that in this rural-agricultural part of the city. Hehehe!" Mr. Santos said.

"Yes, I can see it. Me too. I am wondering!" Mrs. Santos said.

They did not think much about it and went on enjoying the family's bonding. They consistently visited the area, but their visits became less frequent as the years went by.

Chapter LIII

The joint law enforcer unit composed of the Police National Police headquarters, the local police jurisdiction; The Baguio Police and The La Trinidad Police, The National Bureau of Investigation and the Philippine Drug Enforcement Agency received some intelligence information that an abandoned large building in the outskirts of the boundary of Baguio and La Trinidad was used as a drug den. In fact, it was the large building that was being put up several years ago when the Santoses used to visit the property Mrs. Santos purchased in the Longway area. Mr. Santos and his men did a great job of not divulging the information to the other law enforcers. Many of the law enforcers surveillance the area for six months and confirmed the big-time player before going in. Many of the residents around the area kept silent with the fear of being involved. It was discovered that a Filipino-Chinese businessman used the building as storage for "shabu" (the Philippine and neighboring country's term for crystal meth). Tons of the illegal substance was recovered during the raid, and many dealers and several of the building care-takers were arrested but sadly, the main fish was never arrested and fled out of the country. Among those arrested was the nephew of Elizabeth that used to stay with the Santoses. He was one of the caretakers of the building. The job he acquired right after he left the Santose. The issue became a hot item nationwide, and it was the discussion of different news agencies and publications for months before it trickled out into oblivion.

Mr. Santos was drunk the night after the operation. He, with other police officers and some law enforcers involved in the operation had their relaxation at the bar owned by the relative of one of his police officers. He went straight to bed to find Mrs. Santos.

"Mama, I think we should sell the Longway property. It is very near the drug den. Besides, it is very far from the city center," he said.

"You are just drunk. Go wash-up, and let's go to bed," Mrs. Santos said.

Mr. Santos went to the CR, cleaned up then went to bed fast asleep without uttering another word.

Irene tried to reconnect with Sally many times through Sally's cell phone number and social media account, but Irene never got answers. She constantly texted and called Sally's number, but nobody answered. She tried to find her on social media, but nothing showed up. There were many other first names with similar family names, but when she asked if they knew Sally, many of them did not respond, or they claimed they did not know somebody with the name of Sally. In the midst of her search, somebody was consistently sending her a friend request.

"Who is this lady? Why is she consistently requesting me to be her social media friend? I don't even know her and she does not have a picture that shows who she is," Irene said.

"Maybe it is a scam, and she thought I could fall for it, whatever it is," She added.

Every time she opened her social media account, the same friend request appeared. She wanted to ignore it again and tried to see if the account could be blocked. Her plan was changed when she received a message confirming that the account belonged to Sally. The chat between the two was long. Both were engulfed in their conversation they forgot how long they must have chatted. The two friends continued to communicate regularly. They were constantly up-dating what was happening with their lives. Mr. Santos wanted to visit the beach during the summer as the highlanders always craved the warm weather and the seaside waters. Mr. Santos thought about his coming retirement and his health issues; he decided to search for a parcel of land near the sea for relaxation purposes. It was a bit early to plan for his mandatory retirement, but he executed it anyway. He brought the entire family for the beach vacation. While they were preparing to return home, an idea surfaced on Mr. Santos' mind.

"Hey, Irene, you said you have a friend living here in this area?" Mr. Santos asked.

"Yes dad. Why?" Irene asked.

"Let's visit her." Mr. Santos said.

"Yes, I kind of miss Sally but why do we have to visit them?" Mrs. Santos asked.

"Besides, we are all ready to go home. And Bart is here," Mrs. Santos added.

"They are not even prepared for us to go to their house, and besides, my friend is not even living with her family anymore, she has her own life," Irene said.

"Let's just go straight home. There is no reason for us to disturb them," Mrs. Santos said.

"Irene, can you tell Sally to find an available property for sale near the beach? It is not necessarily at the immediate side if they are not available. It could also be meters away from the beach, an area near enough to enjoy the beach." Mr. Santos said.

"Yes, Dad, but I don't guarantee she would agree. I have to ask her first," Irene said.

"Anyway, Dad, what specific details do you want me to ask her?" She asked.

"Just the basics; the selling price, the area, and if the owner or seller is willing to get an installment payment would be nice. Those sorts of things," Mr. Santos said.

"Just don't forget to tell her the next time you have a chance to communicate with her ok," He added.

"Yes, Dad. I will," Irene said.

There was no problem with Bart during their trip back home, with the exception of him needing to pee or take a dump. It was a different story when they arrived. He began screaming that disturbed their neighbors.

"Bart! What! Why are you so noisy?" Mrs. Santos asked.

"We just arrived from our trip, and here you are, too noisy," Mr. Santos said.

"Bart! Be quiet! You are disturbing all the people in the community! Keep quiet!" Martin said.

A few hours had passed when Bart abruptly stopped making noise. His loud screams were replaced by loud snoring that could be heard from his room to the living room.

Sally was informed about the intention of Mr. Santos. She made an appointment that coincided with Mr. Santos' availability. Mr. Santos was accompanied by Martin and Irene to the meeting with the lot owner. The problem was the person they were in meeting with was one of the children of the deceased, owner whose name appeared on the legal documents of the property. The situation was complicated because the Philippine law required the other siblings' agreement with the planned sale through a duly notarized document with their affixed signatures. More problems arose when it was revealed that one sibling was overseas and the other one was in a faraway region of the country.

"Make this happen. Let the transfer to us be successful. Or look for another lot for sale with clean titles. Don't worry you have a commission on this transaction," Mr. Santos said.

"Yes, thank you uncle. I will do what I can. I guarantee," Sally said.

It was almost lunch, and they needed some place to eat. Sally recommended an eatery with a comfortable space. They had conversations while waiting for their orders. Mr. Martin asked personal matters about Sally and her background. They had further discussions about the lot or locating another for sale while Irene and Martin were listening in. After they were done with the lunch, Mr. Martin handed Sally some cash for the restaurant bills and for her troubles and the Santoses went home while Sally stayed.

"We are not very rich but those are the people worthy of our help, not those demanding people who always come to our house," Mr. Santos said.

"Yes dad, we totally agree," Irene and Martin replied in a chorus.

Chapter LIV

ally contacted Mr. Santos after almost a month after their last meeting. She informed him about another property that was smaller than the original one for sale. She also mentioned the asking price and the area was ready for inspection. Mr. Santos asked a police officer to drive him on his trip to the property. They all met in a fast-food restaurant to discuss the property with the owner. It included the policeman as a witness of the transaction. Mr. Santos was so glad that most of the papers, such as the lot survey, the tittle, the drafted deed of sale and the drafted lot transfer were prepared. After their meal, they went to the site. Everybody was satisfied with the agreement, and Mr. Santos handed 70% of the total selling price and the owner was trusting enough to hand Mr. Santos the property papers. Sally's commission was also given even if she and Mr. Santos hadn't agreed on the commission's price.

I hope Bart will enjoy his stay near the beach. I sure want to enjoy my retirement with my Bart near the beach, enjoying the warm atmosphere and the waves of the water. Mr. Santos thought.

Mr. Santos made a government loan to complete the property payment and to erect a bungalow type structure complete with fences and an outside Bathroom. He again asked for Sally's assistance and presented the proposed building plan. Sally recommended her cousin to head the construction for she claimed that he was an experienced carpenter and knew a lot of guys in the area who do construction work. The permits and the house construction itself were completed but every time Mr. Santos went to visit, Sally's cousin always asked for money for the materials or any payment pertaining to the construction. Mr. Santos listed all the money that went to the construction and discovered that Sally's cousin overpriced many of the construction materials. Sally contacted Mr. Santos with her apology on behalf of her cousin. The funny part was the cousin did not even apologize and never faced Mr. Santos again.

"Dad, I am sorry, but I hope you still have trust Sally in spite of what her cousin did," Irene said.

"I can see that Sally is a good lady, and she didn't even ask for a high commission and she apologized immediately to me. The problem is her cousin, and the rest of the carpenters are either her relatives or neighbors. Maybe they tricked me. Maybe she is in connivance with them. We never know," Mr. Santos said.

"But dad, Sally is different, I know her," Irene said.

"Yes, I am sure but she is part of the family. This is the last that we will have some kind of business transaction with her or offer them some work. If we continue to be connected in that manner, maybe her family will abuse her again, or we don't know, maybe Sally herself will take her family's side because she is blood. I don't prevent you from ever being friends with Sally but be extra careful," Mr. Santos said.

Irene did not respond on her father's last remark. She still thought that Sally was an honest-to- goodness-person. She connected with Sally on social media and informed her about what her cousin and crew did to the construction with her father's sentiments. Sally appeared so shocked and apologized through her responses to Irene. Their communication was disturbed when a strong smell was all over the house. Irene went to check it out, and she found clean toilet tissues on the toilet bowl. She went to Bart's room to find him lying with his blanket. She called him to the CR to give him a shower.

"Bart, my brother Bart. Trying to do things his own way. He is doing his best. Hehehe,"Irene said.

Bart was laughing throughout the bath till the time he was dressed. He seemed happy that day. Maybe a rainbow of feelings within him as the Santoses thought he might have. He had his meal of pure vegetables and rice without any complaints. No special "lechon" or stake or deep-fried chicken.

"Good boy Bart. He ate his veggies. No problem," Mrs. Santos said while clapping.

Bart lay on his bed without uttering any words. After a few minutes, the erratic moments came to play. He screamed from his bed. He stood with the sweaty fat body jiggling as he jumped up and down. The noise was again in the Santos' atmosphere. With them trying to make Bart quiet because it was late at night and the world was asleep.

The Santos needed a new help because Irene was preparing to migrate and work to Australia with the help of her aunt. Sally was supposed to be the first choice but due to his cousin's wrongdoing, she was not considered. They sourced help from the ever-reliable "Bagao, Cagayan." Liza was a shy young adult who never had much experience outside her hometown. She was never familiar with the city life and only knew the people from her hometown that were in the city and the neighboring municipalities. Every new help was always good in the beginning and showed their true colors as time went on. Despite Mr. Santos being the city police chief, he never demanded many requirements from the applicants, and the Santoses always based their qualifications on other's experiences and information about the applicant. Sometimes it was good, and sometimes it bit them right to their bottoms.

Irene finally submitted all the requirements for Australia and was confirmed that she was qualified for migration. The Santoses were delighted for her and, at the same time, sad about missing her. Irene was happy but was kind of turned aback deep inside because she will leave her brother Bart.

"Mom, Dad, Martin. I am kind of sad because I will be leaving you with Bart. I will not be able to take care of him," Irene said.

"Don't worry about us. We can manage. The important thing is being good on your life path. We want you to experience life," Mrs. Santos said.

"Sister, it's okay to grab the opportunity to live your life," Martin said.

"Everything is okay for as long as you enjoy life." Mr. Santos said.

The Santos waited for Irene's flight schedule to plan their trip to the Manila airport. Mr. Santos reserved a van for its availability to be used for three days. The Santoses went with Irene to the airport except for Bart and Tina, the new all-around help who stayed with Bart. They waited for more than an hour before Irene's flight was announced. Irene said goodbye to each of her family without any obvious tears or signs of sadness, for "Igorots" were not known to show emotions in public.

"Huh! I hope she will be successful in her endeavor," Mrs. Santos said as they were leaving the airport.

"I am sure she will! And I am still hopeful," Mr. Santos said.

The trip coming home was a safe one with a couple of stop overs that allowed the driver to rest a couple of hours before resuming. They finally arrived early in the morning, and they were so exhausted from the trip. Energies were drained from them even if they only sat as passengers. Bart welcomed them back home with hugs and kisses and looked at each of them like they owed him big time. They went straight to their beds and took naps before having their lunch at the family's favorite restaurant.

For some reason, the restaurant was closed and had to proceed to the available one. They had a long wait for the food that agitated Bart. He was screaming and biting his hands. The other customers were also a bit pissed at the restaurant's service and they understood Bart's rant.

"He must be pissed because waiting for the orders takes forever!" A customer said with a sarcastic smile.

"Give them their orders! Prioritize him! This must be a lesson for you to speed up your food preparations! Look at what is happening!" Another customer said.

The waiter informed them that their orders were next, but the Santoses prompted for their orders to be taken away and proceeded to the car.

"It is your fault! Tell your kitchen crew that next time, they must prepare the orders faster! We have been waiting for so long that even the other customers expressed their dissatisfaction with your services!" Mrs. Santos said.

"Bart! Keep quiet, dad is driving! "Martin shouted while pulling Bart's hands away from their father's face.

"Bart! Your dad is driving! We will have an accident if you continue what you are doing!" Mrs. Santos said.

Chapter LV

It was already five years since Irene arrived in Australia. I was the right time for everybody was home checking their social media account. Irene face-timed her family, and the Santoses communicated with her with smiles on their faces. It was not their initial communication with her through social media, but it was the first time they all got to communicate with her in live face-time. The Santoses asked Irene about her life in Australia, and they also informed her of what was going on with them in the Philippines. After a few minutes, her Aunt joined in and was glad to communicate with them. She just said a few words and left because she had to go to work. Irene was still living with her Aunt, but she revealed that she was planning on having her own place once she saved enough money for her expenses. They ended their communication with goodbyes after talking for more than an hour.

Mr. Santos had only two years before retirement. His health was presented with many problems. The primary problem was gout. There was his heart problem, high blood cholesterol, and high blood pressure, and his occurring high blood sugar in ear stage. A relative attended an occasion at Mrs. Fecora's residence. He had company with him, which everybody thought was also Filipino, but in actuality, he was from Myanmar. The reason was looking like a typical "Igorot." The relative introduced him to everybody at the party, and he heard that Mr. Santos needed a full-time driver. He introduced his companion from Myanmar again to Mr. Santos and mentioned that he was a student who needed a source of income while studying in the country. Mr. Santos expressed his interest of hiring Mr. Myanmar as his driver right on the spot and can start any time.

Mr. Myanmar did not stay with the Santoses for he also had his own place. The arrangement was okay with Mr. Santos for he would call him any time he needed a driver. Mr. Myanmar would also drive Bart around every day. He would run errands for the Santoses and drove Mr. Santos to and from work. He even developed friendships with the policemen. Nobody knew how he was able to manage his time for school and for the Santoses, but he did an excellent job.

Mr. Santos' health condition was deteriorating. He needed assistance due to his limping steps and his overweight body. He was impatient about his incoming retirement to rest and stay away from stress. A memo from the National Headquarters informed him that he was appointed as the OIC Police Chief in one of the municipalities in the lowlands eleven-hours drive from his city of jurisdiction, two months before his official retirement. It was an unusual arrangement because the police chief died of natural causes, and they could not find an immediate replacement that was qualified. He would have his duty on Monday's till Wednesday in Baguio City, and Thursday till Saturday in the lowlands. The situation took a toll on his body as it went on. The more positive side was he became closer with Mr. Myanmar by being his driver. He didn't give him a fixed salary, but he provided payment for his apartment and an allowance. The Santoses and everybody who knew Mr. Myanmar was wondering how he managed to stay in the Philippines for so long with his immigration status of being a student, but they did not focus on it.

Mr. Santos opted for another check-up because he could barely breathe. He suspected that his mild asthma was the culprit but he found out that he was on the brink of a major heart attack. Further examinations revealed that he needed a bypass surgery. The Santoses and the Mrs. Fecora with family were shocked by the bad news. He needed to be hospitalized in the ICU because his breathing and blood pressure were unstable.

"I told you before, dad, that you must watch your diet but you didn't listen and now look what is happening to you," Mrs. Santos said.

Mr. Santos was conscious and could still talk, but he did not have the energy to do so. The specialist strongly recommended Mr. Santos to undergo under the knife, but the it it was too expensive and he was worried about his chances off recovery because of the risk involved.

The Santoses went for a second opinion and sent the MRI reading to the National Heart Center in Manila to see if other options can be done rather than the bypass surgery. In the meantime, Mr. Santos regained his strength back and was prescribed more medications for his heart condition. He rested only for a few weeks before returning to work. The Santoses received a call that a stent procedure could be done. A tube-like wire called the stent will be inserted in the affected arteries, and a thin balloon will be inflated to push the stent against the arterial walls that would stay permanently. It is to push the blockage on the wall for the normal flow of blood rather than opening the chest and creating an artificial vessel bypassing the blocked arteries.

One day, Mr. Santos decided to attend Kabayan's Foundation Day even without any major role in the program. A police officer could drive him, but he opted for Mr. Myanmar. The trip was smooth sailing. They even met some of Mrs. Santos' relatives and friends by chance at a stopover restaurant and had a little chat. They arrived late in the evening and were welcomed by his relatives. They had a great time having a simple gathering of "pulutan" and alcohol until late at night. The next day, Mr. Santos and Mr. Myanmar had their breakfast. Mr. Santos sat in the living room while it was Mr. Myanmar's turn to take a bath. Mr. Santos tried to reach for his medicine box when he fell with his face first on the floor. Mr. Myanmar checked on him and let him lie on the sofa. Some of the foundation employees renting the Santos' residence in Kabayan applied the Cardio Pulmonary Resuscitation. Mr. Myanmar ran to the dispensary clinic, but the doctor was in the city because it was an official holiday. The health workers present were not responsive and did no further emergency interventions. The ambulance driver was also absent, so a relative volunteered to drive. They rushed Mr. Santos to the nearest hospital while the foundation employees did the "ambubag" and continued CPR but when they arrived, it was too late. Mr. Santos was motionless and rigid, without signs of breathing and heartbeat. Mrs. Santos was informed through a call that her husband had a heart attack, and they are on their way to the hospital in the city. Mrs. Santos was nervous and praying that it would be another mild attack. She rushed to a hospital where her husband's heart specialist was employed to, reserve the ICU unit and prepare the emergency team for his arrival. She received another call when she almost arrived at the hospital. She sat on a sidewalk-railings, almost going to collapse, but she picked herself up and went back home crying. Martin was in the house with relatives who got the news of his father's passing. Many were shocked and crying.

"Why Lord? Why did you take Mr. Santos for he is an honorable man!" One of the relatives said.

"There are many bad people in this world, but the one who left is a good one. Why?" Another relative said.

Bart was still asleep, oblivious to what was happening. Many expressed their condolences to the Santoses and gave comforting words. Mrs. Santos arrived crying while being welcomed by words of encouragements and comforts from relatives, friends, coworkers, and neighbors. Irene was informed about the incident through social media face-time, and her face was flooded with tears. Bart woke to a mourning and sad atmosphere, looking at the people with wet faces.

"Bart! Your papa is gone and never coming back!" Mrs. Santos said as she and Martin gave him a tight hug.

Martin posted about his fathers' passing on his social media account. The Santoses were surprised by the overwhelming expressions of their condolences. There were even tons of countrymen from abroad who were video calling through social media. Irene called her mother with her face covered in tears. She even informed her that she was directing a stage play about Autism that was, of course, inspired by Bart. Sadly, she had no appetite to continue her project. She and her Aunt's flight home were also disclosed. Irene's call was not over when another call tried to connect. It was Mrs. Santos' surprise that the caller was Melvin, the same as Irene, with his face covered with tears. He revealed that he moved in the U.S. to a Filipina wife and they had a six-year old child. He and Mrs. Santos chatted a little and asked how Bart was taking the news. He also informed Mrs. Santos that he could not be in person for the wake and funeral. He opted to send some cash to help with the expenses. Others called to either Mrs. Santos or Martin, expressing their condolences, and some even promised some cash to send.

The Santos' residence was full of mourners and the Santos family was astonished by the people's love for Mr. Santos. Many people from all walks of life were present. Even personalities that the Santoses and Mrs. Fecora were not familiar with came revealing how they came to know Mr. Santos and the good thing he had done for them.

"It is so sad that Mr. Santos has passed. I can't imagine how Bart takes the passing of his beloved father," one of the mourners said.

"Not that I don't have a conscience, but for me, it is better for Bart to leave the world first than Mr. Santos," another one said.

"Poor Bart, he might not be aware of his father's passing," another one said.

"What will happen to poor Bart now that his dad is dead?" Another one said.

Many other similar speculations and sentiments were roaming during Mr. Santos' wake until he was laid to his final rest.